FRIGATE COMMANDER

by

Tom Wareham

Pen & Sword
MARITIME

First published in Great Britain in 2004
and republished in this format in 2012 by
PEN & SWORD MARITIME
An imprint of
Pen & Sword Books Ltd
47 Church Street
Barnsley
South Yorkshire
S70 2AS

Copyright © Tom Wareham 2004, 2012

ISBN 978 1 84884 859 7

Typeset in 11/13 Sabon by
Phoenix Typesetting, Auldgirth, Dumfriesshire

Printed and bound in England
By CPI Group (UK) Ltd, Croydon, CR0 4YY

Pen & Sword Books Ltd incorporates the Imprints of Pen & Sword Aviation,
Pen & Sword Family History, Pen & Sword Maritime, Pen & Sword Military,
Pen & Sword Discovery, Wharncliffe Local History, Wharncliffe True Crime,
Wharncliffe Transport, Pen & Sword Select, Pen & Sword Military Classics,
Leo Cooper, The Praetorian Press, Remember When,
Seaforth Publishing and Frontline Publishing

For a complete list of Pen & Sword titles please contact
PEN & SWORD BOOKS LIMITED
47 Church Street, Barnsley, South Yorkshire, S70 2AS, England
E-mail: enquiries@pen-and-sword.co.uk
Website: www.pen-and-sword.co.uk

To Howard S. and Graham J.
and Old Comradeship

Contents

Acknowledgements

I must first of all express my thanks to Mr Christopher Heath who is, to the best of my knowledge, the last descendant of the Moore family and who kindly gave his agreement to the extensive use of quotations from Graham Moore's Journals.

Similarly I must register my gratitude to the Syndics of Cambridge University Library for giving me their permission as current owners of the Journals. The reading of the Journals themselves could not have been achieved without the good-humoured assistance of Godfrey Waller and his colleagues in the Manuscripts Department of the Library.

For illustrations I would also wish to thank the appropriate staff in the National Portrait Gallery and British Library; Andy King at the Bristol Museums and Art Gallery, and especially Eleanor Heron and her colleagues at the National Maritime Museum for their continued assistance on this and other projects.

Finally, my eternal thanks to Chris for her ongoing forbearance.

Tom Wareham, London, 2003

'Memoirs are most to be depended on and certainly they must give the truest account of the manners of the times . . .'

Graham Moore.

Foreword

In my last book, *The Star Captains*, I produced a study of the Royal Navy's frigate commanders during the Great Wars with France, 1793–1815. The basis for this work was the employment records of the officers concerned, and in the interests of academic research, the work focussed on the statistical evidence drawn from those records. With the exception of one chapter, I largely avoided describing the military activities of the officers concerned or the strategic aspect of the wars themselves.

During the writing of *The Star Captains* I became increasingly conscious of the voices of the men themselves. Apart from the many, sometimes ponderous nineteenth century memoirs written by or about the officers at some time after the event, my research uncovered often tantalizing snippets of 'unedited' personal correspondence or journals which conveyed a much more realistic account of the experiences of the men involved. Although I tried to include some of this in *The Star Captains*, the nature of the work precluded this. Indeed, one reviewer commented, fairly, that the book did not really take the reader close to the spirit of the frigate captains themselves. Part of the aim of this current work, therefore, is to try to redress this, but, I hope, it is also much more than this.

During the course of my research – and probably like all similar historians – I acquire old or rare books on my subject. Several years ago I purchased one book in particular which struck me as being of special interest and curiosity. This was *A Memoir of Admiral Sir Graham Moore*, written in 1844 by Major General Robert Gardiner. The book, a slim volume of less than fifty pages, was largely formu-laic, reminiscent of a great many books produced during the 19th century, after the death of their subject. What caught my attention very quickly was the inclusion in the memoir of a series of highly interesting and revealing quotations from Moore about his experiences as commander of a frigate during the war against Revolutionary France. Unlike many other similar quotations I had come across, these spoke with an immediacy which insisted they had not been written at any period after the events to which they referred. Very little searching revealed that Graham Moore had kept a personal journal and, hoping to find additional interesting material, I made my way to the library at the University of Cambridge to read it. To my dismay, when staff at the library produced the journal for me, I found myself confronted with all thirty-seven volumes of it. A rapid inspection of the neat, easily written pages made me realize that what I was looking at was way beyond the scope of *The Star Captains*. Choosing one volume at random, I began to read, and soon became totally entranced, at the end of the day realizing that Graham Moore's journal was an historical gem.

Moore gives us what is, I think, a unique insight into what life was like for a naval officer on active service during the Great Wars. Following his career from his peacetime service as a Lieutenant, we follow him closely through various commands until he becomes one of the navy's star frigate captains, commanding one of the most powerful frigates in service. However, what is most important is the detail that he provides about the exigencies of commanding a warship at the end of the eighteenth century. As his career progresses, we see him observing and learning from his experience of bad commanders, and then we see him implementing his own ideas about crew management. Of course, Moore did not always get it right, but his ideas and practices are enlightening and cannot fail to endear us to Moore as a man. Furthermore, much of what he says and does contradicts the traditional assumptions about life in the Royal Navy in the period.

There is, though, another unique side to Moore's journal, because the pages record in consistent detail the social aspects of his life. We learn of the balls and assemblies that he attended, the dinners with brother officers, the intricate network of connections that attended the operation of 'interest', and the young man's yearning for love and a happy marriage. This degree of portrayal of naval life is, as yet, available nowhere else outside the pages of fiction. Happily, what follows is not fiction.

Introduction

'I see a number of the people who had cut their hair short and left off wearing hair powder, are now powdering and letting their hair grow again; they say the former fashion is looked upon with an evil eye by the People at the head of affairs, and that they consider it as a badge of Democratic principles. I am certainly neither a Democrat nor an Aristocrat, but I shall take the liberty of continuing to wear my hair short, which is more to my taste and I find it far more convenient.'

Graham Moore

Graham Moore was born in Glasgow on 14 September 1764. He was the fourth of six surviving children born to the well-respected physician and author Dr John Moore and his wife Jean or Jeannie. Graham's grandfather, Charles Moore, was a church minister and Dr John Moore, born after Charles Moore relocated to Scotland, was educated at Glasgow Grammar School. He studied medicine at Glasgow University, where he probably met his future wife Jean Simpson, daughter of a professor at the University and a niece of the geometrician Robert Simpson. In 1747, Dr Moore befriended Colonel Campbell of the 54th Regiment, and appears to have served briefly with that regiment in the Low Countries as surgeon's mate. He then went to Paris to complete his studies, in the process becoming the surgeon to the Earl of Albemarle.

The Moore boys benefited from a family environment where education was respected and, certainly as far as the boys were concerned, encouraged. John, the eldest son, born in 1761, was sent to Glasgow High School where he was encouraged to study history, poetry and literature. He was almost certainly followed by the other boys and it is abundantly clear that Graham's studies followed a similar course.

John subsequently chose a career in the army and was destined to become a greatly loved General, killed at the Battle of Corunna in

1809. In keeping with contemporary expectations, medicine and the church provided professions for the other two sons.

In addition to being a physician, Dr John Moore was also, as the naval biographer John Marshall described him in 1823, 'an author of some celebrity'. In fact Dr Moore produced several novels and three books about European countries – although of the latter more will be said later. His first novel *Zeluco*, published in 1786, was described as 'a glorious story' by his friend, the poet Robert Burns. It was also apparently read and appreciated by Lord Byron. In fact, Dr Moore's creative output was greatly helped by his normal profession. He appears to have won the friendship and confidence of Elizabeth Gunning, the Duchess of Hamilton, almost certainly acting as her physician.

In 1772, the Duchess proposed sending her second son, the fifteen-year-old Douglas Hamilton (later to become the 8th Duke), on a Grand Tour of the Continent and Dr Moore was asked to accompany him as tutor, guide and physician. This connection with the Hamiltons was to be important in two respects: firstly, the tour of the Continent was to provide Dr Moore with the material for his first major work, *Society & Manners in France, Switzerland and Germany* which was published in 1779[1]; secondly, Elizabeth Gunning was to provide powerful patronage for the Moores over future years. The Duchess' husband, the 6th Duke of Hamilton, had died some years before, and she had subsequently remarried. Her new husband was John Campbell, Baron Sundridge, who was shortly to become the Duke of Argyll[2].

When the party set off for the Continent, they were accompanied by the eleven-year-old John Moore, who had already set his heart on a career in the army. When, in 1775, the twelve-year-old Graham announced his choice of career to be the navy, John wrote from the continent:

> *I am pleased, my dear boy, that you wish to be a sailor, for I am sure you will be a brave one. I hope that, in some years after this, you and I will thresh the Monsieurs, both by sea and land; but I hope we won't make war with the Spaniards; for the Spanish Ambassador is the best and kindest man I ever saw*[3].

The irony of this last statement could not have been anticipated.

Just weeks later, John learned that the newly created Duke of Argyll had obtained an ensigncy for him in the 51st Regiment of Foot and, leaving his father and Douglas Hamilton, he returned alone to

London, where the family were now in residence. It is important to dwell for a moment on John Moore, because he was to play an important role in the life and career of Graham Moore. In many ways John Moore was a controversial officer; he was certainly blamed by those who saw the Peninsular campaign as a disaster, but others recognized qualities in him that made him an admirable commanding officer – especially in his attitude to the common soldier. However, the care which he took towards the men under his command may have given, at least, the impression of a cautious approach to military strategy. It was certainly this aspect which some of his critics latched on to following the withdrawal of the British army from Spain in 1809.

This cautious nature was equally present in Graham. However, whereas John appears to have been idolized by his father regardless of this characteristic, Graham received criticism for the same. In fact there is some evidence that Dr Moore regarded Graham as 'too good' i.e. 'soft' or 'nice', for a career in the navy. Certainly he may have looked upon Graham's bookish interests, and romantic leanings, as contrary to the robust nature necessary for success in the Georgian navy.

During one particular bout of depression during 1798, while Graham was in the process of accumulating some success as a frigate commander, he pondered upon what would happen to his journal if he were killed, and what would be the response of his parents upon reading it. He realized firstly and pragmatically that it would reduce his mother to tears. But also,

> My Father too, who sees me with so partial an eye, will see here more than perhaps he might wish, fondly thinking me worthier than he would find me; but my friend Currie of Liverpool [see below], who loves me as 'if I had given him stuff to make him love me', what will he say of his departed friend? He will say and he will think, this fellow has not made the most of himself. But my dear Currie, who has? This fellow Graham Moore, was in many things as weak as water.[4]

There is some evidence that Dr Moore's attitude towards Graham may have damaged his son's self-confidence and left him with an underlying feeling of unworthiness. It is certainly true that Graham always felt inferior to John. Among the surviving family correspondence, for example, there are very few letters from Graham to his father but there is a curious one written in December 1795, when Graham was Captain of the frigate *Syren*. It refers to his hope of meeting John at Portsmouth:

*. . . It will be a joyfull meeting to me with a brother whom I esteem as
much as I love him. I think him a better man for the country than myself
and I am well pleased it should be so rather than that he should come
down to my level, although that would not lower him much*[5].

One could quite reasonably have expected a degree of resentment to
develop between the two brothers but, on the contrary, Graham idolized his elder brother and probably attempted to emulate John's
'style'. In turn, John seems to have been very protective towards his
sibling.

By 1777, a place had been secured for Graham as Midshipman on
board the fourth-rate 60-gun *Medway* commanded by Captain Phillip
Affleck, and he was sent out to join her at Menorca. By January 1780,
he had transferred to the third-rate 64-gun *Trident* in the West Indies;
however, his new position was not a happy one. He wrote home to
his mother, expressing some dissatisfaction at the treatment he was
receiving from his new Captain, Captain Anthony James Pye Molloy.[6]
It is possible that Dr Moore found in this another example of his
younger son's weakness, but John came to his defence:

*Midshipmen are often raised from common seamen & Capt[ains] of
Men of War who are not the mildest people, continue to treat
Gentlemen in the same manner, which can't help being disagreeable . . .*[7]

Seemingly days later, Graham was present in his first fleet action when
a British squadron under Admiral Byron engaged the French fleet
under D'Estaing. There was no news of Graham after the action and
John, serving in North America, appended a concerned note to his
letter home, perhaps hoping to prick Dr Moore's conscience:

*as they have had few killed & wounded I hope he has escaped, he is so
young that I think even a wound would be dangerous.*[8]

Graham had indeed survived the engagement, though his personal
record of the event has not. His experience was not limited at this stage
to combat. In October 1780, the *Trident*, together with the other ships
of a squadron under Rear Admiral Rowley, was caught by a hurricane
off St Domingo. Several ships, including the *Trident*, were dismasted,
and the 74-gun *Thunderer* disappeared without trace. The year 1780
must have been a memorable one for the sixteen-year-old Midshipman.
Later that year the *Trident* returned to England, and Graham found
himself serving in the Channel Fleet, happily closer to home.

The Moore family had moved to London in 1778, and by this time the family had moved into an elegant town house in Clifford Street, just off New Bond Street. It was to this house that both Graham and John were to return whenever they were able, until a few years after Dr Moore's death. Clifford Street was close to the centre of fashionable society, and it gave the Moores ample opportunity of meeting and mixing with the great and the good of Georgian London – as will become evident.

In March 1782, Graham sat and passed his Lieutenant's examination, and he was appointed as Fourth Lieutenant of the *Crown*, a third-rate ship commanded by Captain Samuel Reeve. In September 1782, the *Crown* was part of Howe's fleet, sent to escort a convoy of transports carrying stores to Gibraltar, which was under siege from a combined French and Spanish force. On 10 October, they encountered an enemy fleet in the Straits of Gibraltar and an inconclusive action followed after days of manoeuvring. Moore recorded the events of these few days in a journal which has not survived, although extracts are included in Gardiner's *Memoir*. Unfortunately, the extant account is too impersonal to convey anything more than the official histories. However, shortly thereafter, Graham was promoted to Third Lieutenant of the *Crown*.

With the end of the war against America and her allies, Moore found himself as a junior Lieutenant in a shrinking navy. The number of officers receiving promotion fell to almost nil, and with it declined any reasonable prospect of career advancement. Only another war could improve this situation – and there seemed little chance of this occurring. The *Crown* appears to have been decommissioned and Moore returned to London. After consultation with his father, it was agreed that he should travel to France, to spend some time there completing his education and, in particular, acquiring a strong grasp of the French language. In a note at the beginning of his journal, Graham adds wryly that one of the other aims of the sojourn was '*of making what other improvements I could*'.

Within the year he was back in London once again, eager for active service. It is at this point that the surviving journals begin.

Graham Moore's Journal

'. . . *as to a companion, it is what I do not look for, it is so rare. A Captain is well off if he has those with him who are tolerably able and willing to do their duty, and who are not Blackguards. The void, the*

*Besoin, I feel for something more, drives me to this journal, where I
sometime amuse myself in tracing a thought. I find it difficult, however,
to give to this irregular work the life and spirit of my familiar letters,
from its being addressed to no body, and from its being intended to be
kept almost exclusively to myself during my life. Perhaps I may draw
amusement and some instruction from the perusal of this Hodge Podge,
the former part of which I have not seen since it was written; indeed I
never keep more of it than the book I am writing with me, sending them
to a place of security as fast as the Books are filled up. This, with a man
of genius, would be the true way to "catch the Manners living as they
rise" . . .'*

Graham Moore, September 1796

Moore's Journal is held in the collection of the Manuscripts
Department in the Library at the University of Cambridge and it is
shelf-marked under the reference Add. 9303. The journal consists of
thirty-seven bound volumes, each written in Moore's clear, reasonably neat handwriting. Chronologically the journal begins towards
the end of 1784, some two years after he had been promoted to
Lieutenant, and when he was twenty years old. From comments he
makes in a later volume, it is clear that he attempted to keep a journal
before this time, but never managed to maintain it. In fact, the first
extant volume of the journal appears to consist of a reused volume
from an earlier time in his life, as a large number of pages have been
cut from the volume, and it has been reversed so that the current
contents could be inserted. It is also evident that he purchased a
number of blank volumes whenever he was due to go to sea, in theory
sufficient to see him through any particular voyage. Although he
clearly attempted to keep the volumes uniform, this was not always
possible, and sometimes the dimensions of the volumes, quality of
paper etc varies. On completion of a volume, he would dispatch or
deliver it into his mother's safekeeping, with instructions that it
should not be read until after his death, whenever that might occur.

Certainly, after his death, the journal was read by Major General
Robert Gardiner, because he quotes selectively from it in his *Memoir*.
Tucked inside one of the volumes there is also a later letter from the
Rev. William James, vicar of the parish of Cobham in Surrey, to
Moore's widow, Lady Moore, thanking her for allowing him access
to the work. The journal was also read, prior to 1963, by someone,
as extracts relating to Moore's time at Cobham were published in the
Surrey Archaeological Society Collections. One reader has inserted

some page references inside the rear cover of many of the journals – fortunately in soft pencil. The problem with these references is that they reflect the subjective interest of that reader and are of very limited value to other researchers.

At some point in time, some significant excisions have been made from the journals. It is very clear that, at times, Moore allowed himself to express views on paper which, upon reflection, he did not wish to share with anyone. Paragraphs, and sometimes even pages, have been heavily scrawled through in what appears to be the same pen and ink used by the originator. However, a certain number of pages and part-pages have also been cut out of the volumes, suggesting censorship at a later time by a family member. These excisions are, of course, extremely regrettable, as they suggest that Moore was expressing views which were either very personal or which were controversial in some way. This is certainly the case in one example where he had clearly committed to paper strong views about his senior officer; the discovery of these views could have seriously blighted his career, and it is therefore understandable why Moore should, in the cooler light of another day, have decided to obliterate any dangerous statements. There are also occasions when the entries in the journal cease for a period. These gaps are always explained. For example, there are many gaps when Graham is in London, and an account of his activities is sometimes given in retrospect when he returns to his ship. This reinforces the idea that he used the journal as a substitute for society, whilst at sea. On other occasions his musings were simply banished by the impossibility of applying pen to paper in rough weather, as on 30 October 1793, when an exasperated Moore notes:

> *... The ship is rolling about so much that I can write no more.*

In spite of Graham's strictures about the privacy of his diary, he admits that he has given his father permission to read the journal – this being around the middle of 1797. Whether this permission was granted under pressure or not, we cannot be certain, but it is clear that Graham was unhappy about it being read, because

> *... it is written at all times, in all humours and in different situations, there are ignorances and weaknesses displayed which I would rather keep behind the curtains during my life, but which I do not wish should be concealed after my death.*[9]

Conventions

Given the extent of the original journals, selective editing has been unavoidable and has necessitated a degree of narrative intervention, the aim being to enable the reader to follow the events as they occurred – sometimes adding information or comments which explain or put into context what is being recorded. Nevertheless, this book follows the chronological progress of the journals, and the quoted extracts follow in the sequence as written by their author. Those used to working on contemporary source material will already be aware of the stylistic eccentricities of writers of this period. For the uninitiated I should explain that punctuation and capitalization were often random, and of course, spelling and names have often changed over the past 200 years. I have therefore changed what appear to be genuine spelling mistakes – though there are very few of these – simply to make the quotations easier to read, but I have usually retained what appear to be eighteenth-century forms of spelling, and period place names. On the other hand, where I have made an editorial insertion, said insertion appears in square brackets.

Following modern convention, the names of all ships are italicized. Occasionally throughout the text some ships, especially those larger than a frigate, appear with a number following either in parentheses; this relates to the number of cannon carried on board the vessel.

1

Smuggling Patrol – HMS *Perseus*
(1784 – January 1786)

For the vast majority of naval officers – i.e. those who did not attend the Naval Academy at Portsmouth – there was no formal training in the skills, techniques and knowledge that were required to command a ship of war. Such training as there was took the form of observation of senior officers with whom one served. 'Young Gentlemen' were quickly broken into shipboard life, an experience which many officers later recorded as being a rather shattering experience. They were then put through the rigours of a basic training which involved hands-on experience of learning about the rigging and the practical activities of running a ship. By the time they were midshipmen, many of these potential officers were aware of the duties that were required of an officer and, in frigates in time of war, it was not unknown for midshipmen to undertake the watch-keeping duties normally required of a lieutenant. Moore received a grounding in these experiences, but it was really only when he was appointed as a commissioned Lieutenant that his development as an officer began.

However, it would be a mistake to think that an officer – and a good officer, at that – was created solely by his experiences on board ship. Naval officers were men who were still very much part of their society, and Graham Moore's journal makes it clear just how important it was for them to have a social existence.

Graham Moore hurriedly returned from France towards the end of 1784. The Moore family were acquainted with Lord Arden, and just a few months earlier Arden, as part of Pitt's new administration, had been appointed to the Board of Admiralty. It can have been no coincidence that shortly after his return, Moore met Lord Arden and

1

then received orders to join the 20-gun HMS *Perseus* only days later. The *Perseus* was smaller than a frigate, but commanded by a Post Captain, in this case Captain George Palmer, who was in his mid-twenties and had commissioned the ship two years earlier. The *Perseus* was bound for an anti-smuggling patrol off the north-west coast of England, and in this activity Moore was unknowingly joining a number of the navy's best future frigate commanders.[10]

With little regard for comfort, the *Perseus* sailed from Plymouth on 27 December bound for Dublin. The ship called briefly at Cork where Moore chose to remain on board while the other officers went ashore, because '*I was rather short of cash, and of course could not have much amusement*'. Days later, on the way to Dublin, being the only Lieutenant on board, Moore found himself responsible for the safety of the ship. Coming on deck one night he found the ship's binnacle poorly lit. Asking the reason, he was told that the ship's Purser had refused to issue all the necessary candles on the basis that this was wasteful. Moore was furious and confronted the Purser in the Gun Room. The Purser, who may have been drunk, refused to obey Moore's order to issue the candles and the Captain had to be summoned. Palmer promptly confined the Purser to his quarters until he came to his senses.

The depth of Moore's responsibility was brought home to him again shortly after. On the night of 30 January 1785, the *Perseus* sailed into Dublin Bay in a gale, and anchored. As the crew was tired from fighting the winds, '*All the ship's company were allowed to turn into their hammocks excepting me and the midshipmen of the first watch*'. A lonely and troubled vigil ensued from 8pm until midnight, by which time the gale was increasing strongly and a worried Moore had the crew woken. Captain Palmer arrived on the quarter deck to survey the situation but, after a few moments, he decided that it was safe to allow the ship to ride at her anchors until daylight and the people were allowed to return to their hammocks. Thankfully, Moore was also able to turn in to his own small cabin. '*I lay down on my bed with my wet clothes on, I was afraid to undress as I expected to be called very soon, however I was not disturbed 'til 8 in the morning, when with some difficulty we hove our anchor up and ran into the Bay*'.

Moore was not impressed by his first experience of Palmer's encounter with smugglers. On 15 February, the *Perseus* surprised a suspicious-looking cutter that fled at their approach. The alarm on board the cutter clearly indicated a state of guilty panic and Palmer gave chase, ordering one of the ship's nine-pounder guns manhandled onto the foredeck as a bow chaser. However, to Moore's growing frustration, Palmer then decided to bring the ship's broadside guns to bear instead; and every time the *Perseus* yawed to bring the guns to bear, the cutter sailed further away. After a great many shot had been wasted, the cutter disappeared into the growing darkness and Palmer abandoned the chase. It was not a good start and Moore's relationship with his commanding officer was soon to deteriorate.

Without the urgency that was generated by wartime duties, the ships on anti-smuggling patrol were able to adopt a surprisingly leisurely routine with regular stops at local ports. Palmer was clearly not averse to this, and the *Perseus* spent many weeks at Liverpool where the officers indulged in the various pleasures that the city's society could offer. Often these involved all-night 'Balls and Assemblies'. Entering an Assembly one evening, Moore found an unknown naval captain standing just inside the door. The officer was introduced as Captain Isaac Coffin

> . . . *who on seeing me, very politely offered to procure me a partner, which he did. After the first country dance Coffin and I had some conversation together, I found he had known my eldest brother John very intimately in America, on which account he showed me marks of friendship which without that circumstance I could have had no pretensions to.*

The twenty-five-year-old Coffin was an interesting and controversial character. Promoted two years earlier he had fallen foul of Admiral Rodney by refusing to accept three of the Admiral's protégés on board his ship. The midshipmen concerned were mere boys, and Coffin refused to accept them as his lieutenants because of their lack of experience. A furious Rodney had Coffin court-martialled for disobedience and contempt – but the trial backfired on Rodney who was found guilty of making appointments which were 'irregular and contrary to the established rules of the service'.[11] Now, although Coffin was on the beach, he was highly regarded and welcomed in society and through Coffin, Moore was introduced to William Boates,

> . . . *a very capital merchant in Liverpool, who has three very amiable daughters, one of them is esteemed a great beauty. That is the house where I am on the most agreeable footing.*

Ironically, Boates had made his money from the slave trade, to which Moore was opposed. It may be for this reason that the source of

Boates' wealth is not mentioned in the journal. Moore also had a brief flirtation with *Miss 'F__y Pet__rs, a great toast in Liverpool'*. After spending several days in her company,

> *I was really a little smitten with her, she is very handsome, seems to have had a pretty good education; and I think she has a tolerable share of understanding.*

Perhaps Moore was becoming just a little too intimate. The lauded Miss Pet__rs was suddenly whisked away to the country. He returned to console himself with the charms of the beautiful Ellen Boates, and engaged himself to accompany her to a ball in honour of the King's birthday, though he feared that the *Perseus* might be back at sea by then,

> *. . . and of course I shall be then dancing with Davy Jones, to whom, notwithstanding my profound respect, I freely own I would prefer the lady.*

Moore's success in Liverpool society was, however, not going down well with his commanding officer and he became aware of a certain dryness in Palmer's behaviour:

> *he rather treated me with a distance and hauteur . . . he agrees very well with me when we are abroad, but could easily dispense with my company ashore.*

Once they were back at sea, however, this tension eased for a time. Palmer was almost certainly jealous, and perhaps he had reason to be. Arriving at Belfast in June 1785, Moore was sent on board Commodore Gower's ship, the frigate *Hebe*, to collect Palmer's orders. On board the *Hebe*, Gower recognized him as a friend of Lord Arden's and he was immediately invited to return for dinner that night with Captain Palmer. That evening, as they climbed the side rope of the *Hebe*, Moore

> *was received at the Gangway by one of the lieutenants, who entered into conversation with me in an easy stile; I had a suspicion who it was but as I had never before seen him I spoke to him and addressed him in the same manner I would any other lieutenant.*

Later that evening, his suspicion was confirmed. The Lieutenant was Prince William, later to become King William IV. After dinner, the Prince invited Moore to the Gun Room for a more informal session drinking grog, where the Prince

. . . was very at ease and familiar with all officers, calling for songs and joining in the chorus.

This was not to be the first evening that Moore ended carousing with the Prince!

In December 1785, the *Perseus* returned to Plymouth for a refit. The passage was rough and Moore experienced most of it from his small cabin, to which he had, reluctantly, been confined by the ship's surgeon because of a severe cold. They arrived at Plymouth to find a court martial in progress on the boatswain of the *Fortune* who had been formally charged with striking both the ship's Lieutenant and surgeon. A sentence of death was passed on the man, and Moore was ordered to attend the execution with seamen from the *Perseus*. When the signal gun was fired to assemble the witnesses, Moore

. . . took the Pinnace and went along side of the Standard *[64] which ship being the most in the centre of the fleet was appointed for the execution . . . I put some of our people on board the* Standard *to assist at the execution according to the practice in such cases[12], and then joined the other boats of the fleet who lay upon their oars until near 12 o clock when we saw the prisoner taken on the Fore Castle where he after pulling his coat off and praying some time on his knees, had the rope put about his neck, and a gun being fired under him, he was run up the starboard Fore yard arm, I believe the pain he suffered was of very short duration, as [he] went off with such a swing as must have immediately broke his neck.*

Several days later, the *Perseus* was hauled into dock and when Palmer went on leave, Moore decided to ride over to Tavistock to visit the family of an old shipmate, William Bedford. Moore had stayed with the Bedfords several times before and knew he would be welcomed. He had intended to spend only one night away from the ship, but the following day dawned with black skies and heavy rain and he was easily persuaded to extend his visit. However, the decision troubled him:

I was wrong in this as the ship was fitting for sea and it was really improper for the lieutenant to be from the ship, but as I knew that the duty would go on equally as well under the eye of the Master, I remained at Tavistock. Next morning with a heavy heart I left my friends with whom I had been very happy and made sail for Dock with the poems of my favourite Gray[13] in my pocket.

On his return, he learned that Palmer had visited the ship in his absence and although the Captain had apparently expressed his displeasure at Moore's absence, nothing more was said on the matter.

Shortly after Christmas, Moore was intrigued to see the *Hebe*'s barge rowed into Plymouth, flying Prince William's standard. On the following day Moore was strolling down a street in Dock[14] when he encountered the Prince walking in the opposite direction in the company of an officer of the 7th Regiment;

> *As ... I did not expect that the Prince would recollect me I did not stop, but he did and cried out – by God that's Moore – I then turned about and pulled my hat off on which he left the Gentleman he was walking with and running towards me took me by the hand which he shook heartily and after talking some time I took my leave a good deal surprised at his affability and condescension.*

The following night Moore encountered the Prince once again at a very crowded assembly where the dancing continued enthusiastically until 2am. At the end of the night the Prince invited Moore and a number of officers to take supper with him;

> *We were very merry, the Prince seems to have a strong taste for what is called blackguarding and enjoyed some smutty jokes and loose songs which were sung with peculiar humour by an Irish officer of Artillery, he sung some songs himself but that was only I believe to encourage the company to throw off all stiffness and formality and not to charm us with his voice as singing is not his <u>fort</u>.* (The party continued until 7am, when the company broke up.)

Acquaintance with the Prince could not, however, provide Moore with any protection from his Captain's irritation. At the end of January 1786, the *Perseus* sailed again for the north-west coast and during the passage an ugly incident occurred which deeply affected Moore. One evening, the Gun Room officers were hurriedly summoned on deck to find an absolutely livid Captain Palmer waiting for them. The cause of his fury was, apparently, the funnel of the Gun Room chimney which, he claimed, was red hot and emitting clouds of highly dangerous sparks. Palmer immediately summoned all hands on deck and had the two Gun Room servants flogged with a dozen lashes each. Moore considered this grossly unfair, for it was the Quartermaster's responsibility to sweep the chimney on a regular basis. However, as Palmer had ordered the punishment in front of the whole crew, Moore knew that he could not question the Captain's authority. Neverthless, he admitted, his inability to speak up on behalf of the men *'has given me a great deal of pain'*. The incident also provided Moore with a valuable lesson. A commander, he realized, should never order a punishment in haste.

The incident put him in a sombre mood. He transcribed the whole of Thomas Gray's *Elegy on a Country Churchyard* into the journal, and then added:

> *'There is a tide in the affairs of men;*
> *Which taken at the flood, leads on to fortune,*
> *Omitted, all the voyage of their life*
> *Is bound in shallows, and in Miseries.*
> *On such a full sea are we now afloat,*
> *And we must take the current when it serves,*
> *Or lose our ventures.'*

> *If ever I command an English 28 gun Frigate; and should fall in with a French 36 gun frigate, I hope I shall then remember the above.*

2

From Liverpool to London
(March 1786 – May 1789)

By the middle of March 1786, the *Perseus* was back in Liverpool, where several of the crew, given leave on shore, fell victim to crimp.[15] By the time Moore learned of this, the men were on board a merchantman destined for Guinea and the West Indies, almost certainly on a slaver. He quickly rescued the men, to the apparent chagrin of the ship's merchant. On the brighter side though, Moore renewed his acquaintance with the Boates family and in particularly the three daughters

> *all agreeable, but the second is very handsome . . . I am half in love with her, but I do not believe she cares a halfpenny for me. It is said she is to be married to a young gentleman of fortune whose name is Pilson Price . . . an officer in the Inniskillen Dragoons.*

After a brief patrol in the Irish Sea, the *Perseus* returned to Liverpool where Palmer married the eldest daughter of a fellow naval Captain, Richard Smith. Moore, as Palmer's First Officer, was invited to the wedding ceremonies at Smith's house in Cheshire and he was delighted to find that the beautiful but tantalizingly unavailable Ellen Boates was also there. He may have had mixed feelings, however, when Palmer stated that he intended to take his new bride on a honeymoon cruise in the *Perseus* – even if two of the Boates girls were to accompany her. Moore certainly had misgivings about the proposal, and it does seem that Palmer planned the cruise as an event to impress his new wife and her guests. Such plans often backfire, and this one certainly did so.

On 9 July, the *Perseus* left Liverpool bound for the Isle of Man. On arrival at Douglas, Palmer sighted an Irish Revenue cutter flying what transpired to be the adopted pennant of the Irish Revenue Service.[16]

Not recognizing the pennant, Palmer ordered Moore to take a boarding party across and have the offending flag removed. Moore collected a party of seamen and rowed across to the cutter, where his request that the flag be removed was taken as an affront to the national pride of the cutter's crew. Moore took one look at the furious seamen of the cutter, gathering solidly behind the vessel's Master, and the small group of already inebriated men from the *Perseus*, and decided that withdrawal was the prudent option. The matter was not mentioned again. From Douglas the honeymoon cruise continued north to the west coast of Scotland, where Moore spent several days on shore visiting family friends, including the Hon. Keith Stuart and the Earl of Galloway. Hiring a horse, and packing a clean shirt in his pocket, he rode thirty miles to Barnbarrow, becoming deeply affected by the landscape:

> *I never saw a more wild and barren country than this part of Galloway, for miles all round I saw nothing but hills covered with heath and scattered rocks.'*

By August, the honeymoon trip had sailed south again, to Dublin, where Moore once again found himself in trouble with his Captain. Palmer had already become a little tetchy upon learning the identity of the people that Moore had been visiting on shore in Scotland.[17] At Dublin, however, while Palmer and his guests went ashore for several nights, Moore, the Marine Lieutenant and the ship's Purser went ashore to dine with a mutual friend, becoming heavily engaged with *'plenty of good claret'*. As the hours drifted by *'very jovially'*, the party decided that rather than return to the ship that night, they would find beds in a nearby hotel. Arriving back on board the following morning, Moore soon found himself summoned before Captain Palmer. The latter had learned of Moore's use of the ship's cutter and was furious, because he had only used the much less convenient pinnace. There was little that Moore could say to this, because the decision to use the pinnace had been Palmer's own. As Palmer's invective grew more heated he began to comment on Moore's performance as his Lieutenant. Stung, Moore retaliated by demanding to know if he was being accused of neglect of duty – a disciplinary offence – at which point Palmer calmed down somewhat, finishing with a derogatory remark about Moore's attention to duty.

On this rather unsatisfactory note, the discussion ended, but a sour atmosphere appears to have remained as the *Perseus* returned to Liverpool. There, after a few days on shore, Palmer again resolved on another trip with Mrs Palmer and the Boates girls on board. Moore was dismayed when Palmer ordered the ship to sea with unusual haste while the guests settled themselves in the Captain's cabin. Unfortunately, by the time that the *Perseus* cleared the Mersey, she was pitching uncomfortably in a north-westerly wind. Palmer decided to anchor and a deeply uncomfortable night was spent with the ship rolling heavily and the ladies suffering miserably from seasickness. Crestfallen, Palmer ordered a return to Liverpool. After a night recovering from this ordeal, the persistent Palmer announced that they should try once again for a cruise. Moore was aghast. He believed that there was now insufficient wind to give them headway against the tide. Sure enough, outside the harbour the *Perseus* began to drift until she grounded on the Cheshire side of the channel. The crew struggled to strike masts and yards but, in spite of their efforts, as the tide dropped, the ship lay over on its side at an alarming angle. To make matters worse, they were surrounded by quicksand and unable to shore up the ship. This uncomfortable position was endured until 9pm that night, when the ship again began to right herself. The pumps were started, and masts and yards swayed up. Then, following the light of a lamp placed in one of the ship's boats, they slowly groped their way into deeper water. Unfortunately, they quickly ran onto another shoal, and the ship heeled over with startling speed. The tide, however, was continuing to rise, and by midnight the *Perseus* was again afloat. With the pumps going continuously, she limped back into Liverpool.

The following morning, the powder was sent ashore for safety's sake, and the *Perseus* was hauled into St George's basin and lashed alongside one of the wharves.

Here the ship was stripped down for repair and here also Moore, left in charge of the ship, found himself embroiled in an incident with a discontented crew:

> We were obliged to hire a cook room to boil the ship's company's provisions in; when the Pease were boiled they were brought down in a tub, which circumstance displeased some of our lads so much (as they were ashamed to have their Pease brought down before the crowd of people which were constantly about the ship) that they called out to throw them over the wharf, which request was immediately complied with by the marine who was sentry.

As this was happening, Moore was below getting dressed. Hearing the commotion he hurried up on deck and instantly ordered the marine put in irons. The men intervened, trying to explain that the

10

marine was not to blame as he was only doing what they had demanded. The ship's Master, a man by the name of Fryer, fearing that the matter was about to get out of hand, took up a rope's end, and set about the spokesmen, driving the remainder from the deck. It was the first time that Moore had faced such a situation and he had doubts as to whether he had handled the situation well or even appropriately. He sympathized with the men's sensibilities, but also felt that the marine's action had been contrary to his role in helping to maintain order on board the ship. When Palmer returned on board, Moore reported the situation to him and advised that it would be best to let the people have their provisions

> raw as we could not dress it on board. He agreed . . . but at the same time I was happy to hear him express a determination to punish the marine for presuming to throw the Pease off the Wharf. Accordingly after he had been in irons three days he received eighteen lashes at the Gangway. For my own part I was under some apprehensions of a riot . . . however our sentry kept the crowd off and there was not a murmur.

Such actions would not be likely to endear Moore to a crew and he probably knew it. As his career developed, he was to develop a much stronger empathy with the men under his command, and simultaneously a loathing for the use of the cat.

The *Perseus* continued in dock until November 1786, during which time Moore was introduced to the young Dr James Currie, a specialist on the treatment of fevers, who shared his passion for the poetry of Robert Burns. The two became lifelong friends. In February, the *Perseus* was ordered back to Plymouth to be paid off and Moore, lacking employment, returned to his parents' house in London. England was still at peace and there seemed little prospect of a war to improve his career prospects. He decided to devote himself to the study of Latin but found

> . . . that my mind from want of exercise was very languid, and that it was very necessary for me to accustom it to exertion. Then, in September 1787, there was a confrontation with the French . . . on account of the Dutch troubles . . .[18]

and naval forces were mobilized.

At the first sign of a re-armament, Moore applied to the Admiralty for appointment to a frigate, and was made Second Lieutenant of the 28-gun *Dido*, commanded by Captain Charles Sandys. Days later he travelled down to Portsmouth in company with his new commander, only to find that the frigate lay in the harbour without her topgallant or top masts. Before she could be prepared for sea the diplomatic crisis passed and orders arrived from London for many of the ships to be decommissioned. The *Dido* herself was not included in this and it was rumoured instead that she was to be sent to the West Indies. Moore was despondent.

> *I have not made the most of my time, that is certain, for although I am but a very superficial scholar I am notwithstanding by no means a remarkable good seaman. My Father does not wish me to go out in the* Dido *(which it is thought is bound for Jamaica) as he has an idea that a war is not very distant in which case I should stand a very good chance for getting into a flag ship[19], if I am at home when war commences; whereas if I am unluckily abroad I am out of the way of my interest and unknown to the commanding officer on the station. I on the other hand am afraid of giving umbrage to the Admiralty by applying to be superceded. I therefore shall not apply for that purpose by letter but leave it to my friends to work under hand if they can so manage it.* [20]

However, Moore's friends do not seem to have pressed his case, for in December came news which deepened his gloom:

> *Yesterday we heard the accounts of 17 lieutenants being promoted to the rank of masters and commanders and about a dozen masters and commanders were promoted to the rank of post captains, besides a few midshipmen were made lieutenants. My father on hearing this wrote to me lamenting that he had not applied at first on the alarm of war to get me into a flag ship. I certainly must agree with him that it would have been the preferable situation.*

Moore's response to this was, typically, to blame himself for his own lack of promotion:

> *I see numbers of lieutenants who seem to me to possess more useful knowledge than myself, this plagues me and ought to spur me to exertion.*

But somehow, he found this difficult. Like many naval officers, Moore was drawn to the prospect of achieving fame through naval victory, yet paradoxically he also regarded fame as a hollow thing and as a result could put little enthusiasm into achieving it. Kicking his heels, he could only envy the call of other officers to an apparently meaningful activity.

21 December 1787:

The Vestal *frigate sailed this day, she is going on some secret mission, supposed to be bound to China. The Hon. Lieutenant Colonel Cathcart is in her. The ship is commanded by a fine young fellow Sir Richard Strachan.*

Moore's admiration for Strachan was to increase. While waiting for orders, Moore attempted to find entertainment by attending the Portsmouth theatre, but grumpily found the players

tearing Shakespeare's Richard the 3rd to pieces . . . an uncommon silly farce took place of the tragedy at which I found no entertainment.

A different diversion was offered when Moore received an invitation from the banker Robert Drummond, a family friend, to visit his house at Cadland, in Hampshire. Cadland, an estate with grounds which had been created by the landscape gardener Lancelot Brown a few years earlier, lay close to the northern shore of the Solent and Moore was permitted to take one of the ship's boats to land him nearby. There, Moore found himself dining with Sir William Howe, the General who had commanded an element of the British army during the American War and, perhaps more importantly, Philip Stephens, Secretary to the Admiralty. Moore took the opportunity to express to Stephens his concern about being sent out to Jamaica in the *Dido* and learned that his father had already raised the issue. Affably, the Secretary to the Admiralty reassured the anxious Lieutenant that he would manage the matter in some way that would not offend Lord Howe (First Lord of the Admiralty). The visit was therefore apparently useful, and Moore was much impressed by the charm of his host, whom he described as a *'sweet character'*. However, in somewhat Pooterish style, Moore was disappointed by the intellect of his companions:

I was not much edified by the conversation which entirely turned upon trifles. I believe I may say with certainty that from dinner being taken off the table, until tea, the subject never changed from dogs except once when I made an unsuccessful attempt to introduce ships. After supper a dispute arose on the different modes of shaving; I discovered from the infinite weight Mr Robert Drummond laid on every minute circumstance of this operation that he might be rendered the most wretched of mankind by any mistake of his valet.

Moore returned to the *Dido* to await the outcome of his discussion with Philip Stephens. Meanwhile there was much work to be done on the frigate and Moore took a close interest in the way that Sandys managed both ship and crew. Shortly before, the frigate had been supplied with spare fore and main topmasts, and Sandys reasoned that it would be better to try these out while the ship was at anchor, rather than find them unsuitable on a critical occasion at sea. There may have been another reason; Sandys may rather cleverly have thought of this exercise as something to occupy the hands and minds of a bored ship's company.

14 Jan 1788. We began at half past seven in the morning and we had the top gallant masts fidded before three o'clock in the afternoon and we gave them [the crew] their full time to breakfast and dinner at the usual hours. I think this was pretty well done with a new ship's company who do not as yet know one another. One thing gives me great pleasure, which is that we have had no punishment inflicted since the ship has been in commission, neither has there been any relaxation in the discipline. I must except two fellows who were guilty of an un-natural crime, and who were detected very soon after the ship was put in commission and were kept in irons upwards of a month and at last punished with a dozen lashes each, they were then put in one of the boats and an opportunity given them to desert which (in consequence of frequent broad hints that such a step would be highly satisfactory to the Officers) they accordingly did. This was a most disagreeable affair, there was no doubt of the fact as they themselves confessed, mutually accusing each other of enticing. Had I been Captain of the ship I would have turned them both ashore'.[21]

Whilst homosexual activity was not unknown in the navy, it was not common – or at least it was not frequently either reported or recorded. There was little privacy in a ship of war, so it would have been highly unlikely that anyone practicing what Moore termed *'unnatural acts'* would have been undetected for long. Furthermore, Sandys' treatment of those involved in homosexual activity is actually not uncommon. Many officers, who had the issue brought to their attention, were shocked, then embarrassed and uncertain what to do with the culprits. A dozen lashes was probably a rather lenient punishment at the time, and Sandys, like those other Commanders who had to deal with the issue, found the simplest solution was to get rid of the men involved – thus getting rid of the problem.

At the end of January 1788, Sandys received orders to fit out the frigate for foreign service. Moore decided to wait no longer. He wrote directly to Philip Stephens asking to be superseded and his request was

14

granted. Once again, Moore returned to the family house in Clifford Street and found himself kicking his heels and occupying himself partly in reading *'and a great deal in what may be called doing nothing'*. He also attended debates in the House of Commons where he followed political events and anything that related to the Royal Navy. Like other officers, he also paid close attention to the by-election for the constituency of Westminster, when Lord Townshend was returned, beating Admiral Lord Hood. This election aroused particular naval interest, for

> *During his election many battles were fought between the Irish Chairmen on the party of Lord John Townshend, and a body of sailors from Wapping on the side of Lord Hood. I believe the sailors were on every occasion beat.*

Moore followed the street battles with particular interest. The London chairmen, or carmen, were physically very strong, whereas the sailors were generally from merchant vessels in the river, and were unable to match the physical abilities of their opponents. Furthermore, the chairmen, knowing the London streets well, were able to ambush the groups of enthusiastic seamen at every turn. This was made especially easy, as the sailors were quickly recognizable from their mode of dress, whereas the chairmen tended to blend with the ordinary populace.

Moore's professional awareness also noted a couple of other factors: the sailors' ability to fight often suffered because they were quite often drunk; and, because they came from a wide number of different ships, they lacked coordination and were unknown to each other. He doubted if the carmen would have had the upper hand if they had encountered fifty sailors drawn from a single ship. This though, could not have effected the outcome of the election. Moore thought he knew the reason for that!

> *There is not a doubt of the very great influence of the houses of Cavendish, Russell, Bentinck and some others, those three are particularly important from the great property they possess in, and about London, as the Metropolis no doubt leads in a great degree the rest of the country. But the voice of the people in the great trading and manufacturing towns, such as the City of London, Manchester, Bristol, Glasgow etc, I think will be less influenced, from their dependence resting on that which no Nobleman can give or take away – I mean foreign trade. The shop keepers about Westminster were really afraid*

to vote any other way than one, for fear of losing the custom of those overgrown families.'

Shortly after, Moore learned that Captain Cornwallis had been ordered to take a squadron out to the East Indies and he hurriedly applied for an appointment, only to be told that he was too late; the squadron's Lieutenants had already been selected. Moore's only recourse was to appeal to his patron, the Duke of Hamilton, who arranged a meeting with the new First Lord of the Admiralty, the Earl of Chatham. The First Lord was affable but non-committal. Moore could only wait, for in truth he was only one of a vast number of unemployed naval officers whose prospects were bleak unless another war broke out. Still kicking his heels, his attention was caught by an advertisement in one of the London papers during the first week in November, inviting naval lieutenants to assemble at the Cannon Coffee House for

a meeting for the purpose of taking into consideration a plan for procuring an augmentation of their pay.

This seems to have been something of a radical step, and although Moore supported the cause he was wary. Nevertheless, curiosity drove him to walk past the Cannon Coffee House at the time the meeting was taking place and, being recognized, he was obliged to enter. The meeting did not allay his fears:

I own I do not wish to put myself forward amongst a small number, as I see no good purpose it could effect immediately to myself, on the contrary my name being brought forward as an agitator might very possibly hurt me, I therefore certainly had I known what was going on would not have entered the room; but after I was in, I must have appeared ill affected to their cause had I left the room. I therefore remained. Some resolutions were proposed, amongst others a form of memorial to the Earl of Chatham setting forth the case of the lieutenants, and soliciting his countenance to their petition.

It was also proposed that letters should be addressed to the lieutenants of ships lying at the various ports around the coast, inviting them all to attend a larger meeting in a month's time. This was generally endorsed and when it was proposed that the names of those present should be listed, '. . . *I did not hesitate to set my name down with the rest*'. However, he was alarmed that his involvement might be misconstrued and privately resolved not to attend the next meeting which, he reasoned, would do just as well in his absence.

The fact that the Lieutenants' plan is not mentioned again suggests that it did not get much further. In fact, Moore's attention was soon drawn elsewhere by the news that the King was ill. Moore, like many other naval personnel, was particularly interested because it was widely believed that the King's death would lead to the collapse of the government and such

> . . . a change would be fatal to my present views in the Navy, as my friends are for the most part attached to Mr Pitt.

Even when it became clear that the King's illness was mental rather than physiological, Moore felt his future threatened:

> I am much afraid that the King's illness will ruin the chance I had of going out in a Flag ship early in the Spring, as in case of a Regent, a total change of Administration seems inevitable.

As the crisis rolled on, Moore continued to fret about his career, fearing that he was beginning to get out of touch:

> I begin to think that I ought to be at sea again. A man ought to be knowing in his profession. Theory, in order to be useful, should be accompanied by Practice . . . A Sea officer should not be long out of employment, or he is apt to acquire rust.

Yet at the same time he was afraid of weaknesses in his own character which could retard his professional advance:

> I am very apt to be diffident of my own abilities, and have always a fear of not acquitting myself well, it is a melancholy thing that this fear does not spur me on to the greatest exertion; but indolence is the bane of many a man possessed of a tolerable share of good qualities.

Then, on 10 February, came news that he had been hoping for; he was appointed Second Lieutenant of the 50-gun *Adamant*, which was currently fitting out at Sheerness. It took him several weeks to assemble all of the clothing and equipment that he needed, but on 2 March he travelled down to Chatham and dined with the ship's Third Lieutenant, William Hope, who was to become a firm friend. The following day the two Lieutenants took a boat down river to join the ship. Sheerness was not a popular port, as many officers were to comment over the following years. Its facilities were poor and the town was regarded as unhealthy. Moore found it depressing and referred to it as *'this wretched place'*. The *Adamant* was soon joined by her new commander, Captain Knox, and men were subsequently arriving to form the crew. But there was nothing for them to do and Moore soon found himself getting homesick, even though he was not far from home.

Then, on 14 March, came devastating news. Admiral Sir Charles Douglas, his patron and imminent commanding officer, had died suddenly of '*apoplexy*'[22] in Edinburgh. Moore was stunned:

> *I never met a sea officer who gave me the idea of being possessed of half his science; and independent of the loss I sustain in being deprived of such a friend, I believe I should, by sailing with him, have acquired much useful knowledge in my profession which now I am not so likely to obtain. His death is certainly a National calamity.*

The problem was that whoever replaced Douglas would probably demand his own choice of Flag Captain and Lieutenants – or at least their own First Lieutenant. He could only wait and see what happened. Meanwhile he was having to sleep in an uncomfortable cabin in the sheer hulk and he was desperate for a break. When Grosvenor, the ship's First Lieutenant, suddenly arrived one evening to relieve him, Moore set off immediately for London. A longboat from the *Scipio* was leaving Sheerness for Chatham that night and, requesting a ride, Moore landed at Chatham at one o'clock in the morning. It being a fine spring night, Moore decided that rather than try to find accommodation at this late hour, he would set off for London – on foot! It was a long and not altogether easy walk, especially as parts of the road had been the haunt of highwaymen and were infamous for footpads.

> *I was rather afraid for the first four hours as the road between Chatham and London, by Gravesend, is sometimes dangerous, however I walked unmolested to London, where I arrived at ten in the morning . . .*

an extraordinary feat for even a young naval officer.

Eight days later, Moore returned to Sheerness by boat. His stay in London, however, had been very useful, for at a ball at the Pantheon, given by White's Club, Moore had met Lord Chatham, First Lord of the Admiralty. Chatham informed him that Admiral Sir Richard Hughes was appointed to replace Douglas but that Moore need not worry because he would particularly recommend the Lieutenant to the newly appointed Admiral. However, Moore still had qualms.

> *I was at that time rather uneasy, as I knew that Sir Richard Hughes had a son whom he wished to have promoted from the situation of a*

midshipman to a lieutenancy in the Adamant: *and I was under some apprehension, that, he might stand between me and the only chance I at present have of promotion. My father had an opportunity of speaking to Lord Chatham, soon after I came to Town: his Lordship assured him that I should remain in exactly the same situation as if Sir Charles had lived, and that I was certainly the second on the station for promotion.*

Moore's fears were justified, but not in the way that he had anticipated. Sir Richard Hughes' choice for First Lieutenant of the *Adamant* was the Hon. Henry Curzon, son of Lord Scarsdale. Moore was flabbergasted because Curzon was junior to him on the Lieutenants List. Dr Moore was sent hurriedly to the Admiralty to seek an explanation. The Admiral, it was discovered, had assured the First Lord that Moore was junior to Curzon. In fact there was a Lieutenant Moore who was lower on the list, but it was not Graham Moore. Chatham was deeply embarrassed and immediately offered to rescind Curzon's appointment. However, at this stage the influence of a very pragmatic mind asserted itself. Henry Curzon was known to the Moore family and well liked, added to which he was a very fine officer. Having his appointment revoked would benefit nobody and could make life difficult for Graham who would be serving on Sir Richard Hughes' flagship. Agreeing to let the appointment stand would, on the other hand, implicitly put the First Lord in Moore's debt – albeit in a very modest way. With this resolution, Moore's position on the *Adamant* was also secured, and on the last day of May 1789, she slipped from her moorings and set sail for Nova Scotia.

3

HMS *Adamant* and Nova Scotia
(May 1789 – April 1791)

Contrary winds in the English Channel extended HMS *Adamant*'s passage across the North Atlantic, but at least the additional time enabled Moore to make an initial assessment of Captain Knox (who had been retained by the Admiral). Moore was pleased to find the *Adamant* was a happy ship:

> It is an extremely agreeable thing to me to find that Captain Knox is not a Flogger, there has been only two men punished since the ship has been put in commission, one for theft, the other for insolence to his Officer. Neither of these men could reasonably [have] been let off, from the nature of their offences.

He also began to wonder whether he himself would be the sort of commanding officer that seamen were attracted to:

> If I become a Captain in the course of a few years I firmly believe that I am of a character to gain both esteem and attachment, I am also inclined to think that the faults which my Father has often reproached me with in my manner will leave me on my promotion.

Those 'faults' he identified as a tendency towards the frivolous and a lack of serious application to his profession. In fact it is arguable that, his very awareness of these 'faults' substantially negated them anyway.

On the 31 July, having crossed the Newfoundland Banks, where the crew supplemented their diets with freshly caught cod, the *Adamant* arrived at Halifax, the headquarters of the Nova Scotia station. Moore, who always took a lively interest in his surroundings, noted in his journal:

The Trade of Halifax consists entirely of salt fish and whale oil. The fish are chiefly Cod, Herring and Mackerel; the Whale Oil is the produce of the Southern fishery which I learn is by far the most lucrative branch, and is gaining ground here considerably, it is carried on in vessels of various denominations, and bulk according to the finances of the adventurer to whom they belong. These vessels commonly touch at the Cape de Verde Islands for live stock; they then proceed to the southward towards the coast of Brazil where they meet the Spermaceti whales many of which are worth five hundred pounds. The crews of these vessels are interested in the success of the voyage as they all go on shares; some ships which arrived lately were so successful on their last voyage, that the foremast men shared fifty pounds each. They are seldom out longer than eleven months.

In addition to the *Adamant*, Admiral Hughes' squadron consisted of the frigates *Penelope* and *Thisbe*, and the sloop-of-war *Brisk* and it was soon joined by Moore's old ship, the *Dido*. With the Admiral's arrival, several urgent items of business needed to be sorted out, including a court martial which affected Moore deeply. A seaman had been charged with striking one of his ship's Midshipmen. The offence of striking a senior officer attracted the death penalty under Article 23 of the Articles of War and, as the Court duly found that the seaman *had* struck the Midshipman, the sentence was carried out. However, the circumstances had not been straightforward. The Midshipman had been in one of the ship's boats, overseeing the embarkation of a shore party. The seaman involved in the incident had, probably among others, returned to the boat drunk. Whether by accident or design – and Moore implies it was an accident – the Midshipman struck the seaman as the latter was getting into the boat. The seaman reacted instantly and returned the blow, probably without being fully aware of who he was hitting. The act was witnessed and there was no denying it. With hindsight, it is questionable whether the Midshipman should have brought or supported a charge under the circumstances. However, the matter was referred to a court martial, and although the seaman was able to call on all of his officers to give him a good character, the letter of the Articles had to be followed. Moore was not alone in regretting the inflexibility of courts martial and, like other officers, he realized that if the matter had been dealt with speedily on board a ship at sea, the accused would probably have got away with a couple of dozen lashes. It was a waste of a good seaman and, as in this case, probably unjust, but

Moore knew that his views on this could cause him difficulties in the future:

I think if ever I become a captain, I shall have many a long dispute as member of a Court Martial

Before long there was other news to cause disquiet. On 19 September a Packet arrived from England, and with it came a parcel of letters, newspapers and packages from friends and family;

By the Packet we have the news of the surprising turn affairs have taken in France. I have not a doubt that the ancient form of government of that country is now totally overturned since the standing army, the great support of despotism, have shewed themselves on the side of the people. I think the King in throwing himself into the arms of the national assembly has probably acted the most prudent part, though I cannot believe that it will have any effect in stopping them from forming a free government . . . The conversation here has turned a good deal on the idea that Great Britain may be a sufferer by the French becoming a free people: for my part I cannot see the matter in that light, I believe that let them be ever so free we shall probably be able to hold our own against them. There may be great advantages in a free constitution but I scarcely think that it is better or so well calculated for the purposes of war as an arbitrary Monarchy.

Little did Moore realize the extent to which his thoughts were to be put to the test.

For the officers in Halifax, the events in Europe seemed disturbing but distant. Ships from the squadron were routinely sent out on anti-smuggling patrol, seizing ships when their papers revealed irregularities in clearing out from the Custom House. There were also more enjoyable expeditions – though, as seemed to happen rather often – these sometimes ended badly. A week after the news arrived from France, for example, Moore decided to take a trip to Laurence Town, a settlement several miles along the coast to the north of Halifax. He was accompanied, on this occasion, by the Captain and Lieutenant of Marines and two servants. While Moore was keen to see the sights and enjoy a country he had never visited before, the marine officers set out loaded with fowling pieces and a fishing rod, intent on a different object. On their return journey they arrived at the shore opposite Halifax to find that the boat, which they had earlier arranged should meet them, was nowhere to be seen. Rather impatiently the officers decided that, as wind and tide were favourable, they would requisition a small boat drawn up nearby and row themselves back to Halifax, generously leaving the servants to follow as and when they could. Moore and the marine Lieutenant took up the oars, whilst the Captain of Marines, who was rather corpulent, sat in the stern steering with a paddle. Unfortunately,

> . . . we found he did more hurt than good as the least motion endangered the oversetting of so small a boat which I am convinced was never intended to carry three men; the water came in so fast from the extraordinary weight of the Captain of Marines in the stern, that I was under the necessity of quitting my oar repeatedly in order to bale the water out with my hat, indeed the water came in so fast at one time that we found it necessary to push for a small island at some distance to discharge the water clear out of her and begin on a fresh score. I took this opportunity of taking off my coat and unburthening myself of two or three pounds of shot, to be ready in case of oversetting. I was then perfectly easy with regard to my own safety as I knew I could swim ashore, but the Captain of Marines could not swim at all, and the Lieutenant was very indifferent at that work; with a good deal of ado we at last reached Coal Harbour after an hour and a half struggling, another larger boat soon brought over the two servants. During our passage I found the boat at one time aground on a sand bank, on this occasion telling the other two of it with a degree of fretting – By Christ, says the Captain (who is an honest Irishman) I am glad to hear of it, while she remains so, there is no fear.

Despite his earlier satisfaction with Captain Knox, Moore soon found himself changing his mind:

> October 5th. There has been of late a good deal of flogging; the men have deserved it, but on this occasion I must remark that there has been an essential fault in the discipline; so many faults were at our first setting out looked over in the hope that they would not be repeated. That a general relaxation by degrees took place, the hope of impunity rendering the seamen less cautious of offending; and now it requires more severity to drive them out of their acquired habits, than would have been necessary to keep them at the beginning in any mode of discipline which might have been at first adopted. People who act without system have always reason to repent it. Set out on a Plan. Two Captains both averse to flogging, will find very different effects from the same quantity of necessary punishment by the one administering it as it becomes expedient at the beginning, and the other by putting it off until

23

dire necessity obliges him to drive his men from habits which his lenity had encouraged. But the fact is that the Officer who begins very strict will prevent the necessity of punishment after the first month, the men knowing the certain consequence will be careful of infringing upon the adopted regulations. It has an excellent effect to have it in your power to relax a little; but to find it necessary to taughten the cords of discipline after a relaxation has a much worse effect than the same degree of strictness at first.

It was a lesson which Moore learned well. He loathed the use of the cat, but he was also well aware of the consequences of the loss of order on board a ship. It was better, he realized, for a commander never to lose control, never to let order slip in the first place. It was a crucial element in the method of command.

As the year began to draw towards its close, the ships of the squadron began to prepare themselves for the Nova Scotia winter. It was not expected that ships would be put at risk by operating during the winter months; instead they were made snug in harbour, with upper masts and all their yards lowered onto the decks. By the middle of December, Moore was confident that the winter could be little worse than some he had experienced in England. But there were days when a biting wind called 'The Barber' scythed across the harbour. He described it as a

. . . hoar frost blown along by a strong NW wind; this Barber has on the water the appearance of a vapour and on these two days was often higher than our own mast heads; nothing that I ever felt can equal the bitter sharpness of it.

Like all those trapped in some form of confinement the men in the ships or garrison at Halifax sought ways of entertaining themselves to keep up morale. A regular routine of theatrical performances was established by the army officers on the station, assisted by the Midshipmen of the squadron. With mixed feelings, Moore recorded in his journal that *'they play wretchedly'*; but the money raised from the performances was charitably donated to assist the poorer inhabitants of the colony. By February the water in the harbour had frozen over and several adventurous souls went out walking upon it, until an officer of the 20th Regiment fell through into the freezing waters. Crowds of people gathered but were unable to approach the struggling man because of the disintegrating ice that surrounded him. A boat from the *Penelope* frigate was lowered, but could not break through the ice to get close enough. Eventually, a courageous seaman tied a rope around his own waist, and sliding forward upon two oars, crawled towards the desperately struggling officer. Tragically, just before the sailor reached him, the officer became too weak to hold on, and slipped out of sight and reach.

Perhaps it was the effect of the Nova Scotia winter, but as the dark months continued, Moore became increasingly despondent. There were growing rumours about an imminent European war, and he was in Nova Scotia, far from the centre of any possible activity. Furthermore, he was beginning to feel that neither Captain Knox nor Admiral Hughes were officers of sufficient distinction to be able to forward his career prospects. Ironically, his gloom was dispelled somewhat in May, when Captain Sandys of the *Dido* fell ill and formally asked to be superseded. This excited considerable speculation in the squadron, because it might result in a general promotion on the station. After some thought, Hughes appointed Buller, the commander of the sloop *Brisk* to temporary command of the *Dido*, and Curzon to temporary command of the *Brisk*. The letters of recommendation had just been dispatched to the Admiralty when Moore, Curzon and their fellow officers realized that as he was already a Commander, Buller would most likely be promoted soon anyway. If the Admiral waited, two of the officers on the station might benefit from promotion to Post Captain instead of one, and everyone else would advance two ranks. Curzon and Moore were deputed to raise the matter with Hughes who, happily, saw the logic of the case. Unfortunately, the letters had already been dispatched in the Packet for England and, even though Curzon took a boat and caught up with the vessel, a frantic lamplit search of the hold failed to locate the mail. There was nothing that could be done about it.

In due course the promotions went ahead as predicted. Moore had to be satisfied with promotion to First Lieutenant of the *Adamant*. There is no indication that he felt bitter about Curzon's promotion which, rightly, should have been his. Nevertheless, he was becoming increasingly disenchanted with his senior officers. The problems began when Hughes decided to take the squadron on a cruise around Cape Breton passing through the narrow Gut of Canso. Moore, who was increasingly proving his ability in ship handling, had conned the ship through this passage before. But on this occasion, the Admiral decided that it was more appropriate for the Master to take this responsibility. Moore was furious. The Admiral, Moore confided to the privacy of his journal, '. . . *is made up of trifles, and G_d knows I am tired of him'*. There had been another example of Hughes' concern with trifles a few days earlier. He had complained publicly that only two seamen had been detailed to assist him up the side of the ship when he came on board. So on the next occasion he boarded the ship, Lieutenant William Hope, the Second Lieutenant, rather mischievously detailed six sidesmen to assist him, to Moore's great delight. However, the relationship between Moore and his senior officers continued to decline, and a series of events soon exacerbated the situation. Returning to Halifax, the Admiral decided to send gangs of seamen ashore to dig for coal for the ship's galley. In the process of bringing this on board, some forty chaldron of the coal was diverted for use in the Admiral's own house on shore. At the same time, Captain Knox requisitioned over a dozen chaldron of coals for the use of '. . . *an old lady of easy principles to whom he devotes his time at Halifax'*. Moore was outraged to find that in the end, none of the coal was delivered to the Purser for distribution on board the *Adamant*. Furthermore, the Admiral decided that the seamen employed in this task should be rewarded with extra grog, which Moore knew could only lead to disciplinary problems. He went to the Captain and tried to persuade him that the men would be better rewarded with new clothing instead of spirits – but Knox refused to listen. Moore became increasingly frustrated by the senior officers' attitude, and by the middle of June he was writing,

> *I am heartily tired of doing the duty of first lieutenant; I think nothing of the ship's duty, but there are so many private jobs to attend to that I really am sick of the business.*

There was soon news to distract him from the behaviour of his seniors, for the officers of the fleet were 'overjoyed' to hear of a dispute between England and Spain. Letters arrived from England, including one from General John Moore, reporting on the details of the Nootka Sound crisis (popularly known as the Spanish Armament[23]). A fleet was being prepared for hostilities and rumours spread that there would be a general promotion to find officers for this. Everyone was anxious to know who had benefited. Moore decided that there was little chance directly for himself, but he fully expected that Curzon would be promoted. The thought prompted Moore to think again about his current position as First Lieutenant and his future prospects:

26

I believe if I have the charge of carrying on the duty in this ship long I shall run some risk of becoming peevish, for there are so many little petty objects independent of the ship's duty to attend to that I cannot help fretting. O that I were a Captain.

And then days later he inserted into his journal:

I certainly have a strong desire to distinguish myself in war, and if I did not believe I possessed the energy of soul to carry me through the terrours of battle, I should be wretched, for my desires do not point at riches, but to the eminence in life acquired by martial exploits; and, having the reputation of skill and courage, will not at all gratify me, unless I shall have earned it by many conflicts. In short I wish not only to be a great naval commander in the public esteem, but in my own: both of which cannot, however one may, exist, without fighting for it.

It was not long before Moore became aware of another scandal, and one which good officers knew could undermine both crew morale and order. It began when Moore received a complaint from the crew of the *Adamant* that they were being issued with rotten bread. He supported their complaint and referred the matter to Captain Knox who agreed to a formal Survey of the bread. In accordance with common practice, the Masters of the ships in the squadron were summoned to inspect the bread, which they duly condemned as unsuitable. The complaint was then referred back to the victuallers who had been contracted to supply it to the squadron. They, in turn, appealed directly to Admiral Hughes by sending him a sample of their bread, claiming it was of exactly the same quality as that issued to the ships. The Admiral sent the new sample on board the *Adamant* with a request that it be compared with the bread already issued. At this point Moore dug in his heels and pointed out that the supply of bread had already been formally condemned by a survey of the Masters of the squadron. Comparing the condemned bread with the sample would be pointless, as he could not go back on a formal condemnation. Admiral Hughes responded angrily and decided to circumvent Moore by ordering the Masters to reassemble to inspect the new sample. Unable to refuse this direct order, the Masters inspected the sample only to find, as Moore had suspected, that the sample provided to the Admiral was of better quality than that issued to the ships. However, the Masters also took the opportunity to point out that even the newly provided sample was of very poor quality. Thwarted, the Admiral ordered the contractors to replace the

27

condemned bread. However, the replacement too was surveyed and condemned as substandard.

At this point the Admiral lost his patience completely. He issued a direct order that the new bread be accepted on board the ships as it was exactly the same as the sample accepted by the Victualling Office, on the basis of which the contract to the victuallers had been issued. There was little that the junior officers could do, except grumble. Moore was furious, and firmly believed that the Admiral could get into a *'cursed scrape'* for such irregular conduct. Furthermore, he raged

> When Government pay the price for good provisions the Contractor ought not to be suffered to supply indifferent, and put the difference in his pocket.

It was a common complaint and one which marked a changing attitude towards the old way of doing things – an attitude which was to become more important in a few years' time. In wartime, officers, and frigate commanders in particular, had enough problems to deal with, without the men under their command being supplied with substandard provisions. Despite his perpetual admissions of indolence towards his professional duties, Moore was an officer who cared both about the men under his command and the ability and efficiency of the ship on which he served or commanded.

The selfish interests of both the Admiral and Captain Knox were evidently beginning to have an effect on the *Adamant* and its crew. Moore found that he was unable to exercise the crew at sail handling and setting because so many of them were being constantly sent on shore to undertake work at the houses occupied by the Admiral or Captain Knox. The Admiral's own bargemen were frequently sent off from the ship at 6am on some comparatively menial business which prevented their return until after sunset, and their absence from the ship meant that they often missed out on meals. Furthermore, Moore was well aware that skilled seamen were discontented with the sort of work they were being given, feeling that it was demeaning. As First Lieutenant he was concerned about the simmering unhappiness that was being created: *'I am continually on the fret about these things which I cannot remedy'*.

The row over the supply of rotten bread soon resurfaced. It was discovered that the Admiral had written to the Victualling Board in London complaining that the Masters were guilty of some form of partiality in condemning the locally-supplied bread. He had dispatched this complaint with a sample of bread which the local vict-uallers had provided specifically for this purpose. The Masters immediately dispatched their own letter to the Victualling Board, accompanied by some of the real bread which they had surveyed and condemned. While this was going on, Collins, the Master of the *Adamant*, was presented with a receipt from the contractor and asked to sign it to certify that the ship had now been supplied with bread of a satisfactory standard. Without the signature, the victualler could not be paid and Moore realized that the Admiral was taking an unusual interest in trying to get the payment made; *'I shall enjoy a piece of such pimping iniquity being properly exposed'*. To his eternal credit, the Master of the *Adamant* refused to sign, and various attempts were made to intimidate him. Shortly before, Collins had submitted a request to be transferred to the *Dido* and the Admiral's Secretary now responded that his request could only be considered if he signed the outstanding receipt. The *Adamant*'s Master retorted that if that were the case he would happily stay where he was. He was then summoned on shore to the Admiral's office, where he was confronted by the Admiral himself, his Secretary, Purser and the contractor. To their demand that he sign the receipt there and then, Collins responded that he would sign to the amount of bread deliv-ered but not the quality, which in his opinion was not composed of wheat flour, but some unidentified mixture of meals. The Admiral flew into a violent rage, threatening to complain to the Navy Office about Collins personally. Collins was unmoved, so the Admiral tried a different approach. He pointed out that Captain Knox had already signed the document, so by withholding his signature, Collins was disputing his commanding officer's judgement. Collins still refused to concede. Why, the Admiral wanted to know next, would Collins not sign a document which would have no effect on his own pocket? Moore noted with some satisfaction the Master's response that

> . . . *although it might not hurt his pocket it would materially affect his conscience.*

Moore summed up the incident:

> *He was treated excessively ill . . . he stuck to his text and retired leaving the Admiral foaming with rage.*

In the end the Admiral altered all of the relevant documentation to state that he had ordered the bread to be taken on board, even though it had already been condemned by survey. With this proviso, Collins was fully prepared to sign the receipt, although the Admiral was left frustrated and furious. There was a postscript to this incident which Moore recorded with glee: a month later the Admiral received a letter from the Commissioners of the Victualling Office in London stating that the bread issued to the ships was *'by no means fit for the service'* and that the sample supplied by Admiral Hughes *'seemed to have been baked for the purpose of sending to them'*. The Commissioners had, in turn, referred the whole matter to their Lordships at the Admiralty. Whether Hughes was alarmed or irritated by this news cannot now be known. It was of little importance to him, for by the same Packet he received news of his promotion to Vice Admiral of the Blue.

Moore too soon found himself the butt of the Admiral's anger, albeit indirectly. As the year slid towards the end of November, the weather again turned very sharp. Moore, observing the crew of the *Adamant* at their tasks, became increasingly concerned that the men were in danger of getting frostbite by working up on the yards while they were in harbour. When the weather turned cold it was normal practice to strike upper masts and yards and cover the upper works of the ship with some form of roof or 'house' which took no more than half an hour to dismantle. Moore therefore found himself anxiously waiting for the general order from the Admiral to prepare the ship for winter. Finally, he decided to put a written request to Captain Knox seeking permission to bed the ship down and Knox gave his approval, also in writing. The masts and yards were struck the same day, probably by a delighted crew. That same evening, Moore received a brisk letter from the Captain claiming that he had exceeded the orders, leading Moore to believe that Knox had probably been berated in turn by the Admiral for pre-empting his orders. However, he was unmoved because his own growing anger exceeded that of his seniors, for this was not the only indication of the Captain's lack of care for his crew; the fresh bread ordered by the Commissioners had still not been issued.

The arrival of the first Packet of 1791 brought dismaying news. With no prospect of war with Spain, fleets were being disbanded and ships laid up. Moore's depression was deepened and his health collapsed. Over the Christmas period he had developed a complaint from which he was to suffer intermittently all his life – *'This cursed rheumatism'*. He also contracted an inflammation of the eyes that prevented him undertaking any strenuous activity and often confined him to his cabin. Then, quite suddenly and unexpectedly, the situation changed. Another Packet arrived bringing news that the First

Lieutenants of all flagships in commission, which included Moore, had been promoted to Master & Commander. Even before he received official confirmation from the Admiralty, he received letters of congratulation from friends and family at home. His friend William Hope was confirmed as the new First Lieutenant of the *Adamant*, and Moore joyfully packed his belongings to be ready to leave on the next available Packet, for promotion also meant that he had to leave the ship. There was happiness all round as the Packet set off on her return journey, which turned out to be an agreeable passage:

We are very sociable, laugh a great deal, eat more, and drink our allowance.

Also, it seemed that his eye condition was beginning to improve.

I was a good deal alarmed by the condition my eyes were in, they are now, however, infinitely better but not yet as I would have them.

4

Commander of the *Orestes*
(April 1791 – May 1792)

Moore arrived at Falmouth on 28 April and went ashore the same evening. His heavy luggage was sent on board a London-bound brig while he travelled overland arriving in London on 2 May. To his surprise, the riverside communities of the capital were swarming with press gangs. A fleet was being assembled to send into the Baltic to persuade the Empress of Russia to make peace with the Turks. As soon as he was able, Moore sought an interview with Lord Chatham at the Admiralty – where he was received *'with great civility'* – and asked for the command of a fireship if war broke out. He thought that he had little right to expect more than this, especially as he knew none of the active admirals well enough to apply for their support.

With no professional occupation, Moore spent a week with his friend Charles Locke at his family's estate in Surrey.[24] He thought Locke's father, William

the most amiable and enlightened person I have ever known. I left his house with great regret, and with an intention of repeating my visit [at] *the first opportunity.*

Shortly after, Charles joined Moore in London and they went to see an exhibition by the painter Fuseli. Locke had been a pupil of Fuseli and it was almost certainly through Locke that Moore became acquainted with the artist. Moore was totally captivated by his work. He thought him

the most sublime genius . . . his ideas are vast and terrible, and whether his execution is unequalled by the other Artists or not, is more than I can determine, but he certainly fills the beholder with grander ideas than

the works of any painter alive or dead whose works are extant . . .
I know of few men who are better fitted to comment on the genius of
Shakespeare, and none who are so worthy to paint his scenes . . . Fuseli
I am sure will be admired when he is once fairly out of the world; at
present he is certainly undervalued to a degree that disgraces the age.

Moore also followed political debates closely, although he was not
particularly interested in party politics;

I am accused by my nearest and dearest friends of being an Aristocrate,
because their arguments have not convinced me that the destruction of
Nobility is an event to be wished in our own country. The fact is that
I am neither an Aristocrate nor a Democrate, but a man who has no
great opinion of human foresight and who detesting demagogues and
not feeling any humiliation at seeing a Duke strut past him or (what he
thinks worse) a Nabob; fears changes, and the dominion of the many
headed monster. I think there is that in the British Constitution which
enables it to correct evils and abuses when they come to press and I care
not for the names of things if their essences are good. I do not care a
fig for the absurdity that may exist in the abstract idea of an hereditary
Judge, so long as I find that justice is well administered.

Moore was able to exercise his romanticism much more when he and
his father travelled to Wales, paying a visit to Golden Grove, the seat
of a Mr Vaughan, near Llandeilo in Carmarthenshire. Golden Grove
sits on the opposite side of the Vale of Towey to Newton House[25] with
its mediaeval castle and spectacular landscape. They dined there with
Lady Dinefwr and took an evening walk through the Capability
Brown landscape to the romantic hilltop ruins of Dinefwr Castle.
Moore found it quite beautiful:

The prospect continually varying as you traverse this favourite hill
presents beauties of different kinds; at one time you catch a glimpse of
the rivers glistening through the oak branches, then you see the bare
mountains contrasted with hills covered with verdure and wood and
cultivated to the very summits, presently descending a slope you are
arrested by the awful towers of a Gothic castle the walls of which, time
has covered with ivy, and the interior part, with trees and wild shrub-
bery. I entered this venerable fortress, which is older than any records
of the country, and from its only entire tower looked along the vale of
Towy to the west which was reddened by the sun having just dipped
below the mountains.

Unfortunately, his romantic trance was rudely interrupted by what he described as his 'mundane' companions:

> *The rest of the company lamented the lateness of the evening having obscured the prospect, but in the frame of mind I was in what then presented itself was more grateful to my soul than what day's garish eye could look upon . . . I was looking for one of Fuseli's terrible warriors on the battlements, but I saw what Ossian calls little men, the sons of the feeble.'*[26]

Moore was fascinated by the Gothic ruins that abounded in the area and visited a number of castles, including the dramatic Carrick Cennon which he described as *'a very beautiful ruin'*; and another near Kidwelly which, almost complete, was *'more perfect'*. Clearly reflecting work that he had read on the *'Sublime'*, he noted in his journal that a clear sky was unsuitable for appreciating the picturesque. There must be clouds and wind to create *'irregularity'*. Walking on his own, he climbed to the castle on Dryslwyn Hill in the middle of the Vale of Towey, stopping frequently to admire the different prospects that the climb presented to him but, disappointingly, *'the sublime was kept back until mounting the ruined wall my prospect was terminated by the black mountains'*.

In October, Moore arrived back in London, with a yearning to be back at sea. He had received envious news from his friend William Hope, who was still on the Nova Scotia station. Linzee, the Captain of the frigate *Penelope*, had resigned his command following accusations of tyranny and oppression against the ship's surgeon. By a stroke of good fortune, Hope had been next in line for promotion and was now the Captain of the *Penelope* in Linzee's place. Moore wished Hope well, but could not help realizing that the promotion should have been his.

By January 1792, after eight months without employment, Moore was again debating whether to request an interview at the Admiralty, but could not choose which station would be the most advantageous and decided it would be best to *'lie upon my oars for a while'*. It was as well he did, for his romantic interests took a turn for the better. Attending a ball in Dorking, Moore's attention was caught by two pretty young women who turned out to be the daughters of a rich London merchant, Joseph Dennison. A short while later, he and his friend Charles Locke (who he described warmly as *'exceedingly eccentric'*) paid a visit to Denbies, the Dennison's country estate, which lay only a few miles from Locke's. There, in the grounds, the two young men became involved in a flirtatious game of hide-and-seek, with

Maria and Elizabeth Dennison apparently attempting to avoid them, but somehow contriving to bump into them at every turn. Eventually, Locke decided they should present themselves at the house and ask after their tormentors. On announcing themselves at the front door of the house, Moore and Locke were aware of feet running on the stairs in excitement, but, when the two young ladies obeyed the summons to present themselves, they teasingly pretended never to have seen the two young men before. The elder of the two was twenty years of age and to Moore *'the most exquisite creature I have ever seen'*; the younger sister was eighteen.

Another of Moore's close acquaintances at this time was Captain Edward Riou, a naval officer who had achieved great acclaim by bringing his severely damaged frigate, the *Guardian*, back to Cape Town after it had run into an iceberg en route to Australia loaded with convicts. Riou had remained on board the ship with the convicts and a small number of the crew and, after an extremely arduous voyage, brought everyone to safety. It was Riou who was later credited with establishing the principle that it was the Captain's responsibility to either remain with the ship – or be the last to leave. Riou was at times a serious and melancholic character, and it is easy to understand how Moore would have been drawn to him. Together they went to see

> *Lawrence the excellent Portrait Painter, he was so struck with Riou's manly countenance that he earnestly requested him to allow him to make a Portrait of him. Riou thanked him but politely excused himself. This is a man of whose acquaintance I am proud, I always thought him a superior man even before he distinguished himself in the* Guardian. *He is certainly very different from the common rout.*[27]

Then, at the end of January, Moore was unexpectedly summoned to the Admiralty for an interview with the First Lord. Chatham explained that Captain Harry Burrard[28] of the *Orestes*, who was also a Member of Parliament, was urgently required in the House (where the government needed his vote). Moore could, therefore, have temporary command of his ship on smuggling patrol until a better position became available. Moore leapt at the chance and hurried down to Portsmouth to join his new command. The *Orestes* was an unusual looking brig-sloop with a high sweeping stern. She had been built by the Dutch as a privateer and had been captured by the Royal Navy in 1781. She carried 18 nine-pounder guns and a crew of 120 men. Moore recorded his immediate impression:

She is the finest vessel of the kind I ever saw mount eighteen nine pounders and is pierced for 24. Sir Harry Burrard thinks that the nines strain her too much, and has applied for sixes. I shall sail as soon as my things arrive from London.

Moore's baggage arrived on board on 4 February and he sailed immediately into a foggy English Channel to patrol along the Dorset coast where smuggling was rife. Almost immediately they gave chase to a suspicious vessel, and although they lost her in the fog, Moore was pleased with the performance of both ship and crew: *'I find the brig works exceedingly well, and the People seem orderly and willing'*. His assessment was confirmed shortly after when they were caught by a hard gale whilst criss-crossing the Channel:

Having set the trysail, main staysail, and reefed fore sail, we stood over to the English coast; and the wind being at NE b E with a very high sea, the brig went as close as she could lay, under that low sail six knots and a half, and seven knots, sending the sea from her bows over the taffrail, she went right through the sea, in a manner I never saw any vessel do before.

His contentedness was soon tested by a storm that raged for days, driving them further and further to the west. From the Channel Islands they attempted to make Torbay or Portland where Moore wanted to give his crew time to rest. He was well aware that they were

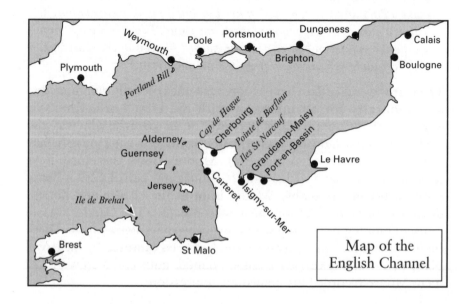

Map of the English Channel

badly in need of sleep and warm food, and was grateful that they had faced the storm cheerfully in spite of being continually very cold and drenched by the sea;

> *When it was hard enough to walk the deck, they were repeatedly furling, loosing or reefing the sails, and supported themselves as well as men could do.*

Finally, the ship dropped anchor in Weymouth Bay and the crew were given time to recuperate. Moore took a break too, wandering along the seafront of the town. Observing a crowd gathered near the shore, he hastened towards them, thinking that he might have the chance to observe a boxing match, a sport he enjoyed. However, he was disgusted to find a crowd of local men amusing themselves *by 'throwing at Cocks'* (i.e. throwing cudgels at a tethered cockerel). He found more of interest in exploring the quarries on the Island of Portland before putting to sea again. However, in spite of chasing more smugglers, including one that threw its cargo overboard in order to escape, they caught none. At the end of February, Moore took the *Orestes* back to Spithead for a much needed refit. There he learned that he had been placed under the orders of Captain Samuel Hood of the frigate *Juno*. While waiting for Hood to return from leave, Moore dined with some of the other captains present in the port. One night, a discussion on

> *the slave trade was started, and they, one and all, attacked Wilberforce as a visionary enthusiast who was bringing most serious calamities on his country by his perseverance in an absurd and impracticable scheme. The old, beastly, confined assertion was made of the slaves being better off than the labourers in England, which if true could only be meant with respect to victuals and lodging, and in these articles a horse I fancy does not yield to either. These men are high in their profession, and certainly by no means destitute of worth or talents.*

Nevertheless, Moore left them, despairing at their narrow-minded-ness. Despite his earlier misgivings, Moore found he was

> *. . . happy to meet the Captains on these occasions as they are all very respectable characters and some of them of high reputation in the service.*

Though it is clear that he was still not over-impressed by some of the officers he had met

> *. . . I have had occasion to observe since I took the Command of the* Orestes, *that people seem to value themselves, in the Navy, and are*

more looked up to for qualities, or the appearance of them, which have nothing to do with their profession. For instance, a pretension to fashion, a smattering of knowledge of the Poets sufficient for pedantic quotation. With these pitiful attainments, they have the impertinence to assume an air of superiority over the plain, assiduous and intelligent sea officer, whose attention has been turned to what is substantial and useful. I have also remarked that these skipping fellows when ashore, and amongst a different set of mortals, assume the Sailor, and in general pass themselves for that which they seemed to despise in the place where such manners are consistent. The reason of this juggle, I think, is that these lads wish for fame at the least possible expense. Among seamen they could not pass for such, so they make themselves conspicuous for what a seaman is in general unacquainted with; and ashore, where they could not shine as Petit Maitres, *or witlings, they become* Rarae Aves *as Seamen.*

Nevertheless, he was anxious to record in his journal that his comments described officers who were by no means very common '. . . *in the Corps* . . .' which was generally '. . . *a most meritorious body of men'*. He was certainly keen to defend the type of officer who was a seaman above all and hated those who took advantage by drawing

an illiterate person into blunders in order to turn him into ridicule . . . When I see it employed against men of simple and modest manners, who have gained the offices they hold, by their hard service, and skill in the useful, though not brilliant, duties of the profession: I say, to see such men made the sport of such reptiles, as are most apt to make them feel their deficiencies, fills me with indignation.

Another subject of conversation in naval circles related to the conflict in India, where British forces were engaged against those of Tippoo Sahib[29]. Tippoo's forces had fought stubbornly against the British under Cornwallis, and there were deep suspicions that the French were secretly assisting them. This suspicion seemed to be confirmed by astonishing news which arrived at Spithead with the frigate *Thames*.

The Thames *brings the very extraordinary intelligence of Sir Richard Strachan in the* Phoenix *having engaged and taken a French frigate which had endeavoured to prevent him from examining two French merchant ships under her convoy.*

38

Strachan had stopped the French convoy upon suspicion that they were attempting to land arms and supplies for Tippoo Sultan. Moore was particularly interested for two reasons: firstly, he had already met Strachan and had been greatly impressed by him; and secondly, the incident could only heighten the tension that was already growing between England and France.

Regardless of the situation abroad, the *Orestes* had her own duty to perform, and Moore soon took her out once again, to patrol along the Dorset coast. They searched a number of suspicious vessels and

> saw lights along shore towards Lulworth, which I believed were signals to some Smuggling vessels expected on the coast; I therefore sent away three boats well manned and armed under the command of the 1st, 2nd and acting Lieutenants, who rowed all night to intercept any vessels which might attempt to run in for the shore. Yesterday morning they returned having seen nothing of what they were on the look out for.

Unperturbed by this lack of success, Moore anchored again at Portland, where his curiosity took him on a long walk to the ancient Iron Age fortification of Maiden Castle,

> which is said to be the completest Roman Fortification in England. It is about a mile on this side of Dorchester, situated upon a hill, and surrounded by a triple ditch and rampart of great depth and height. I could only observe one entrance which is on the east side. I always thought the Roman Camps had four gates but this station is said to have been altered by the Saxons. There is a curious remnant of Antiquity, about 1/2 a mile nearer to Dorchester, called Mambury, which is said to have been a Roman Amphitheatre, I examined it, it stands close to the high road from Weymouth, is of a circular form with one entrance, it did not by any means answer my ideas of a Roman amphitheatre. I could see nothing but a thick earthen wall surrounding about an acre of level ground. There are no remains of any building. I think it well calculated for a Rural place of exercise, as a great number of people might stand on the high bank or wall and perfectly well see whatever was performing within the circle. I wonder the Boxers have never pitched upon it for the scene of their exploits, it would answer their purpose admirably well.

Now that Moore had his own – albeit temporary – command, he could take his own turn at trying to impress his friends. He decided to invite his patron, the Duke of Hamilton, to join him for a cruise.

39

However, no sooner did he receive confirmation that the Duke had accepted the invitation, than he began to have second thoughts:

I have so pimping a cabin, that it was a bold step in me to ask the Duke to go out with me; indeed I would not have done it had I not known that he hates pomp and despises smugness and as I have the warmest affection for him, and know that he loves the sea and is partial to Sailors, I have some hopes of contributing to his health and amusement.

The Duke of Hamilton arrived at Weymouth on 19 April with his two servants, and was welcomed on board the *Orestes* with a salute of *'the usual'* number of guns. Unfortunately, the weather promptly turned very rough and although the Duke suffered no ill effects, the two servants were *'perfectly miserable the whole time'*. As the weather worsened, Moore put into Spithead for shelter and whilst there an unfortunate incident forced him to delay any planned departure. It is once again an indication of the interest that Moore took in his crew that he should have recorded the details so deliberately in his journal.

Whilst anchored at Spithead, Peter Gordon, Boatswain's Mate, was permitted to go on shore to visit his wife.[30] Deciding to bring her out to visit the *Orestes*, he went to hire a boat from the hard at Portsmouth. There he was approached by two watermen, who offered to ferry them both out to the ship in their wherry for a shilling. Gordon said that he would give them no more than 3d (*thruppence*, or three old pence) for the trip and the two watermen agreed. However, half way to the ship they suddenly returned to their original demand for a shilling and repeated this again on arrival at the side of the *Orestes*. Gordon refused, proffering the agreed 3d, at which the watermen attacked him, striking him with one of the sculls and beating him severely. Carried on board the ship, Gordon was treated by two surgeons both of whom declared his life to be in danger, and Moore had to send him on shore to the naval hospital (where, happily, he later recovered). Positively incensed, Moore had the two watermen arrested and committed to prison. He then reported the matter to the Port Admiral who, in turn, passed the matter to the Admiralty. The Admiralty solicitor then prosecuted the accused men on a charge of assault and intent to murder but the trial jury refused to accept the accusation of murderous intent. Moore was furious: *'The circumstances of this outrage were of so villainous a nature that I wonder how they* [the jury] *could act with so little candour.'* In fact, he learned the reason when he next put into port and found, to his disgust, that the two watermen were finally acquitted at the following Quarter sessions *'to the astonishment of every person in the Court'*, when the jury stated that they could not believe the evidence of the witnesses. The real reason was, in fact, that two members of the jury were in the business of leasing wherries to watermen, and they were therefore acting in their own interest in protecting the accused.

When Moore took the *Orestes* to sea again, he had on board not only the Duke, but also Captain Charles Hamilton with whom Moore had served much earlier in his career. He decided to head for Guernsey where they dined with the Governor, enjoying his excellent claret *'which we all did justice to'*. Dinner almost certainly involved a discussion on the current state of Europe for Moore could not see how Britain could avoid being drawn into a war:

> *I am one of those who rejoice in the downfall of Arbitrary power in France, but I by no means go along with those men who wish to make Revolutions in Great Britain . . .*

Moore was consistent in his belief that the English constitution had advantages which

> *. . . are the effect [result] of old custom and habit which have changed the real essences although the nominal are preserved. I think that we are as free as possible, consistent with security, in fact, although not in appearance.*

After dinner, regardless of the claret, Moore returned to the ship knowing that the Guernsey road *'. . . is a very wild one . . .'* where ships were known to drag their anchors and be lost during storms.

A week later, to the sound of a 15-gun salute, Moore landed the Duke and Captain Hamilton back at Weymouth, where they picked up the Duke's carriage, hoping to make Salisbury before nightfall. Moore then sailed back round the Solent to Lymington where a boat landed him near Sir Harry Burrard's estate at Walhampton; *'Sir Harry's seat is a fine one, laid out with great care, and trouble, but in poor taste'*. Over dinner, Burrard announced that he intended to resume command of the *Orestes* in three to four weeks' time. Any disappointment Moore experienced at this news was offset by a letter awaiting him at Portsmouth; William Elliott, the commander of the *Bonetta*, had written to say that poor health was forcing him to apply to the Admiralty to be superseded, and that Moore might want to apply for the command. The *Bonetta* was a 14-gun sloop built at

Perry's Yard at Blackwall on the Thames in 1779 and was smaller than the *Orestes*, but she would be a permanent command. In no time Moore had dispatched a letter to the First Lord and seemingly also to the Duke of Hamilton for on 25 May, he heard from his mother that the Duke had received a letter from Lord Chatham confirming his appointment to the *Bonetta*. The *Bonetta* was bound for the Newfoundland station.

5

Newfoundland
(May – November 1792)

On receiving confirmation of his new appointment, Moore immediately travelled to London to convey his thanks to the First Lord and
express his contentment with the Newfoundland station. Once back
at Portsmouth, he received a request from Elliott that he retain two
of the eight Midshipmen currently serving on board the *Bonetta*. It
was the first time that Moore had to solve the tricky issue of returning
favours by giving employment to other men's protégés whilst simultaneously trying to help his own:

> *I must get rid of three or four of them to make room for my own friends;*
and at the same time he was beset by his usual distress at leaving
England: *I am now in all the dismals of parting from the dearest friends*
> *I have upon earth, this is a distress incident to my profession, which I*
> *never can be so hardened to, as not to feel a great depression of spirits*
> *for several days after it takes place.*

His feelings were exacerbated by the fact that he had again seen the
two Dennison girls and had formed something of an attachment for
the younger of the two, though this was not to last. But

> *Now I must return to my old Mistress the Sea with a heavy heart, which*
> *I struggle to cheer by the consideration that I am doing what is right.*

On 1 June 1792, Moore went on board the *Bonetta*, and read his
commission. As a commanding officer he now had a servant, whom
he described as *'a mere boy'* and who was too inexperienced to assist
him with fitting his mess and preparing for the voyage to
Newfoundland. Once the formalities of introductions and settling in
to his new cabin had been accomplished, he had time to take stock of
his situation:

It will be some time before I find myself quite at home here, both officers and men are entire strangers to me; all this will come round by degrees.

It was a feeling experienced by all new commanders arriving in their ship for the first time. Happily he had been able to resolve the dilemma about the Midshipmen. Two had requested a transfer into other ships. He had meant to discharge a third, but had agreed to retain him on the proviso that the young gentleman's friends persuaded Captain Gower of the *Lion* (74) to take

young Perkins who was under my care in the Adamant; *they have succeeded far beyond my hopes, for Captn Gower very handsomely told me to send for him when I thought proper, that he would rate him Midshipman, and give him a month's leave to go and see his friends.*

On Perkins' arrival at Portsmouth, Moore, who was delighted to have been able to get his protégé taken by Gower, took him on board the *Lion* and introduced him to his new commanding officer. The arrangement meant that Moore was able to satisfy his own interests and retain all of the remaining Midshipmen appointed by Elliott. This was a handsome return of favour, though only time would reveal their quality.

Before three weeks had passed, Moore was beginning to feel more at home:

June 17. I begin to feel myself rather more chez moi; The Officers I think well of, and the men seem to be of the right sort. I shall be glad when our Orders arrive; the sea will roll and toss us together presently.

On the following day, however, one of the more unpleasant responsibilities of command presented itself in unwelcome fashion. One of the *Bonetta*'s lieutenants arrived on board with a man who had deserted the ship before Moore's arrival. He had been one of the ship's Quartermasters and was reportedly '*a good seaman*'. Moore questioned the man and found that he could give no real reason for deserting, but that having stayed on shore a certain time beyond his leave, he had become afraid to return for fear of the retribution which would follow. The ship's complement was already now complete as the man had been replaced, so he could no longer be admitted onto the ship's books. Uncertain how to deal with the dilemma, Moore went to see Sir Andrew Hammond, to explain that although it might be necessary to punish the man for desertion, he would happily enter such a good hand on the ship's books; he certainly did not want to risk the severity of a court martial. The Admiral suggested that another, less valuable hand be discharged into the frigate *Iphigenia*, thus enabling Moore to retain the ex-Quartermaster. Thus far, Moore was satisfied, but he now had to see punishment carried out. As he had previously noted in his journal, he knew that one of the first tasks of a new commanding officer was, from the outset, to establish a tangible sense of discipline on the ship. The Quartermaster had to be punished as an example both of the severity with which the crime was regarded according to the Articles of War, and of the new Commander's determination to establish order on board his ship. Moore's loathing of the event is unquestionable:

> *This morning I had to commence the shocking and revolting business of flogging, by giving this man two dozen lashes, which, much against my nature, I saw severely inflicted.*

It was perhaps of the greatest significance that, at the time Moore had to oversee the first punishment on board his first real command – involving a crew that his own behaviour, abilities and personality would help mould – he should give more than usual thought to the power and responsibility vested in him as ruler of his ship. One thing that he regarded as vital was his ability to control his anger. It was an ability in which many officers failed completely, resulting in an increasing spiral of punishment on board increasingly unhappy ships with deeply resentful crews. The more enlightened officers were already learning of the need to control their feelings,[31] and ensure there was a cooling off period before reacting to a misdemeanour. Moore recorded in his journal a telling memory of an incident which had occurred whilst he was a Lieutenant on board the *Perseus*. One day he had been supervising the reefing of the ship's topsails and had become

> *exceedingly fretted by the stupidity and carelessness of one of the seamen; on his coming down, I ran up with a rope's end to the fellow, determined to thresh him, when the poor man saw my intention, he stood with his hat in his hand and his eyes fixed upon the deck, ready to submit to my brutal rage, but his respectful humility had completely brought me to my senses, and filled me with shame and confusion; I could as soon have thought of cutting his throat as of striking him.*

The incident had taught him a crucial lesson in command and he had never forgotten it.

As the month progressed, more and more ships assembled at Portsmouth, forming a squadron under Admiral Lord Hood, and Moore had the chance of meeting many of the commanders of these ships. Like Moore, most of these were part of a new generation of officers, promoted since 1790. Moore was impressed by what he saw:

there are a great many fine young men coming forward in our service. They vie with each other in having their ships in good order, and I think the spirit of Tyranny and Oppression, which at one time was too frequently visible among the Captains, seems to hide its head.

Shortly after, Admiral King arrived and hoisted his flag in the *Assistance*. The *Bonetta* was dispatched to Guernsey to purchase wine for the Admiral, and the *Bonetta*'s officers took advantage of the opportunity to lay in their own stock. Moore conned the ship into Guernsey himself, as the ship's Master had never been there. Such a task caused Moore no worries, as he had a more pressing issue to deal with. The First Lieutenant, John Eaton, had placed the *Bonetta*'s Captain of the Maintop in confinement, on a charge of neglect of duty. Moore, having considered the case, was determined that the seaman should not be flogged, but was worried how the Lieutenant would respond to having his authority apparently undermined. He wrestled with the problem all night;

In the morning, I sent for the Lieutenant, told him that altho' the man certainly deserved punishment, yet from his good character I was very averse to punishing him; at the same time I asked him his opinion of the former conduct of the seaman, he answered that the man was one of the best in the ship, and that it was for me to determine. I was highly pleased with this, and ordering the hands to be turned up, I pointed out to the people the fault the sailor had been guilty of , warning him how he gave room for complaint in the future, and concluded by informing him that the good character he had, previous to his crime, born saved him on the present occasion; but that he owed his being forgiven to the lenity of the Lieutenant.

Giving Lieutenant Eaton the credit for such leniency was a clever move, for not only did it save face, it credited him with a sense of fairness which was rightly Moore's. Notwithstanding this attempt to smooth ruffled feathers, Moore's problems with his First Lieutenant re-emerged back at Spithead. Once again he found himself spending the night in his cabin raking over the issues:

I do not find that every thing goes on in this ship, exactly as I wish it, the fault, I think does not lie with me, however, I am determined from this morning henceforth, that it shall either be much better or infinitely worse.

The following morning, he summoned Lieutenant Eaton to his cabin and later that day recorded the details of this difficult confrontation:

I have had an explanation with the 1st Lieutenant who has been sullen and dissatisfied ever since I came on board. He remarked to me that he thought the ship was not in such good order as she had been in and every body was taking notice of the changes. I told him that I did not know what state she had been in before I took the command of her, but that [now] she certainly was not kept so clean and neat as she ought, and I saw no reason why she should be thus neglected, as in my opinion blame must lie on the Lieutenant for a ship being in a slovenly state, unless the Captain threw obstacles in the way of her being in a proper state. He hinted, that he did not wish to serve, but did not like to quit the ship when she was on the point of sailing. I said, that I did not wish to lose him, but that he knew best what was for his own interest; but, I told him, as a friend, that he had best not think of quitting the ship at this moment. I concluded by telling him my opinion of the manner that the duty should be carried on. That the common daily duty of the ship should be transacted by the 1st Lieutenant, under my orders, that I looked to him for taking care that the ship was kept clean and in order; and that if I wished anything to be altered I would let him previously know of it. I prest him to let me know if he felt himself hurt by any part of my conduct since we had been together, as I had remarked that he seemed dissatisfied, but had attributed it partly to ill health, and partly to concern for the situation of his friend Captn. Elliot. He declared, that he had no fault to find with me, but was hurt to observe that the ship was no longer in that order that she had been in; I replied that it lay with the first lieutenant to keep her in the highest order, for I did not wish to be giving directions for washing the decks or squaring the yards. We parted apparently satisfied on both sides. I certainly blame myself for suffering him to take things so very easy as he has done, but I was prevented by the consideration of the very excellent character I had of him from my friend Elliot, and by the idea I had of his being in a very bad state of health; but at the same time, I do not stand acquitted in my own opinion for allowing the matter to go thus far without clearing scores. It certainly however was odd enough in him to talk first of a neglect which certainly was his own, and of the relaxation occasioned by his not doing his duty.

It is vital that the modern reader understand that the daily routine of running a man-of-war was the direct responsibility of the First Lieutenant, though within the officer corps there were differing views as to the degree of autonomy which this officer should be allowed in carrying out this role.[32] Towards the end of the Napoleonic wars it was clear that many frigate commanders who had learned their craft during the testing wartime years, understood that it was important for the First Lieutenant to feel he had the full confidence and backing of his commanding officer and that this could only be achieved by allowing the First Officer room to exercise his duties without having his chief looking over his shoulder the whole time. Moore's discussion with Eaton was clearly an attempt to clarify or even re-establish the parameters of the latter's responsibilities, and to indicate where, when and how Moore might indicate if he thought corrective measures necessary. Eaton, for his part, may have been suggesting that Moore was too lax or disinterested, and was leaving too much on the shoulders of his first officer. In many ways this may have been a common situation. Eaton had been used to Captain Elliott's manner of commanding the *Bonetta*. Elliott may well have taken a much closer involvement in the day-to-day running of the ship and, if this had been the case, Eaton's responsibilities would have been lighter. The arrival of Moore, with a more *laissez-faire* approach to command, may have given Eaton more responsibility than he was willing or able to cope with. This seems particularly likely, following Moore's intervention on behalf of the Captain of the Maintop. Moore's sudden intervention would have appeared as a sudden *volte-face*, indicating disapproval of the First Officer's attempts in enforcing and maintaining order on board, which, in fact, was the case. It is also possible that there was an entirely different reason behind Eaton's response. He may, just possibly, have considered that he himself had a claim as successor to Elliott. Eaton's subsequent career seems to confirm that he may have had some difficulties. After he left the *Bonetta* he was appointed First Lieutenant of the frigate *Aquilon* in 1794, before being promoted to the rank of Commander. In 1795 he became Acting Captain of the *Glory*, which, as a 90-gun ship, suggests that he was either acting as a Flag Captain or that the ship was not really in full active service. Whatever the situation, he was not promoted to Post Captain, and in 1797 he committed suicide.

On 4 August, the *Bonetta* and *Assistance* weighed anchor for Newfoundland. Moore was conscious that in taking his first real command off to a foreign station for the first time, he was stepping over an important threshold in his career;

> *I feel some degree of awe when I reflect on the situation I am in at this moment; the lives of a hundred men depend in a great measure on my conduct. My own reputation as an Officer, and consequently my future advancement in the service are much interested at this moment, and may be decidedly marked by the events which may take place within these three months.*

As they worked their way down Channel, Moore went on board the *Assistance* to dine with the Admiral and receive his orders. He was to sail to St John's, re-provision at Trinity, and then cruise between Cape St Francis and Cape St John, protecting the fisheries and collecting Greenwich Hospital Money from the merchants of Newfoundland,[33] for which he personally would receive a one-eighth share of all he collected. He was then to rendezvous with the Admiral at St John's on 6 October. He had also been given a clearer idea about his duties in Newfoundland, which included being given a Surrogate Commission so that he could convene Courts of Justice on the station. This was an inherent part of the Navy's responsibilities, as representatives of the British government, towards the colony. But it was not a prospect that Moore looked forward to: *'I could wish to dispense with this dignity, but there is no remedy.'*

As they headed out into the Atlantic, Moore was still less than satisfied with the situation on board the ship:

> *As far as I have observed of the ship's company, they are in general orderly and quiet, the ship is, however, not in that state of order and method which I wish to have her in; this is owing to a relaxation of the subordinate parts, which I fear will not mend until a change of men brings an alteration of measures. I hate cavilling and jarring, but I must have my eyes about me.*

In fact, he now believed that Lieutenant Eaton would soon asked to be superseded and he was secretly pleased, because he believed that his Second Lieutenant was highly capable and deserved to be made up to First.

On 3 September 1792, after an uneventful passage, the *Bonetta* sailed into St John's Harbour, with its remarkable narrow entrance flanked on either side by high ground. Anchored in the harbour they

49

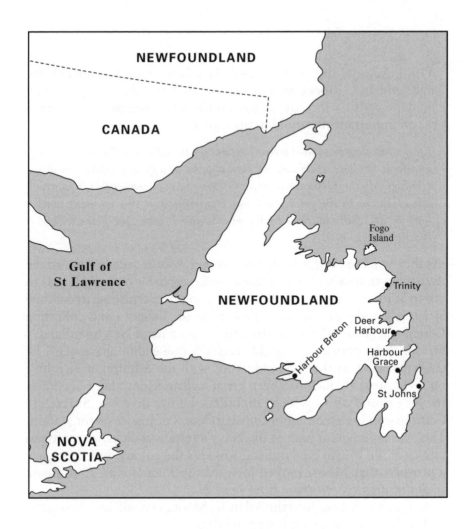

found the frigate *Circe*, commanded by the young Alan Gardner, son of a Lord of the Admiralty.

> *Alan who commands the* Circe *has met with most rapid promotion, I do not believe he is now above 22 years of age and he is more than two years Post Captain. I think him one of the finest young fellows I know in the service, and I believe a most excellent officer at this moment, but if he lives, I firmly believe he will be one of the most shining characters in the Navy. He is at present a lad of fire, with an uncommon flow of spirits, which, as is usually the case, leaves him low and dejected at intervals, in proportion as it had lifted him above the medium. His ship is apparently in excellent order . . .* Gardner himself was full of 'wild pranks'; He has been bred in an excellent school for seamen, and had

the command of a ship when he was barely 17. I love the fellow, and we are very good friends.

Such pleasantries aside, Moore did not like St John's. The harbour was lined with fish stages and 'flakes' for drying fish – *'the smell from which is very offensive'*. However, he had another reason for regretting his stay in the harbour:

While we lay at St John's I had the mortification to find it absolutely necessary to flog three of the best men in the ship. They had got beastly drunk and behaved in a mutinous manner. There is no circumstance incident to my profession that is so revolting to my nature as this business of punishing, but it is absolutely necessary sometimes. The very following day one of the Boatswains mates and one of the marines were confined for drunkenness and rioting; on this occasion I tried the effect of lenity. On our coming into this Port [Trinity] I called the ship's company upon deck and represented to them my displeasure at their conduct during the short time we were at St John's, I assured them that it was a most disagreeable thing to me to punish and I pointed out to them that every one of those who had misbehaved were in the first place intoxicated. I then expressed my hopes that I should see a different conduct for the future, but warned them against drunkenness at sea, or smuggling spirituous liquors on board in a harbour as these were amongst the offences which I never would forgive. I then informed them that one day in the week, the messes might depute a man each in whom they could confide, and these men should have a boat to attend upon them in order to their trucking their provisions against what vegetables or other articles they might want from the shore.

Again we have an example of Moore endeavouring to provide a balanced regime, introducing a restriction whilst at the same time granting a concession. But it is also important to note that Moore was driven to punish the aforesaid men, not for drunkenness but for the offences that followed as a consequence i.e. mutinous and riotous behaviour. The other real problem associated with drunkenness, and the reason it brought forth punishments, was because at sea it was dangerous and led to accident and injury.

Within days the *Bonetta* sailed for Trinity, where Moore opened the Surrogate Court to hear and rule on civil suits and complaints. He sat despondently listening to a succession of cases, beginning with a merchant captain who complained that the drunken sailors on his ship had caused him a large financial loss, and proceeding to complaints from servants over non-payment of wages, disputes over fishing rights etc. Having dealt with the cases, he closed the court and collected over £100 in Greenwich Hospital money from local merchants. He noted that the Surrogate Court had been warmly welcomed by the poorer residents of the town because

> ... the poor people are so oppressed by the rich that they are happy to seek even the rough protection of a Sea despot. I however am strongly inclined to think that our law, or rather our courts of law in England are much better calculated for the convenience of the Rich than the protection of the Poor.

Moore responded to this by tearing up the table of fees which he was supposed to charge for hearing cases and which had been given to him by the Chief Justice at St John's. The fees, he thought,

> ... fall very heavy on many of the poor people, who are in general desti-tute of cash, and will be a trifle to the people with whom they have to contend; it may deter the former from having recourse to the Surrogate and consequently encourage the other to cheat and oppress them.

He had already had some experience of the potential inequality and corruption that existed. Local merchants had inundated him with gifts of fresh vegetables and wild duck. He had no hesitation in recognizing this as attempted bribery and was determined to refuse any further offerings.

Moore's next port of call was Harbour Grace. Here, as soon as the *Bonetta* had dropped anchor, she was besieged by boats carrying people seeking to influence him in cases they wished to bring to the Court. It was not a good sign; '*I shall have much trouble at this damned place*', he noted in his journal. Two days later he opened the Surrogate Court and was deluged with complaints from merchants against debtors, and a smaller number of complaints about '*oppres-sion*'. For three days he sat hearing cases in the Court Room, by the end of which he was heartily sick of the whole business: '*I wish the whole town were at the bottom of the sea; for they seem to be a knavish, lousy, pack.*' He also had difficulty collecting the Greenwich Hospital levy. Merchants tried offering him fish in lieu of the money and, although it had been recommended he accept this, he refused: '*I am no merchant, and the Governor has no right to expect that I am to turn retailer of small wares for Greenwich Hospital.*'

The *Bonetta*'s entry into the next port, Cataline, nearly resulted in disaster. Trusting to directions given to him, Moore entered the harbour, hugging the north side of the Channel. As he did so, people began waving frantically at the *Bonetta* from the shore. In alarm, the ship was sheered over to the opposite shore and began taking in her mainsails. As she did so the stern grounded and, for an agonizing period of time, she hung with the stern and rudder striking on rocks. Moore ordered the ship's stream anchor lowered into a boat and laid out to the southern shore. Fortunately, she was hauled off with little difficulty. Although there seemed to be little damage, a few days later a lump of rock was discovered wedged into the keel and although attempts were made to free it by prodding it with an oar, it remained firmly in place. When the ship left Cataline for St John's, Moore took the precaution of hiring a local pilot to guide her clear of the harbour.

Moore returned to St John's hoping to find orders there directing him to escort a convoy back to England. He was disappointed. The *Circe* had been sent instead, and Moore found himself detained in a port he did not like. He attempted to create some form of social circle by inviting officers from the local garrison [34] to dinner on board the *Bonetta* but to his disgust they got hopelessly drunk and he was depressed by the exhibition of the '. . . *degradation of humanity, which, wherever the army are, is too prevalent'*. Moore himself stayed sober by passing the bottle. It was not that Moore disapproved of drinking in itself, it was just that he tended to suffer from an excess of it;

> *I am very fortunate in having a loathing at wine after swallowing about a bottle, as it generally prevents me from excesses which my easy disposition would otherwise expose me to . . .* [and the] *certainty I have of sickness all the following day, has prevented me from making a beast of myself.*

Moore was particularly depressed by the fact that he had received no mail from home. His father and brother were in France and he was getting anxious about their safety. He could not understand the lack of mail – for his friend Captain Riou had given his mother all the information she needed about getting letters to Newfoundland by way of the ships from Poole. He wanted to go home. Then, on 30 October, a ship arrived from Europe carrying newspapers nearly six weeks old. There was truly shocking news, for in France

> 'The Terror' had begun. *We hear of dreadful excesses having been committed in France. If what is universally said of the conduct of the Parisians is true, they are wretches unworthy to live, and deserve to be*

hunted down as murtherers and cailiffs. Altho I am certainly an enemy to tyranny and a friend to liberty, yet I do hold in horror and detestation, these sanguinary comedians who now play the principal parts in the horrible farce acting at Paris.

Fortunately, the squadron also received orders to sail for home. The Admiral wasted no time, setting sail within days. Four days out, however, they ran into a heavy gale. The *Bonetta*'s upper works began leaking badly and she soon fell behind the other ships. Moore found himself alone. At 4 o'clock on the morning of 11 November, a tremendous sea crashed over the *Bonetta*'s gangways, almost filling the waist of the ship;

I was in bed at the time, and awakened by hearing it roaring like thunder in upon us; when the sea passed us there was a very terrible silence, I never was happier than to hear the First Lieutenant, who had the watch bellow for the carpenters to knock the half ports out to deliver the water. I ran upon deck in my shirt, but the danger was over, and one good spell at the chain pumps cleared her of what had gone down the hatchways.

By next morning, the weather had moderated and Moore removed two of the deadlights which had been fitted to protect his cabin windows. He soon regretted it as a

. . . green sea stove in the cabin windows and filled my cabin, bed and every thing full of water.

Such were the perils of a following sea.

On 17 November, the battered *Bonetta* finally sailed past Spithead.

6

Commander at War
(November 1792 – February 1794)

While the *Bonetta* was docked for repairs, Moore went to London. He was back at Portsmouth on 30 November, when he received urgent orders to make the *Bonetta* ready for sea with the utmost dispatch. Already the *Assistance* and the *Rattlesnake*, commanded by his friend Joseph Sidney Yorke, had been issued with secret sealed orders and had put to sea. Portsmouth was alive with rumours;

> *The reason of this bustle is an utter secret, but the general opinion is that we are about to support the Dutch in preventing the opening of the Schelde. Something serious is certainly going forward . . .*

In London, the militia had been called out and Parliament had been recalled. At Portsmouth, there was frantic activity fitting ships for service, and guardships were waiting for suitable winds to get out of harbour.

By the 4 December, the *Bonetta* had slipped out of harbour and moored at Spithead. Moore now received orders to sail for the Downs and, if there were no orders awaiting him there, to carry on round to the Nore, the naval anchorage off Sheerness. Within hours the *Bonetta* was off of Deal and in the worst gale that Moore had ever experienced, with the serious threat of the Goodwin Sands very close at hand;

> *Our situation was very dangerous, neither the Master being well acquainted nor myself, with this part of the Channel, the narrowest of any part of the English Channel, with a long winter night and dreadful shoals to leeward of us. I did not go to bed until four yesterday morning, when I took two or three hours rest, but not a wink of sleep. The sea ran very high, and not a man had a dry hammock to turn into, which*

together with the great exertions our people had made [to fit the ship in 3 days], so completely knocked them up that yesterday at noon we had twenty working men in the sick list.

When the weather moderated they were able to pick up a pilot to see them to the Nore, though they nearly became entrapped by shoals in the Queen's Channel. The weather had turned bitterly cold and Moore anxiously watched his crew who were *'jaded off their legs'*. Angrily, he partly blamed this on the poor craftsmanship of the dock-yard artificers, as the decks of the *Bonetta* leaked worse than she had before refitting. He felt like complaining but realized that this might further delay their being sent on any profitable active service. Nevertheless *'. . . it is a shameful business, and would prove fatal to many of our people if they were not all of them young fellows.'* Equally badly, much of their stores had been left behind with, criti-cally, the surgeon's medical chest. Around them there were other ships in difficulty and Moore greatly admired the seamen from Margate who ventured out in rough seas carrying anchors and cables to those in need. He thought the Deal men the bravest, as they often put to sea in the worst weather and hardly ever lost a man:

> *They are accused of being very exorbitant in their demands for services performed [i.e. fees], but they run such risks and do so much good that they deserve to be well paid. I never saw men manage their boats so well.*

For the remainder of December, the *Bonetta* was employed ferrying newly raised or impressed seamen from Sheerness to the Downs. Heavy weather set in and the crowded sloop was made additionally uncomfortable. Moore too was suffering:

> *My cabin is so cold and so constantly damp that I cannot sit in it to read or write with any comfort; the stove amongst other things was left behind at Portsmouth.*

To crown it all the ship was woefully short of beer and other provisions.

As if there were not problems enough, Moore's difficulties with Lieutenant Eaton suddenly resurfaced on Christmas Day, very shortly after he had provided his officers with Christmas dinner. Moore was on the quarterdeck as the ship prepared to sail, when there was a sudden scuffle at the capstan. The ship's Master hurried to the First Lieutenant, to report that one of the seamen had spoken insolently to a Midshipman supervising at the capstan. Lieutenant Eaton summoned the seaman to the quarterdeck and then turned to Moore saying,

> ... *in a most insolent manner, that as for himself, he had ceased making any complaints, as they were never attended to, and as he found that a foremast man's word was always taken before his, but that the master had represented to him the insolence of this man and he acquainted me with it; that if he was not punished no duty could be carried on, he added, (with a great deal more stuff, which I have forgotten) that he might do his duty on the Forecastle, or the Top, but he could not carry on his duty as First Lieutenant finding himself unsupported. I was so shocked with this man's folly and impertinence, that, I was on the point of confining him, but recollecting, that, we were all just risen from table, where we had rather exceeded the usual allowance, I thought he must be flustered with wine, and luckily I had the command of myself to say nothing, but to order the seaman who was half drunk to remain aft. All this harangue of the 1st Lieutenant was in the hearing of all the officers, and of the men who were heaving at the capstern; he had, the whole of the day before, been in perfectly good humour, and I had not the smallest reason to believe that he was dissatisfied with me, nor did I know to what he alluded when he said that his complaints were not attended to. After the ship had got into Margate Roads, I sent for the two lieutenants and the Master, into the Cabin and told the 1st Lieutenant before them that I did not wish to carry matters further than was absolutely necessary but that if ever he should take upon him to treat me in the manner he had thought proper to do that evening, I would undoubtedly take public notice of it. I asked him what part of my conduct he adverted to when he said that his complaints were disregarded, and that a Foremast man's word was taken before his, he answered, that, when I first came into the ship, upon any complaint being made, I required a great deal of proof of a man's guilt, before I would punish, and that he had sometimes confined men whom I had not punished, on his representation. I told him that I would pay, and always had, all due attention to any complaint which came from him, or any other officer, but that, I never would punish a man before I had informed myself thoroughly of the merits of the case; and whatever might be his opinion of my conduct, I insisted upon it that he did not inform me of it, in the manner he had done, as it was unlike an officer, disrespectful, and ruinous to the discipline. ... This affair has given me much uneasiness, and a complete disgust at the character of the*

man. . . . I now see, that this fellow has all along been sulky with me. Although, I attributed his manner to ill breeding, and a boorish disposition. God knows, if I have erred in my conduct towards him, and the rest of the officers, it has been on the side of indulgence . . . I will do him the justice to say that he is a remarkably good and active seaman, and his exertion in fitting the ship, after I told him it was necessary to be as brisk as possible, were such as did himself great credit, and gave very great satisfaction to me . . . By the bye, the Seaman's crime was merely on the Midshipman crying 'heave round men' enforcing what the Midshipman said by 'you Bug—rs'.

The incident raises a number of interesting points about Moore and his style of command. From Moore's own account, and from his earlier comments, it is clear that he was determined neither to punish in haste nor to rely solely on the testimony of the accuser before passing sentence. It had become increasingly obvious that Moore and Eaton did not agree on the administration of punishment on board the ship, and the more that Moore attempted to maintain a fair and balanced system of discipline and order, the more Eaton felt that he was being sidelined and his rank undermined. The discontent created by this difference in approach had been growing since Moore commissioned the ship and there was now no possibility of reconciling the Captain and First Lieutenant. To some degree one must understand Eaton's position, for it was unenviable. The more that the Captain refused to acquiesce in his decisions over discipline, the less authority he could wield over the crew. Eaton could be completely wrong in the haste and inflexibility which he applied in the maintenance of order on the *Bonetta*, but it would have been almost impossible for him to backtrack and adopt a different method. As he fell in popularity, the Captain would grow. It was an almost untenable position. What made the matter more serious was that Eaton had made such a public accusation about the Captain's performance. It was something that Moore could not ignore. Finally, to cap it all, when Moore reviewed the nature of the seaman's misdemeanour, he found it to be trivial, if somewhat cheeky. Certainly not something for which a good officer would have a man flogged.

Within three months Eaton had been replaced.

At the end of December, Moore was ordered to the Downs to rendezvous with Admiral Murray's squadron which was bound for the West Schelde to assist the Dutch against the French. On arrival, Moore was informed that the Captain of Murray's flagship, the

50-gun *Assistance*, was ill and he would have to take over as Acting Flag Captain. Moore was jubilant, because although this might only be a temporary appointment, it was more than likely to be confirmed as permanent. To his chagrin, days after they arrived in the Schelde, Captain John Maude arrived with orders to supersede him. Moore returned to the *Bonetta* deeply depressed. He could not help thinking that if so much trouble had been taken to put another temporary officer in his place, he must be held in poor regard by the Admiralty.[35]

Nevertheless, as the squadron lay at anchor in Flushing road, exciting news arrived: firstly, it was learned that French armies were advancing to cross the West Schelde and invade Zeeland and the Dutch navy was mobilizing for war; also that the King of France had been executed. Then newspapers reported that French batteries had fired upon the English sloop *Childers* as she reconnoitred the harbour at Brest. Meanwhile the squadron waited in Flushing road for the Dutch to assemble their defences. Understandably, Moore was anxious to be off. If actual war had broken out, he wanted to be in a more active position.[36] Furthermore, the extended delay and inactivity was beginning to have its effect on the crew of the *Bonetta* and several of the midshipmen had become disobedient and disrespectful to their officers. Moore blamed himself for this, thinking that – despite his determination – he had been over indulgent with them. However, they had now gone too far. He noted in his journal: *'I shall turn over a new leaf with them tomorrow.'* In fact, on the following morning he broke two of them of their rank, though not without misgivings:

> These two young men are powerfully recommended . . . but I must give up every idea of discipline if I pass unnoticed the just complaints of the Officers.

Perhaps it was his brief spell in the *Assistance*, but Moore also had other reasons for being dissatisfied with the *Bonetta*. Now that war seemed imminent, she seemed poorly armed for the duties she was likely to face. He was also beginning to doubt his own abilities:

> I do not feel altogether comfortable in some other respects, there is not that attention to the ship's duty which there ought to be. To be a thorough, Good officer, requires a strict and constant attention, and a spirit of method and routine which I find great difficulty in adhering to.

Four seamen had to be punished, and the Boatswain's Mate had begged to be relieved of the duty of flogging one of them, as they had been messmates together in several ships. Moore could understand the man's position, but he could not afford to have a weakness in the command structure. He pointed out to the Boatswain's Mate that he, as Captain, was the one inflicting the punishment as part of his responsibilities as the ship's commanding officer. The Boatswain's Mate was not acting in a personal capacity but was acting as any other man in obeying his officer's orders. Moore liked corporal punishment no more than any other man, but he firmly believed that such were '. . . *absolutely necessary in order to prevent greater evils*'.

On 7 February, news finally reached the squadron that they were at war with the French and two days later they weighed anchor and headed back across the North Sea for the Downs. As night fell, Moore ordered his crew to quarters in case they should fall in with a French man-of-war. There was no man-of-war; instead the *Bonetta* had to battle with hard gales that blew her far to the north and split her sails. Then the wind changed and she was driven down to Dunkirk where Moore found himself navigating through sandbanks in the dark. It was no wonder he scrawled into his journal:

> *The life of a seaman is certainly one of the most hazardous as well as uncomfortable; if we should strike one of these sands I do not believe a man could escape. We are now kicking about so much that it is with great difficulty that I make shift to write this.*

Days later they arrived at the Downs only to put to sea again immediately, after a French privateer. The latter escaped into Calais and Moore headed back for the South Foreland. Once again, thick weather closed in and the *Bonetta* was swept towards the notorious Goodwin Sands. Moore ordered soundings taken and, to their horror, they found themselves in just 6 fathoms of water;

> *We clewed the sails up and let go the anchor veering to almost a whole cable before we snubbed her. At low water we had a quarter less three where we lay. As soon as the lee tide slackened I hoisted the Cutter out and sent one of the Pilots in her to sound to the SE which was the way we must cast the ship to save her going on the Godwin; when the weather tide began to make she thwarted a little with her stern to the southward which was all against her casting the right way, I therefore ordered a Spring to be clapped on the cable, hove taught, got the top sails set for casting to the southward, cut the cable and made sail. After she had cast the spring being a rotten hauser broke and she had*

very near come back on us again, but by good luck we boxed her off.
This was a very narrow escape.

Back at the Downs, the *Bonetta* was placed under the command of
Admiral MacBride and sent round to Sheerness for new sails and pay
for her crew. Frustratingly, there were no sails to fit the *Bonetta*'s
yards. Moore returned to the Downs, only to be sent to Portsmouth
with a convoy to protect. Every day, accounts were received of French
privateers and prizes being taken by English cruisers, and Moore
fumed:

> *I am losing time. By the Lord, this will be a warning to me never to*
> *hurry out of Port again without having the ship completed in all*
> *respects for the officers I have been under have not paid the least regard*
> *to my representations of the state of the sloop, but have suffered others*
> *to go to Portsmouth who had no real necessity for it. I do wish from*
> *my very heart, that our Convoy may be attacked by something, not too*
> *superior to us, for although I am very short of complement, yet I have*
> *some seamen on board from other ships which makes me stronger than*
> *I am likely to be after I get to Spithead. I think the officers will all fight,*
> *and I believe myself to be staunch.*

At Portsmouth, Moore was able to get new sails and there, also,
Lieutenant Eaton left to join Admiral Elliot's flagship. Moore was
secretly relieved. The days before Eaton's departure had been tense –
'*it is unpleasant to have people in the ship who think every day that*
they are to be superseded'. Unfortunately, Moore also lost Thomas
Maxtone, his Second Lieutenant, whom he had considered very
capable.

At last, on 21 March, the *Bonetta* was ordered to cruise in the
Channel, between Calais and Dungeness. Moore was optimistic. As
he left port there were rumours that Captain George Brisac in the
sloop *Scourge* had taken a French sloop-of-war of nearly equal
strength after what was being described as a '*smart action*'. By the
time the *Bonetta* reached Boulogne, however, Moore was beginning
to regret that his station didn't extend further to the west towards
Cape Le Havre, as he thought there were no significant French ports
east of the Seine. He decided to circumvent this inadequacy by making
a dash to the west towards the end of his cruise. Meanwhile, the
Bonetta settled into a routine, which mainly consisted of stopping
French fishing boats as it was known that some were being used as
privateers. When, however, Moore found himself interviewing the

venerable sixty-three-year-old master of one of these he found himself embarrassed at the role he was having to play. He presented the man with bread and brandy and let him go on his way;

I do not know that I am justified in dismissing her, but I acted from good motives. In the first place, I could very ill spare men to take care of her, in the next place it was lumbering the ship with prisoners, thirdly and lastly, I was actuated by pity for these poor people, who certainly had nothing but their boat to depend upon for the support of their families. Certainly the generous English do not wish to render more wretched, men who have nothing. Had I seen any appearance to induce me to believe her to be a Cruiser, I would have had no remorse.

At the end of his cruise, Moore sailed west to Havre de Grace where he intercepted two American ships putting to sea. They reported that the harbour was crowded with shipping which was afraid to leave port and that several privateers and one 28-gun frigate were fitting-out there. With this news, the *Bonetta* ran back across to Portsmouth to await new orders. There, happily, Moore was joined by a new First Lieutenant, Henry Martin. Martin had not served at sea since the end of the American War, but Moore seems to have taken to him immediately; besides, he was now feeling very positive about both the *Bonetta* and her crew, so much so that he believed he could even try his luck against a ship of superior force. Such buoyancy was dispelled, however, when new orders arrived for the *Bonetta* to return to Newfoundland. Moore had been hoping for either the West Indies or the Mediterranean and he was naturally despondent, thinking that once again he was a victim of disfavour in high places. Although this may have been a natural response to the news, in fact Moore had experience of the coast of Newfoundland and was, therefore, a good choice for the station. His gloom was deepened because the *Bonetta* was twenty-one men short of complement and it seems probable that he had to resort to the Press Gang to fill the places, for he noted in his journal:

I think the necessity for impressing seamen is one of the most glaring although but a partial evil, and yet it is curious here that the people who suffer are not those who complain.

In the middle of April, Moore set sail for Waterford where he was to rendezvous with the frigate *Druid* and a convoy bound for Newfoundland. Sailing west he took a wide sweep to the south of the Channel in the hope of catching something, but all he encountered was a Danish merchantman, which had just left Le Havre. The Dane seemed unable to tell Moore anything about the ships in the harbour and earned himself the epithet 'blockhead' as a consequence. Nevertheless, now that he was at sea again, Moore was feeling happier:

I feel myself much more comfortable in the ship now than I did formerly. The first Lieutenant is a good tempered, agreeable man; who pays attention to his business, and at the same time conciliates the minds of the People under him. The former was a good seaman, but to me, a most distasteful fellow, I always treated him with attention. Much more than he merited at my hands, for he was sulky and careless upon almost all occasions. If I had not always looked upon him as on the point of going away, we should have had a settling; however, God be with him, we shall never sail together again, if I can help it. Mr Maxtone[37], the late 2nd Lt, was a great loss to me, he was very much to my mind, and always conducted himself as a gentleman and an officer, entirely to my satisfaction; I certainly approved of his going, and recommended him strongly to Commodore Murray. I gave up every idea of personal convenience when his interest was concerned. The gentleman who succeeded him, I very much approve of, he is a good seaman, and a well disposed, honest fellow. It may be in my power to be of great use to him, and I shall certainly not neglect any opportunity. He is not [yet] a confirmed Lieutenant.'

Arriving at Waterford on 23 April, the agents for the merchantmen came on board immediately to report that the convoy was very nearly ready to sail. They were closely followed by the masters from the ships who came aboard to receive Moore's orders. However, westerly winds set in and delayed the convoy's departure. Whilst waiting, Moore found himself inundated with hopeful young Irish volunteers, wishing to escape the threat of poverty or starvation on land. Surveying these applicants, Moore was suspicious. Very few were seamen and, cannily, he suspected many of them harboured secret grievances. As a commander Moore knew that *'Complaining is a proof of confidence in those to whom the complaint is made'*. He did not want men in his ship who would be afraid to come forward with problems, nor did he want an undercurrent of simmering resentment to infect the rest of his crew. Nevertheless he picked up a number of *'tolerably good hands'* though three men also deserted and a marine drowned whilst attempting to swim ashore.

On 2 May, the convoy at last set sail and was joined off Cork by the *Druid*, commanded by Captain Joseph Ellison, who was to escort them for part of the voyage. Moore was pleased to have Ellison in company:

> There are certainly some charming fellows in our service among whom I certainly reckon Ellison, with all the frankness which is ascribed to sailors he possesses in great degree the politeness of a man of the world, and that sort of courtesy which seems to flow from a humane and generous heart. His men seem to love him, and are cheerful and happy under him; it requires very little observation to see that, I was convinced of it the second day I was on board his ship. He has an infinite gaiety in his disposition, with some humour, and is a most excellent companion. This gallant officer lost his right arm, above the elbow, when first Lieutenant of La Prudente, *frigate in an action with* La Capricieuse *during the late war. He had received two wounds before, which lost him a great deal of blood, but would not quit the deck until he fell with the loss of his arm and was carried down by the men.*

By 12 May, high seas and heavy squalls had scattered several ships, and the *Bonetta* was twice obliged to take a brig in tow so that she could keep up with the rest of the convoy. The *Bonetta* too was suffering; '*The sloop's decks are exceedingly leaky, many of our men have wet hammocks whenever it comes to blow, but we are healthy, and the people are at three watches*', which meant more time to rest when not on duty. The convoy ploughed on and, as it did so, Moore became increasingly plagued with the problems synonymous with convoy duty:

> Many of the Convoy are exceedingly troublesome, by their total disregard they pay to their Instructions; they are continually striving to slip ahead of the Bonetta *whilst she is obliged to stay by the dull sailors   I frequently awaken their attention with a shot athwart their bows.*

One of the ships, the *Peggy* of Dartmouth, had already deliberately left the convoy behind, despite Moore's orders to the contrary, prompting Moore to jot a reminder in his journal to '. . . *take the first opportunity of writing to Lloyd's Coffee House about him*'. Three days later even more of the convoy had slipped away, whilst the *Bonetta* was preoccupied alternately taking two slow brigs in tow. Moore fumed,

> I find it impossible to keep the Convoy together, there are not above four or five of them that pay any attention to the signals which I make

to them. As I am obliged to wait for the heavy sailors, the others push on, unless we can reach them with a shot which is the only method I have of prevailing upon them to follow their instructions.

Moore ordered the remaining ships to clew up as much sail as possible, to slow the convoy down and allow stragglers to catch up, but by 21 May, only ten of the thirty ships he had set out with were still in sight. Thick fog closed in, and as it did so, seven ships rejoined him. Nothing, though, could lighten Moore's growing despondency. As usual when depressed, he turned to self-deprecation and pondering over the state of the navy:

I do not believe I shall ever have the character of a smart officer, there is too much detail in it; a constant attention to minutiae, much assiduity and method are indispensable to such a reputation, and I have neither the power nor the wish to acquire it, I am far from condemning it in others, I am not sure that our Naval greatness is not in a great measure owing to our excelling in this which I think myself deficient in. But I believe the great superiority which we have over all Europe in maritime affairs is chiefly to be attributed to a peculiarity of character in the common British Tar. Certainly that hardy, active and careless animal has often carried a Commander to Victory in spite of the most egregious blunders. There is not certainly at this moment a man of Genius among our Flag Officers.

Nor was there any joy to be had in the immediate future. His orders were to take the convoy to Trepassy and Placentia, to the south and east of St John's, and then to go north to Trinity for provisions. But it was a hopeless cruising ground;

Lord God, what am I to do when I get there? Sail from one fishing station to another, and carry up and down that cursed country a disc-ontented and repining spirit. I have been languishing for a war, and now that there is a kind of one, I am ordered to the place where there is the least chance of any work ... If I am not to be actively employed as a sea officer against the Enemy, I wish I were a merchant, a lawyer, a Physician, for I never was proud of a cockade for its own sake. It is not for me to grumble as I am very sure that many more deserving men are kept in the background, but I see there is too much partiality. There are few that have more thirst for hard earned military reputation than I have. I really long for a battle, although I know from experience, that my feelings will not be very pleasing when it comes. It is nonsense. It is like a woman's longing. I think it not unlikely that I may be passed over in the next promotion. They may be damned.

Ten leagues from the harbour of St John's, the remainder of the convoy suddenly scattered and there was nothing Moore could do but watch them depart as they headed for their different destinations. Twenty days after leaving Cork, the *Bonetta* sailed into St John's where she reprovisioned and then sailed north to Trinity. The ship itself was not in good condition. Although they had had reasonable weather for most of the voyage, water had constantly penetrated the lower decks from cracks in the deck and even from nail holes. The crew were in need of a period of relaxation, and Moore decided to give them a few days' rest with undisturbed nights' sleep in their hammocks. Happily, he was able to leave much of the care of the crew to Lieutenant Martin who had already demonstrated an admirable concern for their wellbeing.

Although Moore had previously had an unhappy experience with the Surrogate Court at Trinity, he liked the port, finding its poorer residents industrious and simple in their manners. Nevertheless he was unhappy with the treatment meted out to the native Indians. They were now scarcely seen, as numbers of them were frequently murdered by the fishermen, who over-wintered at the colony. They were also attacked by Canadian Indians, who had been supplied with European firearms, which were not available to the native Indians. With great presentiment, Moore lamented this treatment, for

> *. . . great benefit might be derived from these people, if their friendship was cultivated, and the winter inhabitants prevented from murdering them.*

He could only hope that the Government would adopt some means of protecting them before they were annihilated.

Moore learned that the senior officer on the station, Captain Courtenay in the frigate *Boston*, had sailed south in search of a French frigate said to be on the American coast. So he sailed round to Fogo, where there was a considerable cod fishery. The trade of the area was dominated by a single merchant, Lister of Poole. With a virtual monopoly on imported goods, Lister was able to charge high prices for goods and provisions in Fogo, and Moore heard a litany of complaints about him from local inhabitants and fishermen. Then he returned to Trinity and Harbour Grace where the *Bonetta*'s decks were re-caulked to make her watertight.

66

On 22 July, Moore decided to take the sloop out for a cruise between the Grand Banks and 42 degrees north. It was an unauthorized cruise, as Moore was all too well aware:

> I am now acting in a manner which subjects me to censure. If I take a Prize the Admiral will put his eighth in his pocket, and never trouble his noddle about the Latitude she was in. But if in my absence any Privateer or Frigate should molest the coast I should be in a damned scrape.

In the privacy of his journal he reasoned that there was little chance of a French frigate attacking the Newfoundland coast, because there was nothing there to be taken. Furthermore,

> I must run some risk, or the war will slip away leaving me the consolation of having rigidly obeyed my orders.

He was convinced that they could take any enemy merchantman they came across,

> . . . and I would be very happy to meet any Corvette in their service, but I hope we shall not see any of their Frigates, as I should expect to lose many men and be taken at last. I have good men in the ship, but no dashing active young fellow of an officer. The 1st Lieutenant is a most worthy, diligent, good man, the 2nd is a good fellow, and seaman enough, but he is not active, he has no spring in him. The Master is a lazy, indolent, fat, laughing soul, who minds his own business as little as any man I ever knew in that station. The Midshipmen are not the right sort, and the Warrant Officers want much looking after. I believe they would all fight, in the Dutch way, and I have no doubt but the men would do anything which can be expected of English sailors. Oh that I had a two and thirty[38], just manned in proportion as this sloop is. But then I must not have her here.

Moore always felt the loss of any of his crew, which was one reason why he recorded accidents or fatalities with such regularity in his journal. Now, on the passage to the Grand Banks, the cook's twelve-year-old servant became ill with a fever and died after a painful fortnight. With morbid thoughts, Moore noted in his journey, 'It is shocking to see a being in pain, [against which] Death is nothing'.

By the end of the month, the *Bonetta* was hurrying back to her station after a frustrating and fruitless cruise. Moore was still wracked with anxiety after overreaching his designated patrol area. On 15 August they returned to Trinity where, to Moore's chagrin, there was news that the sloop *Pluto* had taken a French brig. While Moore had been straying from his station in the hope of taking a prize, the *Pluto* had been lucky closer to home. There were also confused rumours about Captain Courtenay in the frigate *Boston*. It was said that whilst in search of the French frigate *L'Embuscade*, the *Boston* had lost her mizzen mast at sea and had to put into New York for repairs, where the French frigate was lying under protection of American neutrality. '*I suppose they will be comparing notes*', Moore observed rather sourly in his journal. Several days later, there was different news, and Moore was back to his ebullient self, relishing the possible success of his colleague. The story about the *Boston* being in New York had been a lie; she had last been seen off New York, having sent in a challenge to the French frigate. The outcome was not known, but the officers at Newfoundland were clearly keen to discuss the possibilities;

> The Boston *is one of the old two and thirty's, small and by no means so well calculated for fighting as the new class of Frigates but Courtenay is a charming fellow, and I shall be happy to hear of their meeting. The great danger a small frigate is in from the fire of a larger is in the probability of losing her masts, which when it happens, the most you can expect is to beat your adversary off.*

There was also great news from England, where the French frigate *Cleopatre* had been taken by Sir Edward Pellew in the frigate *Nymphe*, the first such success of the war; '*My friend Pellew has fought a gallant action and has been knighted for it, I would be very glad to fight a gallant action*', observed Moore, adding inexplicably, '*but I would be sorry to be knighted.*'

Meanwhile, Moore had a more immediate problem to deal with in a case of attempted sodomy aboard the *Bonetta*. His response to this was revealing:

> *Yesterday I did what I had no right to do, in flogging and turning a seaman ashore, who had acted in a manner disgraceful to the character of an Englishman. I must either have acted as I did, or taken the fellow round to be tried by Court Martial; it was impossible for him to remain in the ship after it. The horror and indignation which our countrymen have for attempts of that nature could not brook such a man remaining amongst them. Besides I am of opinion that morality suffers by such practices becoming notorious.*

The sudden recall of his attention to the men under his command led him to further observations on the character and nature of the common seaman. More serious misdemeanours were reprehensible and had to be dealt with severely but he also believed, paradoxically, that

> *. . . if they were totally free from the vices and follies which so often lead them into scrapes, some of their peculiar excellencies would quit them at the same time; I believe that the same carelessness of their persons which makes them sell their cloathes makes them patient of cold and wet. Having their swing ashore, and throwing away their money on whores, fiddlers and grog drives them to sea again; and the prospect of another such swagger makes them prefer foreign service that they may have a good haul of money at once. I have a set of famous fellows in this little bum boat, if the Admiral takes any of them from me he will break my heart.*

Moore was evolving into an excellent commanding officer, one who understood and valued the tools with which he worked. His reputation was also spreading and he was constantly turning away men who wished to serve under him, though he attributed this to the fact that they were really discontented with their current employers. He also had a deal of sympathy for both merchant seamen and fishermen on the Newfoundland station because, in order to ensure that seamen on the station returned to England at some point, their employers were prohibited from paying them more than half their wages whilst abroad. Instead, they were issued with Bills of Exchange for the remnant of their wages, which could only be surrendered for cash in England. However, at the same time, the English merchants wanted fishermen to over-winter in Newfoundland, as this avoided the time wasted in getting them to and from the crucial fishing grounds. The result was growing hardship and discontent. It was hardly surprising that many seamen sought escape via the Royal Navy.

On 29 August, the *Bonetta* set sail for St John's, learning on the way that the frigates *Fox* and *Boston* were already there. On arrival, Moore learned that the *Boston* had engaged the French frigate *L'Embuscade* on 1 August,

> *. . . and began a close action at 5 in the morning; after they had fought for an hour the gallant Courtenay and the Officer of marines fell dead by the same shot and the two Lieutenants were carried off the deck wounded, the 1st Lieutenant came upon deck soon after and continued the action for about 20 minutes longer, but having lost the main top mast, cross jack yard, Gaff and not being able to carry any after sail to*

manage the ship, he thought it prudent to make off as well as he could. L'Embuscade stood after her for half an hour and then brought to to repair her damage. It appears that the brave Captn Courtenay engaged this ship under every disadvantage, when he attacked her he had only 190 men and boys on board, one of his Lieutenants and a number of his people being away in a prize; the men that he had were very indifferent, slight hands, and very few of them seamen. L'Embuscade had 450 men on board in the action, the shot from her main deck guns weighed 15lbs and she mounted 4 guns more than the Boston. In my opinion, and it is that of most people with whom I have conversed on the subject, the action was decided by the death of Courtenay, the men looked up to him very much, he was cheering them up with his voice, and singing Rule Britannia at the moment of his death; the fellows crowded round his body and could not be kept to their quarters until the Lieutenant ordered the body to be thrown overboard. It appears that the design of the French was to board, trusting to their numbers, but they could not effect it. The Marines behaved with great valour and their Officer shewed them a noble example until the moment he fell on the body of Courtenay. I knew this valiant and most amiable Courtenay, he was of the right sort, no man could fall more honourably, I am convinced that he was determined to fight 'till he died, and that he never would have struck or run from this frigate.

Moore's retelling of the account of this action is fascinating, because it must have been recorded before the news reached England. The *Boston*, under the acting command of Lieutenant Edwards, had attempted to make the Delaware to carry out repairs after the action. However, on entering that river, Edwards learned that two French frigates were waiting there and he had no option but to press on to St John's, which is where Moore found him. *L'Embuscade* was certainly the heavier of the two frigates and although her complement was not as great as Moore was told, she certainly carried a much larger crew.[39] What Moore could also probably not know was that there was simmering discontent about Lieutenant Edwards' treatment of Courtenay's severely mutilated body. This later emerged as a blatant accusation by the naval historian Edward Brenton, who seemed to imply that Edwards threw Courtenay overboard before he was dead in order to assume command and break off the action. This seems extremely unlikely as Courtenay was killed at 6.20am, and Edwards did not break off the action until 7.07am. Whatever the truth, Edwards had suffered a head wound and had to be sent home to recover[40]. When the news of the engagement broke in England, the King granted Courtenay's widow a pension of £500 per annum, with £50 per annum for each of her two children. Such were the varied rewards for gallantry in action.

At the beginning of September, Moore took the *Bonetta* out to cruise on the Grand Banks once again – where he was also hoping to be the first to meet the Admiral and submit his claim to the command of the *Boston*. Whilst at sea, Moore took the opportunity of putting his gun crews through their paces;

> *We had a general exercise yesterday with the great guns, we fired a six pounder which I took on board at St John's and mounted on the Fore Castle, three times within the minute, with great ease. We now mount 19 guns, the Fore Castle gun being a shifting one.*

Three rounds in sixty seconds was a very efficient rate, though the speed would be expected to be slower for guns of a larger calibre. Nevertheless, there is evidence that Moore was reasonably diligent in keeping up his ship's gun practice. Although this is only the first time that Moore mentions it in his journal, his ships' logs suggest that Moore practised live firing, i.e. with fully loaded guns, at least every five or six weeks. Whilst this was nowhere near as frequent as some of the really crack frigate commanders, it was much more respectable than many officers managed.

To Moore's irritation, the *Boston* with her temporary commander, Richard Morice, was also waiting at sea to intercept the Admiral. Within a week though, the equinoctial gales had set in, and Moore decided to put in to Harbour Grace, glad of the opportunity of spending some time in sheltered water after what was turning out to be a fruitless duty;

> *Lord! What a weary drag these last six months have proved! I have been unlucky indeed, but I have nothing to reproach myself with.*

When Moore returned to St John's, he found Admiral MacBride was already there. His representations to the Admiral met with sympathy, but Morice had been recommended as an officer with excellent credentials (including being the son of a naval officer killed in action) – besides which he had already captured a brig. Moore had been half expecting this and accepted the situation graciously – in any event there was little else he could do. The Admiral, however, sweetened the pill by giving him orders to escort the next convoy back across the Atlantic, thereby releasing him from the Newfoundland station.

Towards the end of October, the convoy of thirty-six merchantmen – most of which were bound for Spain or Portugal with fish – was ready to depart. Moore joined them in company with the frigate *Cleopatra*, commanded by Captain Alan Ball. The *Bonetta* was now in a highly efficient condition. Regrettably, Moore's Second Lieutenant had asked to be superseded but the Admiral had agreed to his replacement by Lieutenant Robert Campbell, '... *a very fine young man, whom I have long known'*. All in all he was now very happy with his officers, and he still had to turn away willing volunteers;

> *I find the* Bonetta *has a most excellent name, which I attribute as much to the care and attention of the first Lieutenant Mr Martin, as to the good treatment they have always received from me. When Seamen crowd to a Sloop of war to enter as volunteers in preference to a Frigate, it is a sure proof that the Officers of that sloop are loved by the men.*

His only concern consisted of fifteen French prisoners of war the Admiral had insisted he should carry back to England. Moore thought that the number was excessive for the size of the sloop. However, he soon found

> *The French Prisoners give me less trouble than I expected, they are fine stout fellows and behave quietly. When they came on board first I told the principal man amongst them who is a smart, chattering fellow that I was perfectly disposed to make their situation as comfortable as possible, that they should be perfectly at liberty to walk about during the day, but that at night, I expected they were to be in the place allotted for them to sleep in. I turned all hands up and addressing myself to our seamen and marines I told them that I expected they would show their generosity to these poor fellows in treating them kindly, and that I should feel grieved and ashamed if they had any cause to complain of us. I then took the opportunity to remark to them ... that we had some chance of meeting an enemy, and that, from my confidence in the ship's company, I had no doubt but we should play our part, and with such men I would be very happy to go alongside of a much superior force. The lads seemed to relish this last touch, as they instantly gave three cheers and one of the quarter Masters damned the Dog that would not stand by me while there was a shot in the locker. Indeed I ought to be proud of commanding such fellows, the ship is better manned than ever she was, and they are attached to me and to the officers.*

On 30 October, the convoy set off in heavy seas. Ball, who was as keen as Moore on taking a good prize, had issued a standing order to

72

chase any strange vessel sighted. In fact he had offered a three-guinea reward to the first of the *Cleopatra*'s crew to spot any prize they subsequently took. However, in the two weeks it took them to reach Portugal, they sighted only one other vessel, and she proved to be nothing of interest. Having delivered their convoy, the *Cleopatra* and *Bonetta* sailed south to Cadiz where they were due to collect a convoy for England. Arriving there on around 20 November, they learned that the convoy would not be ready to sail until 4 December. After a few days waiting idle in port, both commanders were keen to get to sea again, and it was decided they should take a brief cruise to see what they could pick up. The decision almost led to serious trouble. A day out of Cadiz the two ships sighted a squadron of four ships, which included a ship of the line. Uncertain who the strangers were, Moore and Ball cleared their ships for action, and Ball hoisted English colours and signalled by firing a single gun. The strangers responded by hoisting Portuguese colours. Ball signalled to *Bonetta* to tack to eastward towards the Straits of Gibraltar, and then ran alongside to speak to Moore. Shouting across the narrow water between the two ships, Ball explained that he thought the ships were genuinely Portuguese, but given the superior firepower of the squadron, he didn't want to risk being surprised if they were French, so would keep a safe distance from them. Suspicions were not allayed when the strangers appeared to follow the two English ships, keeping to windward of them, and then there was real alarm when the wind shifted and the ship of the line suddenly bore down towards the *Bonetta*. Ball quickly brought the *Cleopatra* close in support of the smaller ship and the stranger veered away. After dark, the *Cleopatra* and *Bonetta* doused their lights and tacking to westward, had the satisfaction of seeing the lights of the mysterious squadron continue to leeward. As senior officer, Ball was in command during this encounter, and Moore was highly impressed with his behaviour. A day or two later he joined Ball for dinner aboard the *Cleopatra* and was again impressed by all he saw on board her and her commander's professionalism;

He spares no pains to improve his ship's company, and to put his ship in the most perfect state for real service, but he has the manly sense to despise the silly refinements which some of our most promising young officers are dazzled with, and with which they are too apt to harass and disgust our seamen. He is blest with a humane and gentle disposition which is not of that nature which is content with doing no harm and mere wishing for the happiness of others, but appears by his

*unremitting attention to the wants, and his active exertions to improve
and meliorate the condition, of that animal to whose peculiar character
I am thoroughly persuaded we owe our unrivalled Naval superiority, I
mean the British Jack tar.*

Four days later, as dawn broke, the two ships sighted a large stranger
to leeward. Ball and Moore both watched the ship closely, agreeing
that she must be a two-decker, but she showed no colours and failed
to respond to the private signal. *Cleopatra* and *Bonetta* reduced sail
until only their topsails were set, and warily watched the other ship
passing on the opposite tack. But then she began to close, working up
towards the two smaller ships. Moore was convinced now that she
was at least a 48- or 50-gun ship, and possibly Dutch. They tacked to
escape;

*Ball asked me, with a half laugh, if I thought her more than a match
for us, I answered that I thought her much more than that. We
continued to run from her with all our sail. At Sun set she was still in
chase, but we wronged her.*

The cruise proved fruitless, for all the vessels they stopped turned out
to be Portuguese and the only real potential prize they saw was a
privateer brig which escaped them after nightfall. On 1 December,
they turned back towards Cadiz, only to have the wind turn against
them. Fretting continually about the delay they were causing the
convoy, they eventually arrived on 10 December to find that the
convoy was still not ready to sail. Finally, on Christmas Eve, they
sailed for England. Moore fully expected to encounter 'St. *Nicholas's
Clerk's*' (i.e. French cruisers) before reaching Spithead. The prospect
did not dismay him in the slightest; in fact he was rather relishing the
idea, commenting

*I see no hopes of promotion but by a desperate fight, and I certainly
would rather owe it to that than to Bum-kissing.*

It was perhaps with this in mind that he had been studying *The Essay
On Naval Tactics, Systematical And Historical*, by John Clerk, who,
being a fellow Scot, he was naturally drawn to.[41] Moore appreciated
that Clerk was not a naval man, but still considered the work one of
the best he had read (which suggests not only that there were more
than a few tracts on this subject but also that he had read them):

*I most completely agree with him in the folly of attacking an Enemy's
whole line instead of bending your force against his rear; independent*

of the infinite disadvantage you fight your enemy at by running along his line, it is most certain that, supposing you could even place your ships, without annoy, alongside of the Enemy, ship for ship, and with the weather Gauge (the point which we have always contended for and which we have so little profited by) we should in all probability make but an indecisive battle of it, as it is next to an impossibility that the whole line should be beat at once, and when any ship in the leeward line finds her place too hot for her, she has only to run to leeward of her own line, when she is completely safe, as the ship which attacked her cannot follow her, to be cut off from her own line.

These were tactics later put to good use by Nelson. But when Clerk observed that *'It is said by many people that the command of a fleet requires inferior talents to those which are requisite for the General of an army . . .'*, Moore retorted that it was an argument not worth entering. He conceded that at sea communications between ships usually broke down once battle commenced, which they were less likely to do on land, but it could hardly be argued that armies were subject to the effects of shifts of wind in the same way that ships were. Moore believed that the most important factor lay in well disciplined (i.e. well drilled) ships, without which even the most perfect naval skills would be of little avail. He thought that the only reason that English admirals had escaped a 'scouring' in earlier wars was due to the excellence of the English seaman. He recognized that in the management of individual ships, there were some excellent officers, but when it came to fleet actions, little of significance had been achieved for fifty years. Although he might soon have reason to change this view, he felt gloomy about the prospects of fleet engagements in the current war, summing up his feelings with the comment *'I do not believe I shall ever be an Admiral'.*

After a painfully slow passage, during which provisions ran seriously short and a Dutch merchantman collided with the *Bonetta*, the two ships arrived at Spithead on 1 February 1794. The war with France was a year old.

7

Post Captain –
Sidney Smith's Squadron
(February 1794 – April 1796)

On arrival at Portsmouth, Moore secured a week's leave and took the mail coach to London. On arrival he learned from his father that, contrary to Admiral MacBride's assertion, Chatham, First Lord of the Admiralty, had been fully expecting Moore to get command of the *Boston*. This made him anxious to see Lord Chatham, to try to rectify this situation. The fact that command of a frigate had been denied him preyed on his mind and he now desperately wanted the command of such a ship. With it, of course, would also go the crucial promotion to the coveted rank of Post Captain.

Like all officers, Moore kept his ear to the ground and along with the usual rumours and news he learned that Captain Joseph Yorke, commander of the *Circe*, was to be promoted to a larger frigate. Moore arranged for a meeting with Chatham on 15 February and asked to be appointed as Yorke's successor. The First Lord made no promises but agreed to keep him in mind. By the time he left London to return to the *Bonetta*, he had still heard nothing, and Yorke himself was unable to give him any news. He arrived at Portsmouth in a state of anxiety, unsure whether he was going to be promoted at all, and fretting that he would not get the *Circe*, upon which he had now set his heart. Above all, it had suddenly struck him that promotion would probably mean he would be unable to take the crew of the *Bonetta* with him. It was a prospect which he found upsetting;

> *I have very little doubt that I am soon to be a Post Captain, but I am*
> *fretting with anxiety at the prospect of losing my men who are as fine*
> *a set of fellows as are to be met with; I have the pleasure of being*

beloved by them, which as it can proceed from no cause that is not honourable to me, is extremely agreeable to me.

His fondness for his crew was reflected in one of the first decisions he made on returning to the ship:

Tomorrow our men will receive about fourteen months pay; I intend to let one third of them go on shore to have their swing, and on their return to let another third and so on until they have all had a surfeit of the shore. I believe by this method I run less risk of losing men by desertions than I should by keeping them ever so strictly on board.

His consideration towards those under his command was reciprocated as virtually all of his men returned on board, in one state or another, though he was a little disappointed that several failed to match his faith in them. Yet any disappointment was soon obliterated:

I have been informed that the ship's company have written a petition to the Admiralty requesting that they may be removed with me, in case of my getting another ship. I thought it would be unbecoming in me to meddle with this business either pro or con, so I let it take its own course.

Moore was deeply touched by this development, but slightly fearful that the Admiralty would suspect that he had put the men up to the petition. He had not, and their unprompted petition reveals the depth of attachment they felt towards their commander – a clear refutation of the old belief that life on board a naval vessel was some form of floating hell.

As the weeks began to drift by, news of other promotions resulted in irritation:

I find the Admiralty have made some Post Captains. If I am not of the number, I think I am slightly used;

and then anger:

Our service is now rendered more difficult than formerly for anything but intrigue or connexion to make its way good. After a man has got a Post Ship, the great stumbling blocks are removed however and he has some opportunities of shewing himself in spite of neglect, and even of making his fortune: The fair prospect I now have of promotion reconciles me to a Profession I had begun to tire of, but so many things happen between the cup and the lip that I am prepared for a new disappointment.

His feelings probably spilled over into a furious tirade onto several of the pages in his journal, which he subsequently thought better to cut out. Fortunately, he was soon distracted by orders to take the *Bonetta* to Deal. Arriving there on 10 April there were a number of letters awaiting him – including the one he most wanted:

> *I received letters on my landing at Deal informing me of my being made a Post Captain into the* Narcissus *20 gun ship, at the same time I am given to understand that I am to have the* Circe *as soon as she becomes vacant.*

Quite how Moore might have celebrated this event is, sadly, not recorded. There was probably little time for social activity anyway, for the *Bonetta* was kept active for the next few weeks patrolling between Deal and Dunkirk, whilst Moore waited with a different anxiety for the arrival of his successor, a fellow Scot, Charles Wemyss. The latter arranged to be at Deal on 23 April to read his commission on board the *Bonetta*, and Moore, taking the opportunity of the sloop's need for beer and water, anchored there on the same day. Moore went on shore to report to the Admiral that Wemyss was to succeed that day but, to his astonishment, the Flag Officer ignored this information, ordering Moore and the *Bonetta* 'over the water' at Dunkirk. Stunned at this reception, Moore left the Admiral's office, believing that some misunderstanding had taken place. Two hours later he ventured back to the Admiral,

> *. . . when I found him on tip toes as stiff as a Crow Bar, telling me that he wanted my sloop over the water, that he thought I had been gone. I stared, as I had not understood that he wished me to go out, notwith-standing what I had stated. But on seeing him on stilts, I told him I was off . . . This old Goose's behaviour to me is extremely illiberal, as he must have seen that I never wished to remain in Port, but he ought to consider the circumstance of my having been made Post near a month past, and, of course, that I must have time to land my things and arrange matters with the new Captain. I have some idea that he wishes to make me quit before I am superseded by Wemyss that he might have an oppor-tunity of putting a person into the ship, but he shall be damned first . . .*

Moore's suspicions about the Admiral's motives may have been well founded. It was not unusual for station commanders to slip a favourite into a temporarily vacant position, as this then gave them more of a lever to secure their promotion – or for the protégé to acquire some form of distinction whilst in command.

Four days later, Moore returned to Deal, and Wemyss boarded the *Bonetta* to read his commission. It was customary for the outgoing commander to address the crew, and in a happy ship this could be an emotional moment. There was no doubt that because many of his crew were attached to Moore, this was the case, but he restricted the entry in his diary to a laden but simple observation: '. . . *I took leave of my men and delivered the sloop up* [to Wemyss]. *The seamen seemed to feel as much as I did on the occasion, which was a good deal.*' On 2 May, Moore received a commission for the frigate *Narcissus* – but he didn't need to go on board as the appointment was merely a device to keep him on full-pay until the *Circe* became available. He was glad, because the *Narcissus* was thought to be '. . . *one of the worst ships in the service*'. As the weeks passed there was still no news of the *Circe*; instead he heard an unhappy rumour that he might be appointed as Flag Captain to Sir Richard King in Newfoundland.

> *The ways of the Admiralty are dark and intricate, puzzled in mazes. I cannot get any information relative to myself. I cannot while in this state attend seriously to anything, I lounge through the streets, dissatisfied with myself, and looking at everything desirable as unattainable. I enjoy the esteem of those I love, without which life would be intolerable to me . . . I am told that I am to be employed but not when.*

Finally, at the beginning of July 1794, Moore was summoned to the Admiralty, where Chatham offered him the choice of the 28-gun frigate *Vestal*

> *. . . completely manned and to retain her men or the* Syren [32] *giving me to understand that her people were to be turned over into the* Apollo *with Captain Manley* [her existing Captain]. *As a 32 is in every respect* [a] *superior vessel to a 28 I did not hesitate in giving the preference to the* Syren *especially as I had reason to think she was in better condition than the* Vestal *which ship had very little repair since she came from the East Indies.*

The *Syren* was an attractive first command for a Post Captain. Launched at Mistleythorn on the Medway in 1782, she carried 26 12-pounder guns as her main armament, and had a complement of 210 men. Moore joined her on 20 July though he was anxious about the future of her crew:

*Manley thinks himself cock sure of all the men, the only chance I think
I have of them is that of the ship being suddenly ordered on service when
I think his accommodation would not be considered.*

Realizing that the Admiralty would be reluctant to strip a ship which
was on active duty, he decided to take the frigate to sea as quickly as
possible and keep her there. He was somewhat reassured when the
Admiralty permitted him to transfer from the *Bonetta* his First- and
Third Lieutenants (Henry Martin and Robert Campbell), together
with his Coxswain and three Midshipmen. At least he would be able
to rely on some consistency in the command structure. By the second
week of August the *Syren* was actively patrolling the French coast and
Moore had a better opportunity of assessing the merits of his new ship
and her crew; *'She is not badly off as to men, but they want to be exercised and methodised.'* Furthermore, he was pleased with the frigate's
sailing qualities:

> *The* Syren *sails well, I did not expect she would have made so good a
> figure, as her copper is very foul . . . I am by no means sure that the last
> class of frigates beat the old 32-gun frigates in sailing, altho' they have
> several other advantages over them and as to the question of the supe-
> riority of the French ships over ours, I have no means the same partiality
> for the French Models that I had. If from their great length they are
> stiffer and more weatherly, they do not work nor answer their helm so
> quick for the same reason.*

This augured well for any chance of distinguishing himself in the
channel, but he was increasingly aware that the ship was inadequately
fitted out and armed for combat, which made him worried that he
might be easily outgunned by an enemy frigate;

> *The* Syren *is not fitted for war as she ought to be, her Quarter-Deck is
> not barricaded, neither has she any carronades*[42]. *Her carronade locks
> are neither good in kind nor complete in number.*

Added to which he still had concerns about the discipline of the crew
and already he had had to order twelve lashes inflicted on two seamen
for contempt:

> *Her men are not well disciplined and from the uncertain state I am in
> with regard to their remaining with me, are not likely to be got into
> good order, until it is decided whether they go or stay.*

Days later, the Admiralty instructed him to transfer the Second

Lieutenant, Master and Manley's Midshipmen, to the *Apollo*. It left Moore with an immediate shortage of Watch Officers.

> *At present I have only two lieutenants . . . and as there is no Master, I keep watch myself, in order to relieve them . . . There are now only two of Manley's Midshipmen remaining, one is son to the Earl of Essex, the other to Lord Boyne, the 1st is a remarkable fine young man, & one whom I am convinced will turn out a meritorious officer; the other is a good young fellow, but as far as I can see an inferior character to Capel. Neither of them remain with me, I shall regret Capel.*

Moore's judgement was correct; within a few years Thomas Bladen Capel[43] became one of the navy's finest frigate commanders.

Anticipating that he would soon lose some of the frigate's better able seamen, he pressed a number of men from homeward-bound merchantmen, including at least fifty from East Indiamen. He was aware, however, that it was unusual for the Admiralty to allow a captain to keep all of the men he pressed:

> *I am now in agonies of fear of losing these men whom we have got, which would be dreadful upon me as I am not to keep the old ship's company.*

In an attempt to retain the men he wrote pleading letters to the Admiralty:

> *I have tried the effect of the pathetic both on Sir Charles Middleton and Lord Chatham, [as] it would be better for me to keep the new men than the old: they are by much the best.*

Bitterly, on his return to Portsmouth, he was obliged by the Port Admiral to hand over fifty-eight pressed men for service in other ships. The loss was slightly mitigated by the fact that he managed to keep fifteen men, simply by not reporting their impressment immediately at Portsmouth;

> *It is a great pity that a Captain of a Man of War, who has no friends in the Admiralty, can never have his ship fit for service if he does not commit irregularities.*

This was a slightly unfair assessment, for Moore clearly did have such friends. Furthermore, they would have been well aware that Moore was in a good position to press more men from homeward-bound ships in the Channel – an opportunity which was not available to the labour-intensive ships of the line.

In September there came reports that a French squadron was preparing at Dunkirk and the *Syren* was ordered to reinforce the Downs Squadron. The Downs was not a favoured station, as Moore noted laconically:

> *The Downs Station in war is in all respects a very disagreeable one, the communications with the shore is* [sic] *very precarious, and we continually are liable to be sent out so suddenly as to leave our linen etc behind, which is my case at present. Then when we are at sea we are on a most dangerous coast surrounded with shoals.*

After an initial cruise off Dunkirk, the squadron was driven back to Margate road by a violent storm and held there for several days. The enforced stay there allowed the officers of the squadron to stretch their legs on shore and

> *Brown, the Captain of the* Active *and myself went on shore yesterday to Margate where I never had been before. We walked to Broadstairs which is three or four miles from Margate, both the watering places are very full at present of the people of fashion from London. We dined at Margate, and were a good deal pressed to go to the Play in the evening, where a Gentleman, a friend of mine, and one of the greatest Originals I ever met, was to perform one of Shakespeare's most capital characters. We had a great desire to see this, but thinking it improper to be out of our ships at night we gave it up and returned on board.*

By the end of October, the scare engendered by the rumoured French squadron had passed, and the *Syren* was ordered round to Sheerness for a refit. As usual, Moore loathed being sent there, the dockyard being poorly equipped and unhealthy, and there were other disadvantages:

> *This is a cursed place, and so near London that there is a very great chance of desertion.* [But] *I think it the most prudent plan to show a confidence in them* [the crew] *by giving them leave to go on shore.*

In fact, he had limited choice in the matter anyway, as the task of refitting the ship meant that numbers of the men had to go on shore at different times, where

> *. . . opportunities of intoxicating themselves are not to be prevented, and every species of disorder follows that beastly excess . . . The circumstances of my profession which is most distressing to me is the necessity of corporal punishment, I believe that our service cannot be carried on*

without it, the seaman being of so careless and dissolute a bent that exhortation is thrown away upon them.

Despite Moore's distress, he had little need to impose such punishment on the crew for drunkenness, although two seamen were flogged for theft.

By the middle of December, the *Syren* was back at sea and on her way to the coast of Norway. On 18 December,

. . . between two and three in the morning, hearing a dreadful noise, I ran upon deck in my shirt and found the ship lying with her sails all aback and the rocks within half a mile of her to leeward; the people were hurrying up in the utmost confusion some crying out that they were all lost. The first thing that struck me, in this horrible situation, was to look if we had room to wear, which appeared to be impossible clear of the breakers. I then ran to the compass and found she was lying ESE upon which I immediately ordered the yards to be braced round and the fore tack hauled on board, sending the pilot forward to look out for rocks and breakers ahead, the men behaved well in this trying situation, making no noise and paying attention to the orders . . . we were dreadfully alarmed several times by people seeing, or thinking they saw, breakers, which we bore up for more than once.

After several nail-biting hours, Moore managed to get the frigate clear of danger, but he was well aware how close they had come to complete disaster:

I never was nearer to Eternity, for as the ship was running between 8 and 9 knots, 5 minutes later in hauling our wind would have had us on the rocks.

When the alarm had subsided, Moore made enquiries about how the ship had been allowed to get into such a perilous situation. The answers he received convinced him that there had been some laxity among the officers of the watch, but as they strenuously denied any culpability he could do no more than issue warnings about being more cautious in the future. It was typical of Moore to avoid publicly allocating blame without genuine evidence of fault, but privately he was angry and frustrated. It was a sobering incident with which to end the year, and left him pondering his future commitment to a naval career:

If a Peace is made I hope I shall be on half pay, I shall have no spirit for employment after the war, for a couple of years.

At the beginning of 1795, the *Syren* was back at the Nore, and Moore travelled to London to see Sir Charles Middleton, at the Admiralty. He was hoping that the *Syren* could be attached to Sir John Borlase Warren's independent frigate squadron, operating out of Falmouth. The squadron, together with a sister squadron commanded by Sir Edward Pellew, was achieving spectacular results and consisted of some of the navy's finest frigates and commanders. It was a highly attractive posting, but Moore was to be disappointed. Middleton explained that '. . . *the* Syren *was not of force sufficient for the service I wished to be on, but that I should not be forgot.*' Moore, though, had no wish to leave the *Syren*: '*We are likely to have hot work in the Spring in the North Sea* [for the French had overrun Holland], *I may account with an engagement or two in the* Syren, *and I do not wish for a larger ship, as I hope to meet with my Match; and if successful my reputation is then established.*'

Nevertheless, Moore's desire for a more active station was soon realized. On 18 February, he received orders attaching the *Syren* to a squadron under the command of the controversial Captain William Sidney Smith. Smith had conceived the idea of putting together a small squadron consisting of several frigates, hoys, schooners and specially adapted gunboats for attacking the French channel ports and coastal trade. The gunboats were fitting out at Wells' Yard at Deptford, and Moore was given the task of supervising their preparation. Early in March, Smith himself arrived to see them and Moore had his first opportunity of meeting him;

> *I like this man. He is bent on the pursuit of reputation, as a military man. He seems extremely active and diligent, overlooks trifling difficulties, and goes the nearest and boldest way to his object. His manner is affable, frank and conciliatory, his conversation sprightly and ingenuous. He has read and studied much on those subjects which relate to his profession, in which he appears well skilled, and as his courage borders on the romantic I have no doubt that he will shine in war. I believe that we shall agree well, for I love the man and esteem his character.*

Meanwhile the *Syren* was moored at the Nore and Moore was becoming increasingly anxious to get her out to sea again, for the extended period of relative inactivity was making the crew bored and slack. At Sheerness work was underway refitting the *Arethuse*, a French frigate which had been taken at the capture of Toulon in 1793, and Moore could not help looking at her longingly:

She is a very fine ship, nine feet upon the lower deck longer than our largest frigates. I wrote to Lord Spencer asking him to appoint me to the command of her and to turn the Syren's *people over to her.*

Spencer declined the request, explaining that Moore had not enough seniority for such a large frigate.

The gunboats were finally ready at the end of April and Moore began a laborious journey to escort them across the Channel. The gunboats were extraordinary looking vessels, with hulls very broad at the bow, and tapering markedly towards their narrow stern. They were flat bottomed, but fitted with Schank's sliding keels.[44] As they made their way, Moore became increasingly sceptical about them, believing there were '. . . *many egregious blunders in the construction of them*', which rendered them unseaworthy and unsuitable for their task. On 2 May they arrived at Spithead,

> *. . . where we heard the melancholy news of the fate of the* Boyne, *which caught fire at Spithead . . . She was in flames instantly and in spite of every effort burnt to the Magazine when she blew up with a terrible explosion which we heard and saw the smoak of at sea 14 or 15 leagues from the place. We hear that few lives were lost . . .*[45]

At Spithead, the *Syren* was joined by Sidney Smith in the frigate *Diamond*, with the rest of the squadron, and they headed across to the Channel Islands where they hoped to fall in with Sir Richard Strachan's squadron. By the time they arrived, Moore had become impressed by Smith's seamanship:

> *I perceive that the chevalier is by no means shy of Rocks, we have shaved some pretty close in rounding Alderney.*

He was therefore somewhat embarrassed when, running into St Aubin's Bay on the west side of Jersey, the *Syren*

> *. . . struck on a sunken rock when running at the rate of 5 or 6 knots and rubbed over it.*

There was worse to follow for

> *. . . as we were clewing the topsails up, John Elphinstone, a seaman, fell from the fore topsail yard on the anchor stock and was killed – Since we struck on the rock, we make water, but not anything considerable; I fear, however, that this accident will very materially affect our sailing as I am sure the Copper must be much rubbed.*

It was not an auspicious start. Strachan's squadron was soon located and it was agreed that the two groups should cruise together down the west side of the Cherbourg Peninsula. They were in action almost immediately for, on the following day, they encountered a convoy of thirteen French merchantmen working along the coast. The ships immediately ran on shore close under a battery at Cape Rozeland and the squadrons' boats were sent in to cut them out, while the *Syren* gave chase to and captured a brig which attempted to run. The battery itself was captured and destroyed, but the operation was costly. Nine men were wounded from Strachan's frigate alone, and Moore dismally noted the effects of the gunnery of the French battery:

Mr John McGuffoc one of our own Midshipmen lost both his legs and died an hour afterwards. One of our best Marines [John Charrington] had his bowels shot out, and two of the seamen were wounded, our capstern is shattered, but in other respects we received very little damage; the Surgeon of the Hebe *and one of the seamen have been desperately wounded, the surgeon of the* Hebe *had his leg shot off and one of the seamen lost one thigh and had his other leg shattered. It is astonishing that three or four guns could have done us so much mischief. Sir Sidney stood very close in and fired grape upon them, and his long boat carrying an 18 pounder Carronade swept the Beach with great effect . . . Guns in a Battery have a great advantage over ships unless the water is deep enough to admit the ships to come quite close, which was not the case here.*

The action brought a salutary lesson which Moore was not to forget.

A few days later, Smith decided to send the gunboats in to attack an armed brig sheltering under a fort. Covering fire was to be delivered by the *Diamond* and *Syren*, but after the gunboats set off, the wind dropped and they were swept sideways by the tide. After another attempt failed, Smith called off the attack, much to Moore's relief:

I own I did not like the business as our success would not have been of any consequence, and we were very fortunate to lose no men.

A similar attack took place on the 17th, though this time Smith ordered the ships' boats to tow the gunboats in to the attack. The boats set off, led by the *Syren*'s Lieutenant Robert Campbell, but half way to their objective, the pilots on board the gunboats refused to approach any closer. Campbell decided to proceed alone, and Moore watched in agony as the boats disappeared as grape and round shot tore up the sea around them. Fortunately, much to Moore's relief,

Campbell abandoned the attack. Like an anxious parent, Moore summoned Campbell to his cabin;

I reprimanded the lieutenant for suffering his zeal and courage to carry him so far beyond his orders. Fortunately none of their shot hit. I was miserable all the time I saw them exposed to such fruitless dangers.

After the departure of Strachan's squadron, Smith continued westwards. The attacks continued and nearly every day, the ships' boats were lowered to chase or cut out French vessels. Entering the Gulf of St Malo, Moore became convinced the French must now send out an overwhelming force from Brest to entrap them. He raised this worry with Smith, who accepted the point, but seemed in no hurry to leave the area. Moore couldn't understand:

These five or 6 days we have regularly anchored along the French shore with all the seeming confidence as if it was not hostile to us . . . Sir Sidney seems to have a passion for danger.

Furthermore, Moore was conscious of the hazardous nature of the coast on which they were operating: '. . . *the fact is that we are all afraid of the dangerous coast which is certainly formidable enough.*'

On 22 May, it seemed as though Moore's fears were justified. The sloop *Childers* arrived with news of a superior French squadron from Cherbourg near the Caskett Rocks between Alderney and Guernsey. Smith decided to set off and meet it, despite Moore's misgivings:

Sir Sidney does all in his power to meet them, knowing their force be so much superior . . . If we meet our match or superior, I think our men will fight, but I wish we had 25 good men more than we have, being short of complement . . .

Alarmingly, when the following dawn broke, Moore and Smith found themselves surrounded by seven or eight sail and '. . . *immediately beat to quarters not doubting that it was the convoy* [squadron] *from Cherbourg . . .*' In fact, the ships proved to be neutrals, and the French Squadron remained in port. Moore could not help speculating on the likely outcome of Smith's impetuosity. With amazing foresight, he concluded that,

From the ardour of his disposition and romantic turn he may adventure on some enterprize too hazardous and which may end fatally, but I think from his active courage, zeal and ability the chances are much in favour of his success.

Despite this, he continued to hold considerable admiration for his senior officer.

Strachan arrived with his squadron, to relieve Smith, on 1 June but the latter was in no hurry to depart and so it was again agreed the two squadrons should sail together to the west of St Malo. En route, the *Syren* was dispatched to chase several gunboats, and Moore followed them until they ran on shore;

> We were within random shot of them when we were obliged to tack for the point of St. Cas. I did not fire at them as I knew they were too far in for us to take them, and I have no taste for killing, or for having shot fired at us.

It was perhaps a curious decision for the commander of a frigate – but then Moore was always averse to the unnecessary shedding of blood.

Towards the end of the month, Smith revealed a new plan. This involved the occupation of the St Marcouf islands, two small rocky outcrops about 500 metres apart and lying some six kilometres (3.7 miles) from the French coast. Smith believed that a small force based here could effectively disrupt French coastal traffic and threaten any French vessels attempting to use the port of La Hogue. He had already dispatched a small party to occupy the islands and Moore was now sent to reinforce them. Upon arrival, however, he found that the position had already been abandoned in a panic at the first hint of a sortie from the French. Moore was sceptical about the value of holding the islands, but he now had standing orders to visit them regularly to keep their garrisons supplied. On 17 July, the *Syren* fell in with the frigate *Sybille*, which had been sent to join Smith's squadron and which Moore described as '. . . *one of the finest frigates in Europe*'. The *Sybille* was commanded by Edward Cooke who had been very successful in taking prizes, so it was agreed that the two frigates and the sloop *Childers* should share any prize money. Moore set off for a short cruise between Le Havre and Cape Barfleur, quickly taking two prizes. One, an American bound for Le Havre, carrying cotton, sugar and rice; the other, captured near La Hogue, was carrying foodstuffs, shoes and cotton. Despite these successes, however, Moore's duties were beginning to affect his health:

> I am very unlucky in being in bad health at this time when employed in the most active manner and likely to have an action. This may have the effect to break my constitution up, as I am liable to catch cold being necessarily much exposed to the weather.

Moore's constitution was never robust, and the obligations of a frigate commander were not going to improve matters.

On 28 July, patrolling off Le Havre, the *Syren* captured another American ship, a schooner, attempting to break the blockade with a cargo of flour. Dispatching the prize to Portsmouth, Moore returned to St Marcouf where he found the rest of Smith's squadron. Smith himself was busy supervising the mounting of a battery of 24-pounder guns and 32-pounder carronades behind an 18-foot earth rampart. Despite his belief in the overall weakness of the French navy, Moore found himself incredulous that the French could disregard this establishment of an enemy position so close to their coast. The squadron itself was causing a serious disruption to local coasting traffic and Smith was convinced that the island would soon be attacked, hence the resources he was throwing into the defences. Moore was doubtful:

> *We know that in Havre de Grace alone they have a superior force to our squadron, but they nor no other power in Europe have got English Sailors.*

At the beginning of August, Smith decided to launch an attack against a French camp near La Hogue but was forced to abandon it in bad weather. Moore, who was still unwell, was unenthusiastic about the attack and was even more perplexed when Smith suddenly disappeared across the channel to Brighthelmstone (Brighton) without leaving any explanation. Days later, however, Smith was back and the *Diamond*, *Syren* and *Sybille* sailed eastwards to Le Havre. Here they could clearly see two frigates and a number of smaller vessels building on the stocks. Smith summoned Cooke and Moore to the *Diamond* and informed them that he planned to row inshore that night in his wherry, taking four men to set fire to the vessels. The two captains were horrified, and persuaded Smith to let Lieutenant Pine of the *Diamond* lead the attack. The party duly set off at 11pm, rowing with muffled oars so as not to arouse any attention from the shipyard but when they arrived at the shore they found themselves on a stony beach and, as the night was very still, every footstep could be heard. Nevertheless, the five men made their way as stealthily as possible towards the ships where, unfortunately, they could find no ladder or any other means of climbing into the hulls. At this point they were challenged by a sentry and, fleeing back to the boat, put off from the shore. Several minutes later they realized all was again quiet and turning the wherry about they began to make their way back, only to see or imagine four men waiting for them on the shore. Obviously thinking discretion the better option, they returned to the *Diamond*, abandoning their attempt. Moore did not record Smith's reaction.

Two days later Smith, ordered the squadron to sail to Brighthelmstone, and Moore soon realized why they were there, for the Prince of Wales was in residence. Smith ordered the squadron to make a great display, saluting the Prince with twenty-one guns, firing off rockets and blue lights. The frigates then sailed to Portsmouth to re-provision, but whilst at Spithead a storm blew up and the *Syren* was damaged when her anchors dragged and she collided with an East Indiaman. While she was being repaired, Moore took the opportunity for a flying visit to London. He was just a few weeks short of his thirty-first birthday and, like many other young men and naval officers in his position, he was beginning to think that life was passing him by – especially in the matter of marriage and family. The question of love began to assert itself in his mind:

> It is curious that every time that I have been in love, which, by the by, has been pretty often, I have acted in a way which has afterwards appeared to me perfectly ridiculous, and of which I have consequently been ashamed. I am at present very fond of a girl whom I have not seen this year and a half. I have concealed it from my friends and never mentioned any thing that could lead her to believe in any stronger attachment than that of friendship for her and her family. I have not the least reason to believe that she loves me, but I am thoroughly persuaded of her esteem and friendship. I would marry her tomorrow, if she chose, and if we had enough money, but, as I have none and she has not enough for two, I have avoided endeavouring to engage her affections. I would be very unhappy if I saw her partial to any man, and I cannot help indulging a hope of what is very improbable, that circum-stances may so change as to make it a fair thing for me to address her ... have known her from childhood, she being nine or ten years younger than me, and admired her sweet and amiable mind and manners long before there could be any love in the case.

Unfortunately, Moore either deleted or avoided naming the young lady – but for convenience we will refer to her henceforth as Miss M.[46]

From the end of August through the early part of September 1795, Smith extended the *Syren*'s cruising ground to cover the triangle between Guernsey, St Marcouf and Start Point, the headland south of Torquay on the north side of the Channel. Although largely cruising alone, Moore continued to worry when he learned about Smith's activities. The problem remained the same: '*Sir Sidney exposes himself and his people a great deal too much*', and sooner or later something was going to go badly wrong. By the end of September, the *Syren* had taken several prizes and a significant number of the frigate's crew had now been sent off in them. Moore was keen to recover his men from Portsmouth and he set off to rendezvous with Smith, to get the Commodore's permission. Instead, when they met, Smith insisted on the whole squadron going to Weymouth where the king was currently in residence. Moore fumed quietly:

> *I am very sorry for it, as it can answer no other purpose than foolish parade, I think we might be better employed . . . Sir Sidney had been at the Islands as I expected and had amused himself drawing fire from the Batteries along shore with his boats.*

On the following day, Moore's fears were realized:

> *On the 15th we went into Weymouth Road where as the King was at that time each ship fired a Royal Salute. The [frigates] Melpomene and St. Fiorenzo were in the Road attending on His Majesty. Sir Sidney and the other captains waited on His Majesty on the Esplanade in the evening. Next morning it was intended that the King and Royal Family should go on board the St. Fiorenzo, which was to get under sail accompanied by the other ships and perform some Naval evolutions: This plan was prevented by the unfavourable weather.*

Undeterred, Smith decided that the squadron should put on a good display by putting to sea whilst simultaneously firing salutes. Again, however, the weather intervened to frustrate Smith's plans. The *Diamond*, being the furthest from the shore was able to implement the plan, but Cooke decided that it was imprudent to weigh anchor at all given the state of the wind and swell. The *Syren*, although closest to the shore, weighed anchor, but was too busy tacking out of the bay to fire any salutes. By the time the *Syren* had got off the shore, Smith had disappeared off to the west, leaving the other two frigates to rendezvous with him at Cherbourg.

Once back on station, Smith decided to take the squadron to Le Havre. Perhaps as a demonstration of his own zeal, Smith took his own ship in as close to the shore as possible. Moore watched with evident disapproval and determination not to put his own ship and crew at risk:

As I hate this bravado business, I let go the anchor as soon as the signal was made for that purpose.

Springs were then run out from the ships so that they could be quickly manoeuvred in case they were attacked by gunboats. Moore was sceptical about the efficacy of this precaution, for if the French gunboats did come out and kept at long-shot distance

. . . they might finish our cruise with very little risk to themselves. I certainly do wish to have an action in the Syren, *but I mortally nauseate this childish kind of bluster that we are pestered with.*

That night the wind blew up, veering from the south to westerly, but Smith gave no order to move to a safer position and, Moore noted wearily, '. . . *I concluded that we were to continue on this useless and hazardous parade until the wind came in'*. After several days the squadron was withdrawn, but on 15 October, during a patrol along the coast, Smith and Moore returned to Le Havre. This time Smith ordered the *Syren* to anchor closest to the harbour entrance and Moore went on board the *Diamond* for orders. No sooner had he done so than French gunboats made a spirited sortie from the harbour. Shot began to fall closely round the *Syren* and Moore hurried back to her;

Before I got onboard the shot were falling pretty thick about us, the ship had begun to play away among them. This I stopped instantly in order to get our anchor up and the sail set. We hove up pretty brisk (altho' it was difficult to keep the people from firing) and got our topsails set, but as we were lying to, stowing the anchor, what we call catting it[47], a heavy shot cut away the fore top sail sheet and passed through the centre of our Fore yard about 14 feet from the Yard arm.

Moore immediately ordered the frigate to wear and ran out to the *Diamond* to see if Smith wanted him to make an attempt to cut off the gunboats, after they had repaired their fore yard. Smith agreed, but darkness fell before the *Syren* could complete the repairs and then, during the night, the weather blew up so the two frigates were forced to weigh to get a safe distance from the land. Once again, Moore found himself questioning Smith's tactics – especially when it came to attacking gunboats in shoal water;

I like the Chevalier most sincerely on account of his great, good and amiable qualities, but I cannot defend such absurd conduct as this which teases and frets those who love and esteem him, as well as those

92

who envy and wish to ridicule him . . . I am sorry to see a good deal of illiberality in many officers in our service with respect to Sir Sidney; this is owing in a great measure to the singularity of his character, manner and dress, and also to his being passed off in a most ridiculous manner by some very injudicious friends: I do not apply this observation to Strachan who is a most open, generous, brave fellow and a most excellent seaman, but to many others men of merit and others. I have a great deal of respect and real regard for Sir Sidney but think . . . he wants judgement. I love and value him and think I know him better than most people, but there are many of his plans that I totally disapprove of.

Moore found himself fulminating once again on the strategy of occupying the St Marcouf Islands. He was aware of the general attitude of other captains towards Sidney Smith, and couldn't help thinking that the occupation of the islands would be seen as just another of his madcap antics;

I never knew a man who seemed to brave Ridicule so much as my Commodore, I am obliged when at Portsmouth to answer this question two or three times a day – What use are the islands of? The fact is that the plan he is upon, as he never can have it thoroughly and fully adopted, will never turn to much account. Blocking up the Ports of the enemy cannot be completely done without seizing some Posts which will insure a tolerable Road for the different Squadrons on the coast.

In other words, although it was strategically valuable to have possession of some positions on the French coast, they were useless unless adequately resourced and unless the supporting ships had a safe and secure anchorage. So far the government had shown little real commitment to the occupation of the islands. If they were supportive, they would have supplied proper barrack buildings and gunboats which were designed for rowing as well as sailing. In fact, where the gunboats were concerned, Moore sincerely wished that Smith had not been allowed any involvement in the design; he would rather that had been left to '. . . *Captain Schank or some other practical mechanic'*.

Moore had even more cause to question the strategy when he returned to the islands;

The crews of the Gun Boats are excessively dissatisfied, they see themselves cooped up in two barren rocks, neglected and ill fed; kept at hard work of a nature they are not accustomed to, and at the same time violently of the same opinion – cui bono. *Their discontent has appeared by their frequent running away with the boats, sometimes even in*

93

weather so rough that there is great room for believing that they perished . . .

He also found himself wondering what he should do if the *Syren* was surprised by a superior force whilst alone at the islands:

It would become a question what was best for me to do, whether to anchor close in and share the fate of the islands or to attend to the safety of the ship alone. I have no very high opinion of the actual force of the islands, and think that 3 [enemy] frigates ought to settle the business for both us and them; yet considering the probability of succour coming from England, and perhaps on the back of the ships attacking us, [i.e. attacking them from the rear] as also that disabling these Frigates, even if we should be worsted might prove the safety of many of our Merchant ships, upon the whole, I think, it would become me to stand by the islands. Besides, in my profession, whenever it is a disputed point whether to fight or not, it is best to fight.

In the middle of November, Moore set off to rendezvous with the frigates *Amazon* and *Caroline* off Cape Barfleur. Looking into Cherbourg, Moore saw the French frigate *La Romaine* lying in the road. She was not preparing for sea, but as the weather had been so bad this was not surprising. There seemed to be hardly any English cruisers at sea, and the weather conditions were taking their toll on the crew of the *Syren*;

Since we left Spithead we have scarce passed a day and night without being obliged to take in our fore top sail. – Our people are a good deal harassed by fatigue, cold and wet.

But, in his own way, Moore too was suffering:

The want of society is one of the most uncomfortable circumstances in my profession. Among six or seven men, which is the most we meet of that class which we can conveniently have much social intercourse with in a frigate, a man is in high good luck if he meets one person from whose character and conversation he can draw much amusement or instruction; and I fear that being too much either alone or in the company of indifferent, common minded men, must by degrees weaken the energies of our minds, which no doubt, require exercise to strengthen or even keep them at their attained degree of perfection. Want of books is another disadvantage incident to our profession, as a great collection would occasion inconvenience and expense . . . Indolence is one of our greatest failings and the cause of many others.

94

Such were the disadvantages of command.

On 29 November, the *Syren* fell in with a cartel brig that reported that the storms had devastated a force bound for the West Indies under the command of Admiral Christian. The force had been intended to stabilize the position in the Caribbean, for the initial British success of the earlier expedition under Jervis and Grey had been short-lived. Moore believed that he knew the real reason for this because he had talked to many naval officers who had served there under Admiral Jervis:

> *They assure me that our own misfortunes in the Leeward Islands orig-*
> *inated in the alienation of the esteem and confidence of the inhabitants,*
> *and in their hatred of us occasioned by the scandalous rapacity and*
> *extortion practised upon them . . .*

In fact Admiral Jervis (later Earl St Vincent and First Lord of the Admiralty) had completely overstepped the mark in allowing his cruisers to go on a prize-taking rampage, while both Jervis and Grey had virtually plundered the French colonies they captured. The resultant alienation was huge, undermined confidence in British rule and gave encouragement for the restoration of Republicanism.[48]

By the middle of December, the *Syren* was in need of repair and Moore took her back to Portsmouth for docking. She was not ready for sea again until 6 February, by which time she had lost ten men through desertion, and was considerably short of complement. The stay in Portsmouth had also resulted in a disruption to the ship's discipline and Moore was obliged to order a number of punishments on their return to sea. He set sail towing a new launch for the St Marcouf islands and reached the coast of France in a gale. Before he realized it, the *Syren* had run deep into the Bay of La Hogue and they were unable to weather Cape Barfleur. The increasing gale and lee tide threatened them with disaster. Moore though, for all his self-doubts, had already shown himself a cool hand in a crisis like this. He imme-diately ordered the courses set and '. . . *haul'd our wind for Cape Barfleur*', passing the St Marcouf islands about two miles to wind-ward;

> *We were standing towards the Fort at Fatihou and the flood tide on our*
> *weather bow setting us fast in. Had to cut the launch adrift, it was half*
> *swamped. I concluded that the tide had begun to slack and that on the*
> *Larboard tack we should take the Ebb under the lee bow. When within*
> *3 miles of Fatihou, wore ship and by carrying a great press of sail I*

found she went off shore: at low water we wore again and the wind favouring us a little we got to the North East of Cape Barfleur in the course of the night.

The next day they made their way back to St Marcouf, where they were soon joined by the *Diamond* and the *Childers*. Fortunately, the Lieutenant commanding the garrison on the easternmost island had spotted the abandoned launch and had been able to retrieve it. Moore, though, was now suffering physically as the spell of bad weather before Christmas had given him agonizing rheumatism in his shoulders.

Looking into Cherbourg again on 23 February, he found the French frigate *La Romaine* preparing to sail with two armed brigs and a convoy of twenty-seven vessels. He decided that, with an easterly wind, the convoy must pass through the Race of Alderney, so he anchored the frigate there so that he could surprise them if they sailed during that night's ebb tide. As night fell, he had the frigate's topsails loosed, ready to sheet home quickly and axes standing by for cutting the anchor cable in case they had to move in a hurry. Moore was well aware that *La Romaine* was nearly double the strength of the *Syren*, but he was undeterred;

> *I am not afraid of the consequences of a meeting with what we saw in Cherbourg, the wind being off shore, I think the worst that could happen to us would be getting a drubbing, as we could probably get off before the wind if we found them too strong for us.*

Nevertheless, it must have been a relief when, on the morning of the 26th, the crack frigate *Niger* arrived, commanded by Edward Foote;

> *I would feel great confidence in meeting anything that would fight while Foote is with me, he appears to be a remarkably zealous, intelligent officer, and the* Niger *is in very excellent order.*

Then, very shortly after, a large ship was seen approaching through the Race accompanied by a convoy of merchantmen. To everyone's bitter disappointment this proved to be the frigate *Melampus*, commanded by Richard Strachan, with his squadron and a convoy for Guernsey. Moore though, still found some cause for celebration:

> *I was well pleased with the spirit and alacrity which our fellows displayed this morning when they thought they were going into action.*

This bode well for the future. Strachan anchored, for a consultation with Moore, and then took his squadron off in search of the French convoy, leaving the *Niger* and the *Syren* at anchor near Alderney. Once again, Moore found himself admiring Strachan:

> No man can be more zealous, active and daring than this brave fellow;
> it is a real pleasure to me to meet him as he possesses my entire esteem.
> I think his ship one of the fittest for action of any in the Navy.

Almost immediately after Strachan's departure, a heavy gale set in and the two frigates were obliged to remain at anchor for several days. Lack of activity was once again making Moore morose and his thoughts turned once again to home and affairs of the heart, and in particular the young woman of whom he secretly had great hopes – Miss M:

> As the prospect of active service against the Enemy lessens, the desire of revisiting my friends augments; I foresee that I shall cut out matter for chagrin and unhappiness by indulging a passion which has been taking slow, but, I believe, firm root in my heart.
>
> As succeeding, in my present situation as to Money matters, would open but an uncomfortable prospect, I have never yet made any advances, nor, consistent with my ideas of right and wrong, can I; there appears no reasonable ground for hope, there being so very little probability of my being possessed of fortune sufficient to live as I would wish when no longer a Bachelor – If that bar were removed, the rest of the Romance would very soon finish as I think if I found myself unacceptable my mind is so tuned that I could get the better of my disappointment, as I could not bear to be tied to any person to whom I was not as dear as I could wish. If on the other hand I were, what they call, fortunate, we should probably get into the old jog trot way of life that all our brethren before us have followed. The Romantic side of the picture, amuses and teases my thoughts.

Entombed on board his frigate, while bad weather crashed around the anchorage, it is hardly surprising that the bachelor frigate captain's thoughts should eventually turn to the pleasures of the flesh. Yet, as the days passed, the more professional interests exerted themselves. Foote was waiting to be relieved by Captain Lord Henry Paulet in the frigate *Thalia*, and was anxiously looking out for him. Moore was more worried about the situation at St Marcouf. When the weather moderated on 4 March, he sailed for the islands and was relieved to find everything there in good order. He then returned to the Channel

Islands where he was supposed to rendezvous with Sidney Smith, but by 9 March there was still no sign of the Commodore. However, he was soon joined by Strachan in the *Melampus* and Foote in the *Niger*, and the three frigates ran round to St Marcouf where they encountered the frigate *Druid*, commanded by Captain Richard King. Near there, on 19 March, the *Druid* and the *Syren* surprised a sloop and a lugger which took shelter close to the shore. Moore and King decided to try to cut them out, using a launch borrowed from St Marcouf.

At 11pm, the attack was sent in. Moore, in a state of agitation knowing there was little he could do to effect the outcome, retired to his cabin and took up his pen:

> *It is now midnight and I have just sent the Island launch, our large and small cutter, the* Druid's *barge and cutter well manned and armed to the mouth of the river to endeavour to cut out the lugger and Sloop. I am of course very anxious, but if they can get alongside I have no doubt of their success.*

Unfortunately, the lugger escaped in the darkness and the frigates' boats ran aground and remained so until the tide rose. They returned to the ships at 3.30am. Things went even more wrong the following morning. At daylight Moore gave the order to weigh, as the wind had risen and there was a heavy swell;

> *In heaving ahead the Capstern flew round (owing to the heedlessness of the men) killed one man outright and wounded three others slightly.*

It was not the only accident there had been recently:

> *Three days ago as we were coming to an anchor two of our men fell overboard, and altho' we picked them both up yet one of them was so much hurt, having fallen from the main yard, that he died the next day – We are now very weakly manned.*

When Moore returned to St Marcouf, he found that Smith had arrived with storeships carrying supplies and blockhouses for the islands. The storeships also carried arms and equipment for a Chouan army which was expected to assemble on the coast shortly. On his way back to St Marcouf, Smith had landed a spy on the coast to make contact with the Chouan leaders and Moore, who had regularly been charged with the covert landing of spies, was ordered to pick up the spy on the night of 1 April. On the appointed night, the *Syren*, in company with the *Diamond*, ran in to the coast after dark, anchoring about five miles from the shore so as to avoid arousing suspicion. The *Syren*'s cutter was lowered and manned with eight seamen and a midshipman, plus Moore and Richard King – Captain of the *Druid*, who had insisted on accompanying Moore out of friendship – all of whom were well armed. Muffling the oars, they set off on the two-hour haul towards the shore. At first they steered by compass, but as they came closer to the shore they were able to use a church steeple as a mark. Then, some way from the shore, the boat suddenly grounded, and although they pushed her along as quietly as possible, four men armed with muskets appeared on the beach. Moore was initially alarmed, but on calling out the secret challenge he was relieved to hear the correct response. The men began to wade out towards the boat. Moore was still suspicious and stood watching them with a pistol in each hand but as they neared he saw that they were carrying the spy on their shoulders. Once back on board, the man reported that the surrounding country was ready to rise against the Republican government as soon as the arms could be landed.

Before any such attempt could be made, however, news reached the squadron that a French convoy was about to depart from Le Havre, bound for Brest. It was to be escorted by a powerful force of three frigates and three corvettes, which indicated that the convoy was of considerable value. Smith immediately ordered both the *Syren* and the *Druid* to take station off Havre, while the *Diamond*, with the frigates *Magicienne* and *Minerva*, would wait out of sight to the west. Moore and Sir Richard King set off on 6 April, with the *Druid* sailing further in shore than the *Syren*. At 4pm, Moore was surprised when the *Druid* suddenly opened fire, and it was seen that she had fallen in with a convoy of eight deeply laden merchant brigs. Moore closed in with the *Syren*, and the merchantmen ran for cover under the heavy guns of a battery at Port-en-Bessin. Leaving King to maintain a guard over the brigs, Moore took the *Syren* on towards Le Havre. Before he got there, however, he fell in with Smith and his detachment who had overtaken them. It was now agreed that the four frigates should form a screen across the likely path of the Le Havre convoy; each frigate to be stationed nine miles apart with identification lights at the head of each mast. For three days, Smith maintained this position, but there was no sighting of the convoy. It was agreed that the convoy must have slipped past the cruisers, so Smith decided to take both the *Druid*, which had rejoined, and the *Diamond* as far as Cherbourg in pursuit. The next day, however, Moore discovered that the convoy was still secure in Le Havre.

By 11 April, the spring tides had passed and so had the opportunity for the deeply laden merchantmen to cross the bar at Le Havre. Moore, greatly disappointed, was ordered to escort some empty transports back to Spithead.

A week later Moore returned to St Marcouf to hear the most astonishing news: Sidney Smith had been captured by the French. He had led a party of three lieutenants, six midshipmen and twenty-four seamen in boats to cut out a privateer lugger in the harbour of Le Havre. Also with the party were his private secretary and a French émigré, Lieutenant de Tromelin. The party successfully seized the lugger, but the vessel's anchor cable was cut prematurely and, as the tide turned, she drifted helplessly into the hands of waiting French troops. Smith's men tried to resist, but they were surrounded and hopelessly outnumbered. There was nothing he could do but surrender. It was a ridiculous affair but typical of the antics which Smith had been undertaking. There was something of an inevitability to the outcome and Moore, with no trace of vindication, simply noted in his journal that it was

> . . . most extraordinary and much to be regretted that so gallant and accomplished a man should run such risks to little or no purpose . . .

though he could also not help adding that the lugger was an unworthy object on which to hazard both the Commodore and his men.

In Smith's absence, command of the squadron had fallen to Captain Thomas Peyton in the *Minerva*. Moore also had ambitions in this direction and dispatched a hasty note to Spencer, the new First Lord of the Admiralty, asking for command of the *Diamond* and/or command of the station. The application was quietly refused, but on the last day of April 1796, the squadron's new commander arrived and any disappointment Moore felt was instantly mitigated by the fact that it was his old friend, Richard Strachan.

8

Strachan's Squadron, HMS *Melampus* (April 1796 – March 1797)

Following Strachan's appointment, the squadron was reduced in size. Moore had expected this, believing that it was really too powerful a force for the operations assigned to it. One of Strachan's first orders to his depleted group of commanders was an insistence that they were not to attempt senseless expeditions unless there was some clear justification to the degree of risk involved. It is hardly a surprise that Moore confided that he was '. . . *heartily glad of the appointment of Strachan to this command'*. The *Syren* herself was immediately ordered to Cherbourg to watch a large assembly of merchant vessels which was now there in the harbour. The rest of the squadron was deployed ready to intercept the Le Havre convoy once again, but Strachan learned that two of the French frigates had already escaped. With a reduced escort the convoy would not attempt to sail, so the squadron returned to St Marcouf. Lamentably, on arrival there, another accident occurred on board the *Syren* which Moore, who was always so careful of his men, noted in his journal:

> *Just as we were taking in our topsails, one of our best seamen was knocked off the main shrouds by the carelessness of another and although the boat from the stern was lowered down with great alertness he almost immediately sunk. This is the third man we have lost in the* Syren *by similar accidents, besides one who was rendered totally unfit for service.*

The incident depressed him. He was once again fed up with the war; '*I tire of this station, nothing is to be done, and I tire of the scenes around me, where I see nothing to interest me.*' His mood was improved considerably when Strachan stated that the *Syren* was the most effective ship in the squadron, and in a lighthearted moment he copied the full lyrics of the popular naval song 'Spanish Ladies' into the journal.

On a more serious note though, both Moore and Strachan were becoming increasingly concerned about the noticeable change in French naval tactics. Moore again noted in his journal that, *'The French are distressing our trade extremely with their Privateers'* and *'These small craft have done a great deal of mischief'*. He and Strachan discussed this and considered the possibility of switching the focus of their operations westwards towards Brest in the hope of retaking English or allied merchantmen captured by privateers, but Strachan knew that he had to protect St Marcouf and patrol the vital Race of Alderney. Besides, the Commodore argued, even if he left the *Diamond*, *Minerva* and *L'Espion* on the squadron's current station, '. . . Melampus *and* Syren *would be too slight a force to go off Ushant with'*. It was a sensible and responsible decision and one that Sidney Smith might not have reached. A few days later though, Strachan had decided to risk taking the whole squadron to cruise north-east of Ushant for a few days. Moore recorded this as

> *. . . joyful news to me as we have been so long on the worst cruising ground, and where we are going I look upon to be as good a place for meeting an enemy as we could go to. I have long wished to meet with something we could cope with in company with Strachan. The* Syren *at this moment sails very equally with the* Melampus; *the* Minerva *is by far the worst sailer of the squadron.*

Moore's joy was short-lived; on 25 May, near the Isle de Bas, as the *Syren*, sailing close to the wind, turned at speed towards a suspect lugger, her foremast split

> *. . . with such a crack that I thought it must have gone over the side. We called the men from the Mast head and the top as soon as possible and shortened sail in all haste. We found the upper part of the mast under the Cat harpins quite gone, so bad that all the hope I had was to lower the heel of the top mast below the spring and endeavour to secure it by good lashing above and below it.*

After three hours' intensive labour, the mast was jury-rigged and he consulted Strachan. Moore thought he could carry out a better repair at the Channel Islands, but Strachan advised getting the frigate back to Spithead or Plymouth for a new mast. With the wind fair for

Spithead, Moore took the *Syren* there, arriving on 27 May. In ten days the ship was ready for sea again and Moore was greatly encouraged by the eager cooperation of the ship's company whilst in port. For although they received their pay,

> *. . . they had very little enjoyment, poor fellows, as, from the urgency of the case, I could not let any of them go on shore, and not even Sunday afforded them a relaxation from work. Indeed they seemed to acquiesce in my measures as none of them asked to go on shore, but all went through their work with great cheerfulness.*

On 7 June the *Syren* sailed again, escorting another group of transports for St Marcouf. What Moore did next serves to illustrate exactly why he was a superb frigate commander, and one who was increasingly respected by his men. As recorded in Moore's journal it also gives us a rare insight into the techniques which the best frigate commanders used in the effective management of the men under their command – at a time when there were no manuals or handbooks to inform officers about leadership:

> *In the evening after we had mustered the Ship's Company at their Quarters, I called them up on the Quarter Deck and told them that I had found it necessary to keep them hard at it during their stay at Spithead on this occasion as it was my wish, and I was certain they were no less anxious, to fulfil the expectation of that active and gallant officer Sir Richard Strachan who had expressed his confidence in the exertions of the* Syren *in so very handsome a manner. That I thought it was but fair to tell them that I was exceedingly well pleased with their conduct since we had met with the accident that forced us into Port, that it shewed an admirable disposition and a Spirit worthy of English Sailors, and gave me the utmost confidence in their zeal and courage. I concluded with thanking them for their manly forbearance from asking what I could not have granted without injury to the public service, and by assuring them that I would not forget their very meritorious conduct. While I delivered my sentiments to the Lads, I was frequently interrupted by their declaration that not a man of them even wished to go on shore when they knew there was so much occasion for them on board, and that they were all equally desirous with me to meet the* Melampus *again. As soon as I had finished my harangue, I was saluted with three such cheers as went to my heart.*

Moore's increasing popularity was not just evident on board the frigate. He noted with a degree of modest puzzlement in his diary, that he had been generally well received on his last visit to Portsmouth. It was making him more optimistic about his prospects.

Strachan too was proving a popular commander with the crews of his squadron. He certainly seems to have had the right touch. When the *Syren* rejoined his squadron in time to search for a French convoy off Ushant, Strachan came on board to congratulate them on their speedy return

> *... and on his saying that he was very glad to have the* Syren *with him, our People, who like him exceedingly, jumped up and gave him three cheers.*

In fact the squadron itself was growing into a remarkably close fighting organization, with the crews of the frigates developing relationships which, on the whole, served to stand the squadron in good stead;

> *Our People are exceedingly intimate both with the crews of the* Melampus *and* Diamond, *but they have quarrelled with those of the* Minerva *which I am very sorry for; the cause of the dispute is the People of the* Minerva *having spoke disrespectfully of the character of Sir Sidney which was taken very heinously both by the* Diamond's *and* Syren's. *The People of the* Diamond *are very partial to Sir Sidney on account of his bravery and good nature, two very popular qualities with English Sailors.*

Whatever the officers may have thought of Sidney Smith, there can be no doubt that he was regarded with great fondness by the ordinary, generously-hearted sailors. As the four frigates ran down towards Ushant, Moore had cause to record yet another example of both the squadron's closeness and the sailors' generosity:

> *Our Seamen sent a Deputation to me yesterday, to say, that as the* Melampus *and* Diamond *had been a long time without Beer they wished to make them a present of their allowance for two days to be equally divided between the two ships; I told them I was very happy to see so much cordiality between them and their brother Sailors in the two ships & that I would send their present on board the first opportunity.*

We might now question whether the exclusion of the *Minerva* from this arrangement was actually a somewhat negative and divisive move but, for Moore, Strachan and Gossellin, this was a heartwarming gesture and one which gave them powerful confidence in the men of the squadron. Such spirit was vital to the success of both frigates individually, and frigate squadrons collectively – and it was evident in Warren and Pellew's squadrons also.

Strachan's squadron reached the Isle de Bas on 15 June where they found no convoy – but did fall in with Sir John Borlase Warren's frigate squadron. Moore went on board Warren's frigate, *La Pomone*, to pay his respects and was impressed by what he saw:

> . . . she is, by far, the finest frigate I ever saw and, except the Line of Battle ships cut down, of the greatest force. He is an officer of great activity, zeal and courage, and has been exceedingly successful; I endeavoured on first being appointed to the Syren to be attached to his Squadron but could not accomplish it. If I had my choice of service, however, I know no man I would so soon serve with as Strachan, but I wish we had Sir John Warren's station.

The squadrons parted company that evening.

Towards the end of June, Strachan ordered Moore to take the *Syren* back to Plymouth to re-provision. There, Moore learned of the capture of the French frigate *La Proserpine* by the *Dryad*, commanded by Captain Lord Amelius Beauclerk.[49] Approvingly, he noted in his journal,

> Lord Amelius's letter on the above glorious occasion was perfectly consistent with his simple and unaffected character, I think it contains about eight lines of the plainest narrative.

A week later he returned to St Marcouf to find the garrison in an unhappy state. The islands were now occupied by a miscellaneous collection of Royal Artillerymen, artificers, invalids, marines and gunboat crews,

> . . . the whole under the command of the Senior Lieutenant commanding the Gun Boats, who happens to be a bustling active fellow, but overbearing, ill tempered, quarrelsome, vulgar and addicted to drink.

Moore considered the officer to be totally unsuited to command such a heterogeneous body.

Strachan's squadron now consisted of the frigates *Syren*, *Melampus*, *Minerva*, *Diamond* and *Camilla*. Strachan and Moore had hopes of achieving great things with such a powerful force, but they were handicapped, as Moore wearily noted in his journal:

Sir Richard is heartily tired of the station, as he is so hampered with Marcouf on the one side and the Islands of Guernsey and Jersey on the other that we cannot cruise.

Moore too was feeling frustrated. His present station offered little chance of good prize money and yet he was increasingly aware that without greater income he could neither marry nor live comfortably on land. His spirits were lifted at the end of July when orders came from the Admiralty appointing Strachan to the command of the *Diamond*, and Moore to the *Melampus*. This was effectively a promotion, for the *Melampus* was significantly larger than the *Syren*, and armed with 18-pounder guns on her main deck, compared with the latter's 12-pounders. Furthermore, she was '*most capitally manned*' and, although her copper was in a bad way, Moore was delighted with the news. Until the transfers were formally ordered though, there were the usual duties to perform, and by 8 August, Moore and the *Syren* were back off Le Havre for the spring tides, keeping an eye on the frigates and corvettes still trapped in the basin.

Once the spring tides were over, Moore was sent back round to Jersey. What happened next was one of those curiosities that almost characterized the Napoleonic wars; anchored in St Aubin's Bay, the *Syren* was joined on 16 August by a fine- looking ship-rigged private yacht belonging to Lord Craven. On board were the Duke and Duchess of Manchester who, in spite of the threat of French cruisers and privateers were on a pleasure cruise in the Channel. Moore appears to have been completely unperplexed when '. . . *they did me the honour to come on board, wishing to have a peep inside St. Maloes before they returned*'. Moore was ever willing to oblige, especially as he had taken an instant liking to the Duchess, who was a fellow Scot.[50] Moore admitted that she was not a beauty, but he was attracted to her

> . . . *native pronunciation, her frankness, her open countenance, and, above all, by her taste for Scotch music, and her universal and particular acquaintance with all the genuine songs of that country . . . I felt towards this natural and unaffected creature as to a very old acquaintance, and my spirits were sunk at leaving her. How often have I been the dupe of this heart of mine! There is no love in the case, it is friendship.*

Shortly after the departure of his guests, the *Syren* stopped a little French coasting sloop. It was

*. . . a very small thing of only 26 tons, laden with lime stone, and the
sole property of the poor man who commanded her . . . finding that the
sloop was really of no value to anybody but the poor Frenchman who
commanded her I proposed to the Officers and ship's company to
dismiss her, which they cheerfully agreed to. I told him to take notice
of the difference between the French and English Cruisers many of the
former having often captured or destroyed even our fishing boats . . . I
then let him proceed with his vessel.*

The grateful Frenchman reciprocated this kindness by giving Moore
detailed information about French warships then lying in the road at
St Malo.

Four days later, while the *Syren* was lying in Grouville Bay off
Jersey, the *Melampus* arrived and Gossellin was rowed over, bearing
Moore's new commission for the command of the *Melampus*. Moore
had commanded the *Syren* for just over two years and he found the
moment of departure an emotional one:

I took my leave of the Syren's *the next day, I was affected, and the Ship's
Company seemed sorry to part with me: they are a very gallant set of
fellows and a very drunken.*

Yet his comment about the *Syren*'s drunkenness was really an
affectionate one: they were, after all, the same men he had labelled his
'rogues'. In fact, if the Lieutenant's logbooks are to be relied upon,
the *Syren* was on the whole a happy ship. During the 661 days he had
commanded her, punishment in the form of floggings had been
inflicted on just twenty-eight occasions, on average one every 23.6
days – a remarkably low incidence. Of a crew which had consisted of
approximately 400 different men during the course of his commission, only about twenty-four had received a flogging. Of this
number about one-third were marines, who always seem to have
lacked the cohesion and team spirit of the seamen in frigates.
Certainly, the *Syren*'s were not seriously prone to drunkenness, at
least, no more than was to be expected of any other seamen of this
period. Their high spirits were confirmed that same day:

The Seamen and Marines of the Melampus *made our Lads in the* Syren
*a present of two Butts of strong beer in lieu of the two puncheons of
small beer that the* Syren's *had given them.*

Strachan in the *Diamond* arrived before nightfall and a general cele-
bratory party seems to have taken place:

I think it worthy of remark that the Diamond *brought a similar present to the seamen of the* Syren: *there is the strongest attachment among the crews of these three frigates to each other, I have always encouraged and promoted it as much as I could as I think it of very great importance to the service that ships acting together should be on the most cordial terms with each other. While we lay in Grouville Bay the Seamen were allowed to visit each other and the scene of drunkenness that ensued was quite in character of this strange, invaluable animal, a British Sailor.*

Once again we are given a clear indication of the high level of morale and cooperation that existed in the Channel frigate squadrons, and a picture which once again profoundly contradicts the traditional portrayal of life in the navy as some form of floating hell.

On the 28th of August I took command of the Melampus, *Sir Richard had taken 16 men with him into the* Diamond, *notwithstanding which she is a very well manned ship. I took four seamen besides my servants and some of the midshipmen with me, I intend to take three more seamen when the* Syren *goes into Port, but I do not like to distress her now.*

Unfortunately, the Admiralty declined his request to take his First Lieutenant, John Henry Martin, with him to his new command – and he was going to miss his support badly. The following morning, sore heads notwithstanding, Strachan took the squadron towards Ushant. Moore now had the opportunity to assess his new command under sail;

This is one of the finest frigates in the English Navy, but rather out of repair, not having been docked these three years, her copper is bad, yet she sails as well as the generality of ships in all situations, and better than most upon a wind. Her crew is very good, but at present she is considerably short of complement, and there are 39 in the sick list, none of whom, however, are in a bad way being in general affected by the casual maladies the consequences of their drunkenness and debauchery at Spithead and Portsmouth. As yet I feel like a stranger amongst them, but I have much confidence in her capability as a fighting ship, even in her present state.

En route to Ushant, the squadron learned that Spain had declared war on England and that sixteen ships of the line, under Admiral Richery, were preparing to leave Brest to rendezvous with a fleet from Cadiz. It was rumoured that this combined force was going to escort transports carrying 40,000 troops to invade Ireland. Off

Ushant the squadron fell in with Sir Alan Gardner's fleet, which had already been posted to meet this hostile force and was awaiting reinforcement by a squadron under Admiral Colpoys. On board Gardner's flagship, the *Royal Sovereign* (100), Moore sought out his old friend Captain William Bedford, who confided that they were worried that the enemy might arrive before Colpoys, thus overpowering Gardner's fleet. Matters quickly took on the confused character of all such naval campaigns for, the following morning, the 80-gun *Caesar* arrived to report that, far from being in a supporting position, Colpoys had returned to port and nobody knew where Richery was. Strachan took the three remaining frigates of his squadron (i.e. *Diamond*, *Melampus* and *Syren*) back in towards Ushant, while Gardner kept his station to the west. Activities were soon restricted by fog, which seriously reduced visibility and added to the tension, but Moore was feeling more confident now that he had the *Melampus* and her crew:

> *I am very much pleased with the crew of the* Melampus, *they are in general finer men than that of the* Syren *and are in much better order.*

The possibilities arising from a war with Spain were heartening and Moore was excited. Victory, he believed, would depend on the Royal Navy rather than the army, and this prompted him to consider the difference between the English soldier and sailor:

> *The moral and physical qualities of the English Soldier are, in my opinion, equal to the acknowledged excellence of our Sailors, but they have not fallen into such good hands. The same kind of stupid pomp has sometimes, in a small degree, infected the Navy, but the absolute necessity which the Nation has for its defence checks the progress of nonsense and frivolity and prevents their degrading influence in this home bred body . . . Unfortunately the gratification of a false taste has been always the object in the discipline and dress of the English Army, instead of fitting them for the service they are likely to be employed on . . .*

Moore continued to be pleased with the *Melampus*, despite the fact that her copper was in poor condition, but he was still faced with problems with his officers. As already noted, he had applied to the Admiralty to have Lieutenant Martin, the First Lieutenant of the *Syren*, transferred, but they were being difficult about it. The existing First Lieutenant of the *Melampus* appeared to be good at keeping the frigate in order, but Moore was not happy about the way he managed the crew, and he was also aware of shortcomings among other officers. The First Lieutenant in particular had

> *. . . a want of discretion, and ignorance of mankind that I think must lead him to disgust the seamen for nothing. I am much mistaken if, without severity, he does not make himself odious to them. This is extremely disagreeable to me, I wish the Officers to be as much loved by the Seamen as I always am myself; if it is otherwise things never go on well. The Crew of the* Melampus *are really excellent and are capable of any thing if properly managed. I find also that there is very little real zeal for the public service, it is only a minutiae, an attendance to trifles or matters of small importance. There is a constant desire to be in Port, many of the Officers being family men with their wives at Portsmouth; all this will require a sharper look out on my part to prevent the service suffering for their convenience.*

The issue was one that he would have to deal with by and by, but in the meantime he knew it was the commanding officer's lot to make the best of the isolated position of command;

> *The People here seem well disposed. And I dare say we shall agree well enough; as to a companion, it is what I do not look for, it is so rare. A Captain's well off if he has those with him who are tolerably able and willing to do their duty, and who are not Blackguards.*

Strachan's squadron was still off Brest in the second week of September, and Moore stopped and boarded a number of vessels running along the shore, at one point coming under fire from a battery at Le Havre. The shots plummeting about the ship served as a salutary reminder:

> *I expect to get a licking some day from the Batteries here, as if we should happen to be becalmed with the Flood tide setting in we should be obliged to anchor, and if under the fire of one of these Batteries at the time, the matter might be very serious. If I am left to myself I shall certainly never get into such a situation, unless the object will justify the risk.*

Sidney Smith's tactics still rankled.

As there were still frigates and corvettes in the basin at Le Havre, Moore was ordered to sail there and keep the *Melampus* off that port until the spring tides had passed. Lingering in this fashion was a tedious business, hated by all frigate captains who found themselves so employed. Moore was no exception:

110

The business of Blockade is a service exceedingly tiresome . . . I shall be very glad now to see a Peace, I am tired of the War, which is ruinous to the Country, at the same time that we have no service of honour or profit. What I fear is not an Invasion of the Enemy, but internal commotions at home, in consequence of the weight of taxes and the Intrigues of the Seditious.

As the highest tide approached, the *Melampus* was joined by Strachan in the *Diamond*. The two frigates cleared for action and sailed in close to Le Havre road in case any of the French men-of-war tried to break out. The hours passed slowly and monotonously, and after standing the crew down at 1am, Moore retired to the lonely privacy of his cabin. There would be no action on this occasion.

At the end of the month, Moore took the *Melampus* westwards to Cherbourg, where she fell in with the *Minerva*. From her, Moore received new Admiralty orders instructing all cruisers to stop and seize all Spanish vessels they encountered. Moore fumed that such orders were useless on his current station – where there were no Spanish ships to be found;

If we are kept on this cursed station the war with Spain is not at all likely to benefit us, and I see no prospect of getting off it . . .

The best that he was able to do for the present was stop small French coasters, most of which were in ballast or carrying relatively value-less cargoes of oysters from Cancale. In frustration, he dismissed them all. There seemed to be no French men-of-war at sea, and Moore was convinced that the blockade was resulting in a decline of the French navy. It was widely known that the French navy had been purged of its aristocratic officer corps, but he believed that this had little to do with the navy's decline, for these officers bore less of the responsibility for seamanship. Ironically, real seamanship in the pre-revolutionary navy had been the responsibility of auxiliary officers who previously had never had the opportunity of promotion. Once the aristocrats had been removed, these more practical seaman officers had been promoted. Thus, for a short time, the French navy had been im-pressive and

. . . therefore, in that respect I believe their Navy became more effective.

But

. . . they certainly do not defend their ships so well now as they did at the first – witness the engagements with the Nymphe *and* Cleopatre,

111

the Iris *with a ship of nearly equal force*[51] *and the* Boston *with* L'Ambuscade.

Since then, the French navy had suffered a series of *'severe drubbings'* which had the effect of thoroughly demoralizing her seamen.

Despite Moore's lamentations about the lack of Spanish vessels on the station, on 5 October the squadron stopped a Spanish merchant-man that knew nothing of the state of war that existed between England and Spain. She was taken as a very welcome prize and sent back to Portsmouth. Laden with a cargo of various goods, Moore noted delightedly that if she was condemned '*. . . she will be a pretty good Prize even for the four ships'.*[52] Four days later, the October gales began. Moore was obliged to run under just a foresail and two storm stay sails, several other sails having been blown to pieces by the fierce winds. At about 8pm that night they saw signal rockets launched from the *Diamond* but were unable to see any other signal. If the rockets were distress signals there was little the *Melampus* could do, so intent was her crew on keeping their own ship and themselves safe. When Moore was at last able to retire to his cabin he noted briefly in his journal,

> *This has been the hardest gale since last March, the ship complains a good deal . . . I do not know if it is good policy to keep a squadron constantly off Havre and Cherbourg, but if it is I would be glad if any other ships than the* Diamond *and* Melampus *had it in charge.*

Nevertheless, on 16 October, the *Melampus* was back on her station off Le Havre. That evening, Moore retired to his cabin to read. Suddenly at 9pm, Moore's quiet moment was alarmingly disturbed:

> *While I was at my dinner the first lieutenant contrived to run the ship on board of a Danish sloop and did her some inconsiderable damage. This was entirely from ignorance in Seamanship of the 1st Lieutenant who is more deficient in this respect than I at first thought him.*

Fortunately, the *Melampus* herself appears to have suffered no damage from this incident. But the apparent failure in the ship's First Lieutenant on this occasion simply added, in Moore's mind, to a growing list of his deficiencies. Several days later as the *Melampus* was patrolling along the coast, Moore suddenly gave orders to haul to the northward,

> *. . . not liking the appearance of the weather. It was very lucky that we haul'd up in time as the wind shifted suddenly in a squall to the NW so*

that we were obliged to carry sail to clear Cape d'Antifer, it being at that time the first of the Flood tide. It is very dangerous to be caught off the road of Havre with a gale of wind at NW, more especially with a flood tide.

Again, Moore's seamanship had avoided potential danger for both his ship and crew.

When the weather abated, Moore took the *Melampus* to St Marcouf where one of his Midshipmen and a number of seamen were waiting, having delivered a prize to Portsmouth. On boarding the Melampus, however, the Midshipman had to report that many of the seamen had deserted on their arrival in port,

... and went ashore to the Grog and the Girls, from whom with much trouble he got three of them. I punished the three this morning, which is the first exhibition of that kind that has been made since I took the command of the ship[53]. I found it absolutely necessary to endeavour to curb the licentiousness of the Jacks who have tried my patience pretty well since I came among them. When we were in the Downs two of them got drunk when on shore on duty, left the boat and I suppose were crimpt as I saw no more of them. It is a sad thing that there is no way of managing Sailors without occasional examples of this kind being made. I hope I shall have very little of it to go through, as it is the most shocking art of my duty and hangs like a heavy summons on me when I see the necessity of forcing my nature to it.

The *Diamond* arrived off Le Havre a few days later, and as both frigates had only about a week's provisions on board, Strachan decided that they should take a quick cruise near Ushant before making their way back to Spithead. Once in position off the Isle de Bas, they hoped to intercept French privateers with their prizes attempting to get back to Brest. However, all they encountered were small merchant vessels who repeatedly ran into port to escape or took shelter under powerful shore batteries.

After a week, they again encountered Warren's squadron off Ushant, and the sight seems to have reminded Moore how dissatisfied he was with his existing station. He composed a letter ready to send to Spencer, the First Lord of the Admiralty,

... requesting as a particular favour that the Melampus *may be ordered on some other station than that of St Marcouf where I am convinced there is nothing to be done; ... I hope I shall be removed but if not I give up all hopes of further success this war.*

113

It was almost as though he felt his crew deserved a better station because just days before, he had remarked in his diary:

There is much of the true spirit of English sailors in the Melampus, *I observe a marked difference in their making sail when they have an idea of a chase and on ordinary occasions: this morning when the hands were called to give chase . . . every sail was set in an instant. To make up for this noble ardour, they are intolerable drunkards, but I am sure they would fight. We have a great many Irish on board, I am very well pleased to have some from that soil as I think they bring a degree of gaiety and fun with them which enlivens and keeps up the spirits of the Johns. But I always wish the greater part to be English and Scotch.*

Moore doubted that the *Melampus* would be removed to another station at this time, but he hoped that if the war continued,

. . . there may be another Western Squadron of frigates and that Strachan, who is high in reputation, may command it, in which case I think I am very likely to be with him, as I would try for it and I am pretty sure he would like it; we draw very well together and I believe he has a complete confidence in me. I think him one of the most executive fellows we have, and a very original character. None whom I know so well calculated for harassing an enemy with a squadron of frigates. He is active in mind and body, brave, in an eminent degree, zealous and ambitious of honour and well earned military fame.

Despite their shortage of provisions, on 5 November Strachan set off in pursuit of a strange sail, leaving orders for Moore to rendezvous with him back at St Marcouf. Slightly irritated at the position in which this left the *Melampus* and her crew, Moore set off back to the east. Five days later the *Diamond* still had not returned and Moore was aware that his crew were feeling aggrieved about their reduced rations. He privately simmered about Strachan who, although aware of their lack of provisions, had changed his plans suddenly at the sight of a potential prize. Moore entered a sour note in his journal: '*. . . my friend the Chevalier is extremely whimsical, and changes his mind as often as a girl.*' He decided the time had come to ignore Strachan's orders and sail for Spithead;

I have no idea of allowing the Ship's Company to be pinched and abridged of their allowance and of their comforts, merely from the fickleness of any man, unless when the public service requires it.

Before the *Melampus* had completely abandoned her station, however, she fell in with the frigate *Minerva* commanded by Captain John Peyton, who was many years senior to Moore. Peyton was able to supply the *Melampus* with enough provisions and ordered Moore to take up station watching Le Havre, where he would find the sloop *Childers*. Moore doubted he could stay there long as, in spite of the additional provisions, the *Melampus* had only three tons of water on board, '. . . *which is a very small quantity for a ship like us*'. On the following morning, before Moore could depart to carry out Peyton's instructions, a French man-of-war was seen approaching from the east. Both frigates immediately tacked to give chase, but the *Melampus* was by far the better sailor and soon left the *Minerva* behind. The ship, which was running inshore of the two frigates, could now be identified as a French corvette carrying between sixteen and eighteen guns. As Moore closed with her, she attempted to cut close inshore, probably with a view to making Cherbourg,

> . . . *but seeing that we must bring her to action if she persisted, she kept to windward of Cape Barfleur and ran ashore in the entrance of the little Port of Barfleur, the tide being at that time very little fallen. The* Melampus *was very near within reach of her Lee guns of her, but from our being quite light, and, consequently, heeling very much, our shot did not reach her. As the wind was directly on shore, and the tide falling, we could not go near enough to cannonade her.*

Moore abandoned the attack and headed off for Le Havre, but next morning in a light easterly breeze, abreast of Port-en-Bessin, he sighted another corvette some six or seven leagues from the shore. As the *Melampus* was inshore, the corvette had no option to turn north-wards and Moore set off in hot pursuit. By 3pm he gave the order to commence firing with the frigate's bow chasers, and the first ranging shots were thrown over and ahead of the corvette,

> . . . *upon which she hoisted French colours and fired her stern chasers at us. We kept so exactly on the angle of her quarter that she was obliged to yaw to fire even the stern chase guns at us, and sometimes she ventured to yaw to fire her broadside guns at us, she only struck us once which did us no damage. We never yawed the least but kept the ship steadily after her firing the two Bow guns at her when they could bear in order to confuse her: at a little before five o'clock we were within ¼ of a mile of her, and as I was then certain she could not escape us I was going to give her a broadside, lest, by continuing her fire, she might*

115

do us some damage, when she discharged all her guns in the air and struck. She proved to be a National Corvette mounting 18 long 12 pounders and 137 men called L'Etna . . . She had on board a considerable quantity of Naval and Military stores and 100 cases of Jesuit's Bark for St. Domingo. *

Moore took 100 of the corvette's crew on board the *Melampus* and replaced them with a prize crew of thirty seamen commanded by the First Lieutenant. Both ships worked their way into Spithead on the following morning. Strachan arrived two days later, with no prize, and having spent the intervening days battling with contrary winds. When Moore went on board the *Diamond* to report, he was deeply hurt at an implication from the Commodore that he was dragging his heels in port:

It was on this occasion that I had the appearance, for the first time, of a disagreement with Sir Richard, [a] circumstance which was painful to me, and would have been still more so if I had not been conscious of acting right and of his treating me rather ill on the occasion. I however felt more grief than resentment.

Moore responded to this by spending two weeks in London while the *Melampus* was refitting. He met Earl Spencer but decided against asking for a new station; besides he was now more concerned about his personal than his professional life. He noted that although he was now '. . . *on the wrong side of thirty, I have never seen but one woman whom I should wish to marry*'. Moore's financial position was not strong enough to make a formal approach to the lady's father, and furthermore, she

. . . has pretensions to a much better match, from her situation in life as well as her beauty and accomplishments. In fact, I have not the least reason to think that she feels any thing stronger for me than Friendship. Still I have an unreasonable vanity fed, idea that she almost loves me.

Although he convinced himself he would marry her, he lacked the courage to call upon her while he was in town. He left London without having resolved the issue in any way and it would come back to haunt him.

* The *Etna* brought Moore and his crew a very handsome £4,917 in Prize Money, of which Moore received £1,229, the equivalent of over eight years' pay.

The *Melampus* sailed again on 19 December and joined Strachan, with the *Latona* and the *Camilla*, two days later. On the 23rd, the squadron chased a French brig which attempted to run inshore under a battery. The *Melampus* and the *Diamond* sailed in close, hurling shot over the brig so that it could be seen falling on the adjacent shore, and in some alarm the Master of the brig promptly surrendered. The brig proved to be *L'Esperance*, from Dunkirk. On Christmas day the squadron stretched north across the Channel in a heavy storm, with the *Melampus* leading. During the refit, the frigate's standing rigging had been replaced but a week at sea had stretched the ratlines so that every roll threatened to throw the main and mizzenmasts over the side. Fortunately, the crew of the *Melampus* were still alert enough when Portland Light suddenly loomed out of the gloom, and signalled to the rest of the squadron to wear. The next morning, Moore managed to get some of the slack taken out of the rigging, but he couldn't secure the masts and decided to run for Plymouth Sound. However, the gale brought sleet and the land soon disappeared from sight. In desperation, Moore decided to haul to the southward, and in this way was finally able to tension his starboard rigging. The gale continued severely, and on the 27th, the *Melampus* stormed into Plymouth Sound, closely followed by the frigate *Latona*;

> *We lay all that night in a very dangerous situation with two anchors ahead and the wind blowing almost a hurricane.*

As the storm continued with little abatement, the Sound was gradually filled with frigates and other ships seeking shelter. Then worrying news arrived in the form of several battered ships from Colpoy's squadron, who reported that the French fleet had put to sea from Brest and was thought to be making for Ireland. In a classic example of the occasional inadequacies of the naval support systems, Colpoys was unable to give chase because his ships were now short of provisions and water. All available ships were hurriedly prepared for sea again, and the *Melampus* sailed on 3 January, in spite of the fact that she had thirty-three men on the sick list. Most of these were suffering relatively minor ailments, mainly colds or injuries sustained in falls during the recent rough weather – though, as Moore noted grimly, a number were suffering from the effects of drunkenness or debauchery while in port. With the lack of any authentic intelligence about the French fleet, rumours spread that they had landed at Bantry Bay with 20,000 troops. Moore remained sceptical, believing that the weather had been too rough for such a landing. The day after leaving port Moore fell in with Bridport's fleet in the Channel and spoke to their lookout frigate, the *Daedalus*. Strachan was thought to be still off Cape Barfleur, and Moore decided to head southwards to join him, realising that if Strachan's squadron were being held on the station, in spite of the apparent crisis, the Admiralty considered control of the area of great importance. Resignedly Moore realized that, despite the fears over the French landing, as he was

> *. . . pretty well acquainted with the ground, it is likely they will keep me always upon it. It is after all, better than being sent to the West Indies, so I shall trouble myself no more on the subject.*

There was no sign of the *Diamond* off Barfleur, but the *Melampus* was joined by the *Latona* and the *Greyhound*, who had picked up rumours that the French had been driven out of Bantry Bay and were therefore likely to fall in with Bridport's fleet. Surveying seas empty of enemy shipping, Moore could only lament privately, '*Oh lord what would I give to command a 74 with Lord Bridport at this moment*'.

Although the group fell in with the *Diamond* on 9 January, the weather continued to be uncomfortable. With little to do other than patrol back and forth and keep themselves safe, Moore became listless and irritable. With little to occupy his mind he could not help once again pondering what he believed to be his own deficiencies, and those of his First Lieutenant. Moore's thoughts on this give valuable confirmation of the important role that the first officer played in the day to day management of the ship:

> *The common routine and detail of duty which must be a good deal attended to, in order to keep a ship in good order, has something very insipid in it, and I find it rather an up hill work for me to look into the different wheels of the machine to see that they all perform their proper functions. There is nothing more necessary to facilitate this kind of plain work than laying down a certain regular plan of operations to be invariably followed up, in short, acting methodically, which I have never been able to do; by neglecting method I occasion to myself ten times more trouble than a man of method has in doing the same thing better. From this irregularity in my mode of proceeding the ship I command will always resemble her captain, either in a great bustle, or else doing nothing. I have very little assistance, in the general business, from the next to myself* [i.e. the First Lieutenant], *as he wants method totally, is lazy, non effective in a time of difficulty when presence of mind is requisite, as good natured almost as myself, but a tolerable,*

slow, sailor. In this way the ship is hardly ever neat, but always in a kind of hugger mugger way fit for service. In my opinion, my taste for certain branches of Belles letter goes all against the arrangement in the Ship, my mind being almost always intent upon something not immediately about me, until my attention is roused by some circumstances out of the common road.

Moore's self-criticism was hardly justified. It was not the commanding officer's duty to see to the minutiae of running the ship – and indeed, a captain who bothered himself too much with this was more likely to irritate his seamen and become obsessed with appearance etc. Moore knew this and had himself criticized it in others. He was not an officer of that type. However, there was clearly an ongoing problem with his First Lieutenant.

When the weather finally moderated in the third week of January, Strachan's squadron reassembled off Alderney. Moore hoped that he would be detached to cruise in company with the *Latona,* for he had formed a very high opinion of her commander, Arthur Legge, a younger son of the Earl of Dartmouth. Legge was a good example of an officer with an aristocratic background and lots of 'interest' behind him, who had proved himself as a frigate commander of a professionally high standard. He was certainly turning into one of the navy's star captains, and Moore thought the *Latona*

. . . an uncommonly well appointed frigate: her Captain as fine a fellow as I know in our service, and a man whose society I like much. But all these men of interest do all they can to keep clear of this station which is exceedingly harassing without being profitable: I therefore suppose that when the Latona *goes into Port we see no more of her.*

As they continued to cruise off the north coast of Brittany, they learned that the Channel Fleet had had no contact with the French:

I much fear that the opportunity of striking a great blow has been let slip and that our Fleet are cruising off Brest which is little better than being at Spithead at this time. It will be a most mortifying circumstance if these fellows are not met by Lord Bridport. It is certainly a bad plan when our superiority in numbers is so great to keep one squadron until all its provisions and water is expended before they relieve it with another squadron.

Counter rumours that the French fleet had in fact been sent to attack Portugal simply added to the fog of confusion that existed, as Moore noted in some exasperation: *'Our intelligence on this occasion has been very bad.'*

True to Moore's prediction, the *Latona* was soon detached from the squadron, Legge having reported a sprung mast. Moore watched enviously as she went. He was now desperate to leave his existing station, believing it *'. . . the most teasing and harassing of all the home stations'*. By 26 January, the squadron received copies of London newspapers full of confused reports about the French fleet having returned to Brest from Ireland after a series of disasters, and Strachan's attention appears to have turned back to the East. This was essential anyway as the spring tides were imminent. At 8pm that evening, Moore stopped an American vessel which reported that a number of ships were preparing to sail from Le Havre, including a 24-pounder frigate. After a conference with Strachan, it was decided that the *Diamond* and the *Melampus* should wait just out of sight of Le Havre in the hope of luring out the French ships. The prospect of some action enlivened Moore:

> *Since I got this intelligence I have been all alive, I have good hopes we shall meet some of them. Beating about the Channel without any prospect is the Devil, but now we have an Object.*

Sadly, his optimism was to be short lived. For three days the *Melampus* and the *Diamond* hovered off Cape Le Havre, but the French ships did not come out. The spring tides began to fall;

> *We have had a great deal of stormy weather, but that is nothing in annoyance compared to the insipidity that I groan under; would it were peace, or that we had more to do with the Enemy! I am sick of the business I have to attend to, and sick of those who are chained to the oar with me . . . I cannot say that I like the act of fighting, but I like to be in the way of it when it is fitting to be there, and I mortally hate much ado about nothing – I think this Irish Bravado will not be relished by the French Nation, it was too serious a Joke, and they may thank Fortune it was no worse . . .*

Strachan decided to abandon the position, for it was clear that the French were not coming out. He decided that the two frigates should stretch north across the Channel before heading down towards the Race of Alderney. By the time they reached Cape La Hague, a very thick fog was setting in and visibility was reduced to about a ship's length. Sometime between 7pm and 8pm, when they were three or four leagues north-west of the Cape, lookouts at the bow of the

Melampus suddenly shouted a warning about rocks ahead. Moore immediately gave orders to back the ship and box her head around, but before these actions could take any effect, the *Melampus* struck on the rocks and hung by the heel as far forward as the mainmast. Peering through the fog, a line of rocks could be seen extending along their starboard side and quarter, whilst another line of rocks extended on the larboard bow. Moore gave orders to trim the sails in another attempt to back the ship off of the rocks, whilst at the same time guns were fired to warn the *Diamond*. It was something of a relief to hear guns replying about a mile to the south-east. The wind was onshore, but fortunately there was little swell, '. . . *the ship seemed to thump entirely on her keel, and it was dead low water*'. Moore now had the frigate's boats swung out and had the stream anchor carried out to the north to try to pull the ship's head round as the tide rose. The after sails were clewed up, and as the wind was off the starboard bow they kept the head sails 'braced a box' (the headyard braced flat aback to the wind to ensure that the bow moved in the required way). As the hours passed, the tide gradually rose, bringing with it a freshening wind. Eventually the bows began to swing round to the north, the headsails began to fill and as soon as the ship took the wind aft they sheeted home the main- and mizzen topsails and made all sail;

> *To my infinite joy she launched off the rocks. We hailed the boats to follow us and let go the end of the hawser, and steered out to the Northward happily clear of all the rocks. We continued firing guns to direct the Boats by the sound, as not even our Blue lights could be seen through the Fog. We got all our boats but the Launch on board last night, and this morning we got our launch, which had rowed all night and got on board the* Diamond *this morning.*

Moore realized that they must have run onto Alderney, but he could not understand how they had reached it so quickly, as they had been off of the Isle of Wight at noon. According to his calculations, they should have been ten miles to the north-east of Alderney. The emergency over, Moore was able to relax and took some comfort in the fact that he had behaved well during the crisis:

> *I never lost my coolness, but I had not the least hopes of saving the ship, and was very intent on alarming the* Diamond, *which I think, by being to the se of us must have been in the Race of Alderney.*

With daylight, he was able to make an initial assessment of the damage, recording it despondently in his journal:

. . . the lower part of the Rudder appears ragged, and a great deal of the Copper about the keel is ript and sticking out on both sides. We must be docked.

Daylight also revealed the *Diamond*, riding safely a little distant away, and also another (unnamed) ship which had just arrived from Spithead where the port was buzzing with news that Sir Edward Pellew, in the heavy frigate *Indefatigable*, in company with Captain Reynolds in the *Amazon*, had taken on the French 74-gun *Droits de L'Homme* in a heavy storm as she was making her way back from Bantry Bay. The French ship had been driven on shore where, sadly, she had been followed by the *Amazon*. When Moore went on board the *Diamond*, he was shown Sir Edward Pellew's official letter printed in one of the London papers, and heartily approved of the *'lively'* account it gave of the action. Days later, the entire squadron appears to have been *'extremely happy'* to learn that Reynolds and the crew of the *Amazon* had all been saved.

The recent excitement had certainly revived Moore's enthusiasm and now, despite the damage to the frigate, he was anxious to avoid returning to port prematurely. On 11 February, Moore and Strachan stopped a suspicious-looking ship which proved to be an American frigate sailing from Le Havre to New York. The two captains were convinced that she was really a French-owned vessel, but they had no proof, and rather than risk the penalties of a charge of false detention, they let her go. Ironically, Moore had only days before been pondering the relationship between America and France:

> *We have no other way to force the French into our terms but by con-*
> *tinuing to cut off their Trade, which I believe is too slow to be effectual.*
> *The late Revolution they have come to relative to the Americans seems*
> *profligate in a great degree, allowing that the English have treated the*
> *Americans ill, that cannot justify the French in plundering them. The*
> *Americans are in an awkward predicament between the English and the*
> *French, a war with either would be fatal to their Commerce, but with*
> *the English ruinous, altho their privateers would get some plunder. The*
> *conduct of the French on this occasion leads me to think that they wish*
> *to force the Americans into a war with us, or to rob them.*

Eventually, shortage of provisions forced the squadron back to Spithead. Moore reported the damage to the *Melampus* but was told that he would have to wait until the early part of March for a dock to become available. Moore and Strachan decided to put to sea again, rather than linger in port. But before they departed, the frigate *Greyhound* arrived with the second privateer brig she had captured off Barfleur, and paraded her triumphantly past the other ships in the anchorage. Moore watched with gritted teeth:

> *. . . She has not been any thing like so much at sea as the* Diamond *and us, nor had a tenth part of the harassing and fatiguing service. I grudge her her success, as, comparatively with others on the station, she has not deserved it.*

Back at sea, Moore found himself mulling over news that he had received whilst in port. He was especially concerned over the welfare of his brother John, who had contracted fever at St Lucia. He also read and re-read Sir Edward Pellew's official letter recounting the action with the *Droits de L'Homme*. In the letter, Pellew had written, 'The fate of her [Droits de L'Homme's] *brave but unhappy crew was perhaps more sincerely lamented by us from the expectation of sharing the same fate.*' There was something about this statement that Moore felt was not right, and eventually he came to the conclusion that Pellew was not only expressing a sentiment he didn't genuinely feel, but was also philosophically wrong;

> *After the danger was over they might the more sincerely pity the French Crew from the imminent danger they themselves <u>had been</u> in of sharing a similar fate, but I doubt if a single man in the* Indefatigable *pitied them at the time, but if they did it was not for the reason given.*

Only a frigate commander, whose ship and crew had faced the sort of danger experienced by the *Indefatigable*, could have made that distinction.

On 1 March, Moore stopped an American vessel that was seen to depart from Le Havre. The Master of the vessel reported that a large 24-pounder frigate, the *L'Indien*, was in the harbour, but no crew could be found for her. The difficulties of the French navy were growing. Confident that there could be no threat from that quarter, Moore turned north for Spithead, and a dock in Portsmouth.

9

Love and Mutiny
(March 1797 – May 1798)

On 3 March 1797, the *Melampus* anchored at Spithead. Four days later, Moore took the frigate into harbour and was informed that a dock would not be available for at least a week. With little apparent hesitation he arranged a week's leave and travelled to London. For some time his vague relationship with the young Miss M had been on his mind, and he now decided to try to strengthen any bonds that existed between them. Although he had previously kept his distance, he decided it was time to put himself forward. In London, he called at the M family house;

She received me in a manner which convinced me of her warmest friendship, which altho' it is far short of the sentiment I wish her to have for me yet is as much as she ought to have for a man who never made love to her. She appeared more lovely and amiable in my eyes than ever and I feel that I shall never be happy until I have declared my love for her, and put it out of doubt whether or not she loves me. She appears to me to love me like a brother, and I am greatly pleased and flattered by the manner in which she behaves to me. She is the only woman of the number I have been in love with that ever I wished to marry, and I do think her from long acquaintance the most perfect female character I ever knew. I am inclined to think that she rather loves me, and I shall be very miserable if I find myself mistaken.

The signs of affection were as yet slim, but Moore was optimistic, perhaps over-optimistic under the circumstances, but at least it was a start. At Portsmouth there was another delay in getting a dock ready for the *Melampus*, so Moore stayed in London. London society was buzzing with talk of Admiral Jervis' victory over the Spanish fleet at the Battle of St Vincent. [54] Moore considered it

124

. . . a most brilliant achievement . . . although it certainly was by no
means a hard fight . . . The conduct of Commodore Nelson in the
Captain *and of Captain Trowbridge was above all praise. From what*
I have heard of Trowbridge, I think he must be one of the most ener-
getic, and gallant officers in our Navy, as also one of our best practical
seamen. Two days before the action the Colossus, *one of our 74's, ran*
foul of the Culloden [also a 74] *(Trowbridge's Ship) and damaged her*
so much that it was thought impossible for her to keep the sea, however,
by the great activity and resources of Trowbridge he not only did not
go into port but continued to be in such a situation on the morning that
the Spanish fleet appeared that he was enabled to take the Post of
honour and peril, and to lead the English Line into action . . . I am
credibly informed that the Chain Pumps were at work the whole time
of the action, and that sometimes the leaks occasioned by the above
mentioned accident gained on the pumps.

Once again we perceive a ship commander's appreciation of the
battle, in that what he esteems is the ability with which Trowbridge
managed his damaged ship in order to have it ready for combat.

In London, Moore visited the painter Fuseli, spending three hours
in conversation with him, finding his conversation

. . . full of grandeur and sublimity. With regard to his works they interest
me infinitely more than those of any other painter that ever I have seen,
except the most admirable drawings and unfinished paintings of my
friend William Lock who unites expression with divine beauty . . .

Moore had delayed his return to Portsmouth and, knowing that the
Melampus was due to be docked on the 19th, he hurried there on the
following evening to inspect the damage to the frigate's hull. Standing
in the dry dock, he was able to see for himself that almost all of the
Melampus' false keel had been ripped away, and that there was
considerable damage to the main keel. Despondently, he realized that
the repairs were going to take weeks. This was bad news, for any
extended stay in port was bad for the health, morale and efficiency of
a ship's crew. He would have been more depressed, had he not had
something more powerful on his mind. Within three days he was back
at the M family house – the place which he dazedly described as the
place where his *'goddess reigns'*. He was aware of his own condition,
but despair over his financial position now dragged him down into a
turmoil of confusion:

*I am now over head and ears in love, yet refrained from declaring myself
. . . chiefly by the consciousness of my being in no condition to support
her in the event of her consenting to share her fate with mine. I am in
a painful state of suspense with regard to the state of her heart; she may
like me, but I am sure she is not dying for any man. If I could be sure
that she loves me I could go to sea with satisfaction and with increased
ardour, founded on the hope of removing the only bar to the completion
of my wishes by captures from the Enemy; but if I were sure that she
were indifferent about me, I would be extremely indifferent about
riches. I did not tell her how dear she is to me. Dear as the ruddy drops
that warm my heart, but I think she must see it, and I do not think any
of the family can be ignorant of it.*

Despite the longings of his heart, there was another mistress calling him;

I wish to the Lord my Melampus *were fairly afloat again; I am losing
time, yet I do not grudge the time I have spent near the Lady . . .*

The news that the *Melampus* was ready for sea arrived at almost the same time as news from the West Indies, where John Moore had recovered from fever and had been offered the position as Governor of Jamaica. [55] Perhaps inspired by the news of his brother, Graham's thoughts returned suddenly to his naval duties. He resolved to return to Portsmouth, and devote himself properly to his profession, and to his crew;

*I have not been active enough in putting in practice my own ideas
respecting Naval Discipline; when we go out again I shall endeavour to
think of nothing else.*

Perhaps thinking that a change of station would shake him from his current state of mind, Moore made another half-hearted effort to get the *Melampus* transferred to another station. The Admiralty refused and he stoically accepted the fact that he would probably be watching the north coast of France until the end of the war.

On 13 April, the *Melampus* was hauled out of dock and alongside a jetty. She was mastless and was not ready to receive stores. A huge effort was now going to be required to get her ready for sea. To make matters worse, predictably, twelve of the crew had gone missing and it could only be presumed that they had deserted. Then two days later, the crews of the ships at Spithead mutinied. Moore noted in his journal that it began with the crew of the *Queen Charlotte* (100)

126

giving three cheers, '. . . *which was the signal for a mutiny throughout the fleet*'. In an incredibly revealing comment, he noted that the cause of the mutiny was found to have originated some time back with a petition to Lord Howe for an increase in pay. It was passed to the Board but '. . . *they did not think fit to take ~~their responsibility~~ any notice of it*' [Moore's crossing out]. There can be little doubt that Moore watched the events unfolding at Portsmouth with some sympathy and, one detects, even a hint of admiration:

17th April. The fleet are still in a state of Mutiny . . . They behave much better than could be expected, considering that the Power is completely in their own hands. Regular instructions have gone round to all the ships from the Charlotte, *recommending the strictest obedience to their officers in every thing except going to sea . . . Some of the ships have gone greater lengths than others but hardly any of them have shewn any ill will to their officers . . . They have not insisted on the Frigates joining them, on the contrary, they do not wish to detain them if they are ordered on any service. The ships in the Harbour have not declared, but there is no doubt that they are no more to be depended on than the others.*

Moore was well acquainted with the demands of the mutineers – as all officers probably were soon enough.

By 27 April, Moore believed that the government and Admiralty had conceded the demands of the seamen, and all of the ships had returned to duty except four, which included the frigates *Jason* and *Nymphe*, '*Which ships have continued in a state of Mutiny ever since on the score of dissatisfaction against their officers*'. At least Moore had the satisfaction of knowing that his men had no real grievance against him, for some captains had been ordered to leave their own ships. Thinking that the affair had been settled, he observed,

This has been a very extraordinary and a very alarming affair. The fleet were for eight days under the command of the Committees of the Seamen of the different ships. A most rigid discipline was kept up and any disobedience to the Orders and Regulations which they themselves had drawn up was punished in an instant with great severity. They prohibited spirituous liquors and every thing stronger than the common small beer . . . One of the leading men in the Queen Charlotte *received five dozen lashes on board of her for getting drunk, but the common punishment among them was ducking from the fore yard arm, which was practised with very great severity for every fault almost immediately after its commission. The common routine of the Duty went on in the usual way, and in general the Seamen treated their officers with great respect. They disclaimed all disloyalty or disaffection to Government, they declared themselves ready to defend their country to the last, and that they equally longed for an opportunity of meeting the Enemy to convince the Nation that they were no way degenerated from the well known character of English sailors.*

Moore's sympathy for their cause was clear:

The Spirit of the Seamen was aroused by finding that altho' they were so miserably paid, there was no intention of raising their wages and that they never could obtain by fair means what they are so well entitled to.

In fact, he thought that it would not have been unreasonable if they had raised other grievances also. The main lesson though, was that those in a position of responsibility, be it government or Admiralty, had a duty to consider the needs of their seamen. A failure to deal with such responsibility – the word was one which he had inserted in his own journal – would have serious implications. For those in power and authority

. . . have neglected the matter until it broke forth like lightning. They have taught the Seamen how to carry their point. It may have very serious consequences and is a sad blow to the Naval Discipline.

An uneasy calm settled over the fleet. It was well known that the crews of the ships at Plymouth had been following events closely, and Strachan's squadron had avoided the dispute only by remaining at sea. The *Melampus* was still receiving the attention of the shipwrights and more of her crew had deserted. Moore was optimistic about getting to sea again soon, even though he was short of complement.

Then the fragile peace was suddenly shattered. The mutiny

. . . broke out with more violence than ever . . . The pretext for this new outrage appears to be the manner the subject was discussed in the House of Peers on the Motion of the Duke of Bedford, which created doubts in the minds of the Seamen lest the concessions granted them by the Admiralty might be negatived by the Parliament.

On Admiral Colpoy's flagship, the *London*, a seaman was shot by Lieutenant Peter Bover and the angry crew seized their officers, threatening to hang Bover there and then. Many of the seamen were for hanging Colpoys himself, but the majority argued that he should be handed over to the civil authorities. Anger spread through the fleet but there was still a majority who were in favour of giving up the strike but

> *All the frigates were driven to Mutiny by the large ships who threatened to sink them if they did not go to St. Helens*

[i.e. with the other mutinous ships]. Then, at what Moore described as this '. . . *critical and delicate*' moment, the greatly revered Lord Howe arrived at Portsmouth to negotiate with the seamen;

> *the whole business came to be revised again, and every thing was given up to the caprice and licentious disposition of the seamen, all the officers whom they had forced on shore were superseded from their ships. This miserable and melancholy negotiation lasted several days, during which time Sir Roger Curtis squadron came round from Torbay being compelled by their crews.*

As the mutiny subsided, Moore, like other officers, found himself assessing the damage that had been caused. In the immediate weeks after the strike, much of his sympathy for the seamen had evaporated, though it was to return with hindsight. The second, more angry phase of the strike had unexpectedly touched both Moore and the *Melampus*, and this undoubtedly coloured his opinion. There were still ships in mutiny, and whilst most of the seamen were celebrating their success, many of officers were having to cope with the aftermath. Moore witnessed all of the festivity which was being represented as an enthusiastic celebration of Howe's intervention on behalf of the seamen, but could see it only as an unwelcome celebration of the seamen's victory

> *. . . over the discipline of the Navy, which has received a blow which I much doubt of it ever recovering. A few days after this ridiculous and fatal farce Lord Bridport went to sea, a great number of Officers and men being left behind. The* Melampus *was, on the whole, a very quiet ship, however, one afternoon they forced one of the Midshipmen out of the ship whom they had taken a dislike to. I spoke to them the following day and had influence enough with them to persuade them of the folly of some part of their conduct, and gave them to understand that I expected the Midshipman to return to the ship again. As this was in the very height of the mutiny at Spithead, I suffered a few days to elapse, during which I had opportunities of observing that the generality of the seamen of the ship had been merely passive in this outrage,*

however I was advised by my friends here not to insist on the rein-
statement of the Midshipman but to yield to circumstances and to the
temper of the times. The Midshipman was very urgent with me to
discharge him; I therefore called them up a few days before we came to
Spithead which was on the 22nd and asked them if they meant to persist
in the Midshipman being kept out of the ship, they made no answer but
seemed divided: I told them I meant to discharge him at his own request,
but I desired to know if they meant to commit any further violence or
if I was to consider them as returned to their duty as usual. They assured
me they had no grievances and were quite satisfied. I told them if they
meant to endeavour to get rid of any more officers, as I knew they had
no just cause, that I hoped they would apply for another Captain. They
said no we are very well satisfied with our Captain and all of our
officers. They then gave three cheers and we parted very good friends.
On the 22nd the Melampus *came out to Spithead. The ships at Spithead*
are all more or less in a state of Mutiny, the streets are filled with
drunken sailors, in short, I see no end to this dismal business.

The *Melampus*, together with the frigates *Revolutionnaire* and *Virginie*, was now ordered round to Harwich to ferry the Prince and Princess of Wirtemburgh to the continent. Before leaving port, the crews of the three frigates received their pay, with the inevitable result;

It is now eleven o'clock at night and I do not believe there are 20 sober
men on board. They have been boxing at a great rate among the
Irishmen, of which description we have a very large proportion, but I
do not believe they are at all disposed to Mutiny. They are just left off
dancing, and those who are not totally insensible are singing in chorus
the 'Boyne Water'.

Behind this good-natured insobriety, however, there lay a genuine problem which was often the real reason that drunkenness led to punishment on board ships at sea, for a heavily drunken seaman was not a competent one. On the evening of the 28th, the three frigates set sail from Spithead, and the alcohol which had come on board as a consequence of the sailors' wages was still flowing;

We were in such a state of drunkenness that it was with difficulty we
could get the ship under way, and as we were running out we carried
away a Sloop of War's Gib boom without suffering any damage
ourselves.

It was an all too common experience.

Shortly before leaving port, an attempt had been made by the crew of the frigate *Beaulieu* – which was still in a state of mutiny – to prevent the three frigates sailing. This had failed, but this and the preceding events certainly made Moore apprehensive about the future. In his darker moments he thought that a

> *Revolution in the Country is already begun and must go on . . . Those who are for overturning the Government are active and daring, the supporters of it indolent and corrupt in general.*

If the navy had mutinied, he thought it even more likely that the army would turn against the government, which was itself only nominally a government – '*Like the Captains in the Navy, who in the present state of the Navy, only command the ships nominally.*' In such a bleak mood he was afraid of what was going to happen next and it is easy to understand, when he exclaimed that he could take '. . . *no pleasure in the ship*'.

At Cuxhaven, where the Wirtemburgh party was disembarked, Moore was immediately called upon to deal with another disciplinary matter. Whilst anchored here, an Irish seaman on board the *Melampus* seriously abused the First Lieutenant, to the outrage of other members of the crew;

> *The ship's company wanted to duck him, but were prevented, tho' with much difficulty by the first Lieutenant; this morning they were again wanting to punish him and when I went upon deck they were going to reeve a yard rope for the purpose of ducking or hanging him. I ordered all hands aft, told them if they presumed to punish any man of them-selves, they took the command of the ship from me, and were in a state of rank mutiny. I then asked the fellow what he had to say for himself to which he replied with great indifference that he had nothing to say, I then ordered him to the Gangway and gave him 39 lashes; and to another man who had stolen some stock, belonging to the Green Cloth[56], a dozen.*

The squadron weighed anchor, in calm weather, at about 11pm at night. However, the majority of the *Melampus'* crew was drunk, with the result that one of the frigate's best seamen fell overboard and disappeared. Moore despaired:

> *I am sick and disgusted with the conduct of the ship's company, the bulk of them never lose an opportunity of getting completely drunk,*

and I am under the necessity of either winking at their licentious and disorderly conduct, to the ruin of the discipline, or continually punishing them, which is equally revolting.

The answer lay in getting the ship back into more active duty as soon as possible;

I have been under the necessity of punishing a number of seamen since we sailed from Spithead in consequence of their drunkenness and rioting but not a tenth part so many as have richly deserved it. I endeavour to keep up enough of order and regularity to be able to execute the orders we may receive in some way or other, and I believe if we were out of the way of contagion that we should get quite into the old way again.

The problem was that the mutiny had made him unsure of his authority. So far, the crew had maintained their respect for him and his rank; but he knew better than to put this to any real test – and this had a knock-on effect on his ability to properly command the ship. He also felt he had little support from his officers;

This ship is now very much unhinged, we have hardly any good officers in her. The First Lieutenant does nothing more than he is ordered, and that but in a slovenly way, he is good natured and obliging but wants energy and is very little assistance to me when I am on board. We have 35 men in the sick list. O peace, peace, peace.

Without the efficient and energetic support of his executive officer, Moore's hands were tied to a large degree. If he attempted to intervene in the duties of the First Lieutenant, that officer would not only feel undermined, but his authority would be weakened in the eyes of the crew.

Moore was conscious of his depressed state of mind and didn't know whether to attribute this to

... nerves or the affections of my heart, I should suppose the latter. I have been in the dismals all day, but am come round a little since the evening; my business becomes heavy and insipid to me. I could go through service against the enemy, I think, with zeal and alacrity, but the common ship detail is a burthen to me, more especially at this moment when we are only half obeyed and not sure of being obeyed at all.

To make matters worse, news came of a much more serious mutiny among the North Sea Fleet, which had anchored at the Nore. It must have been with mixed feelings that the squadron received orders to return to Harwich to lift any buoys which might be of use to mutinous ships attempting to break out into the North Sea. This operation might invoke the spectre of sympathy with the mutineers, and Moore was glad when, on 17 May the *Melampus* was ordered to report to Admiral Peyton at the Downs. He hoped that this would mean that he was to be transferred from the St Marcouf station – but whatever the result, he knew the ship needed occupation, and didn't want to be held at the Downs for long. Even so, at the Downs there were disciplinary problems. One of the ship's marines got drunk and was insolent to his officer. The man was given two dozen lashes, but appeared to be drunk and unrepentant even as the punishment was being inflicted. Moore ordered him put back in irons. He was however more lenient with

> ... *one of the seamen who had been disorderly when drunk, I thought fit to forgive as he expressed contrition for his faults. This is all extremely disgusting.*

Matters were not helped by the fact that the frigate *Beaulieu* was now at the Downs, and still suffering from mutinous outbreaks amongst the crew. The Captain had now been replaced and five of the mutineers had been allowed to return back on board, but one of these had immediately attacked the First Lieutenant and had been placed in irons. Some of the crew had immediately attempted to rescue him, arming themselves and running the marine sentry through with a cutlass. The frigate's officers had initially barricaded themselves in the gunroom then, arming themselves, they had broken out on deck through the cabin skylight, where the mutineers immediately attacked them with cutlasses. Fortunately for the officers, the marines and remainder of the crew came to their assistance. Whilst this desperate struggle was going on, there was consternation among the other frigates at the Downs, who went to quarters and prepared to fire upon the *Beaulieu*. The mutineers were eventually driven below decks where, given time to cool off, they surrendered. Sixteen men had been wounded, several mortally, including one of the mutineers who had been shot by the First Lieutenant in the process of turning one of the fo'c'sle guns on the quarterdeck. It was a bloody and bitter incident that shook Moore considerably:

> *I am not certain that our men would have stuck by me, but I believe they would. If the Mutineers had attempted to carry the* Beaulieu *to sea*

I would have cut the cables after her and treated her as an Enemy. Captain Hunt in the Virginie *was all ready for acting against her. The day following I spoke to our men and after giving them credit for their good behaviour told them I would not give a curse for them if they were not as ready to attack a ship like the* Beaulieu *as an Enemy.*

The events at the Nore and the *Beaulieu* mutiny had hardened Moore's attitude, though he could not help a grudging respect for Richard Parker, the leader of the Nore mutiny. Parker, who had now been sentenced to be hanged,

. . . seems to be a fellow of great intrepidity and considerable abilities . . . he is without doubt a most dangerous and daring man though dissolute and imprudent in an eminent degree. The sooner he and some more of them are hanged the better.

He had now come to believe that many of the mutineers, like the men of the *Beaulieu*, would really have been prepared to hand their ships over to the enemy; *'They are dangerous knaves and wicked scoundrels.'*

The *Melampus* was now held up at the Downs because Moore was required to sit on the court martial of the *Beaulieu* mutineers. She was joined there by the frigates *Garland* and *Southampton*, the latter commanded by James Macnamara, having just arrived from St Vincent's fleet blockading Cadiz. On 4 July the courts martial began on the *Beaulieu* mutineers. The man who had struck the First Lieutenant was found guilty, but because of some favourable circumstance was recommended '. . . *to the mercy of a lesser punishment'.* Another man was ordered to receive 100 lashes '. . . *from ship to ship'.* The rest of the mutineers were tried two days later, and seven of the sixteen were condemned to death – though Moore thought that, in the end, only four would be executed. Perhaps in an attempt to escape from the horrors of the courts martial, Moore found himself thinking more and more about Miss M. Once again he reminded himself that he was not in a financial position to propose marriage, but he decided that if he could win the lady's affections he would certainly marry her,

. . . for I find myself wretched without her, or at least until I am rejected by her. I do not, however, intend to hang myself, although she is dearer to me than all the world besides.

In desperation, he sat down and wrote a declaration of his love, *'. . . which I do not believe I will ever send to her.'*

To his disappointment, in the middle of July, Moore was ordered to rejoin Strachan off the coast of France. Still, at least he was away from the Downs and the turmoil of the Channel Fleet; and he could always console himself with the fact that he was not being sent to the disease-ridden West Indies, where brother John had buried more than three-quarters of his men in less than eighteen months;

He himself has several times been dangerously ill, but fortunately survived what has proved fatal to thousands under his command. He is my dearest friend and the man in the world I love and value the most; if he had died I scarce think my Mother could have borne his loss, he is now at home and she and my Father never can be happier.

On the 24th, Moore fell in with the frigates *Stag*, *Pearl* and the sloop *Cynthia* off Le Havre. In Strachan's temporary absence, Captain Joseph Sidney Yorke, in the *Stag*, was senior officer, and had been ordered to remain on the station until the *Diamond* returned. He explained to Moore that he only intended to remain off Le Havre during the Spring tides, and as soon as these subsided he would give the frigates leeway to cruise. Moore was greatly reassured by the remarkable rapidity with which the crew of the *Melampus* settled back into the usual routine, once they were on active duty:

Our men are getting quite into the old way again, I do not believe they have any mischief in their heads, and I am much mistaken if they would not behave with great spirit if we met an enemy.

By 29 July, the spring tides had passed, and Yorke gave Moore permission to cruise on the western edge of the station, returning again for the following springs. Eagerly, Moore ran westwards, scarcely heeding the onset of heavy weather. The frigate rounded Cape Barfleur during heavy rain squalls, lit by continuous flashes of lightning and with her crew shuddering under the impact of large hail stones. Moore wisely ordered all sails clewed up and, shortly after, the wind slammed round to the opposite direction, taking the ship aback even without her sails. Fortunately, little harm came to her. Sailing on to St Malo, Moore found the seas empty.

On 10 August the *Melampus* rejoined the squadron off Le Havre, to find that Strachan had returned. The squadron, which now consisted of the frigates *Diamond*, *Melampus*, *Flora* and *Syren* – which Moore considered '. . . *a very respectable light squadron*' – set off to patrol the coast as far as Ushant. They were joined off Guernsey by the frigate *Pearl* and on arrival Moore climbed to the frigate's masthead in the early morning to see Bridport's fleet in the distance. They then returned to Le Havre where the *Syren* stopped a French corvette which turned out to be a cartel carrying English prisoners of war. By extraordinary coincidence, many of the English prisoners turned out to be the seamen from the *Diamond* who had been captured along with Sidney Smith and these were hurriedly signed back on the *Diamond*'s books. Strachan had also now received orders to send the *Melampus* back to Spithead, and Moore was ordered to escort the corvette there. As he sailed northwards leaving the squadron behind, Moore could not help wondering what lay in store. He had hopes that the Admiralty would at last send him to join Warren's squadron, perhaps in place of the *Artois*:

> *I am very glad to leave the unprofitable station of St. Marcouf, but it is with regret that I part with Strachan a man whom I love and esteem and who always had great confidence in me.*

At Portsmouth there was, indeed, wonderful news. The *Melampus* was ordered to complete her stores and sail for Falmouth, the base used by both Sir John Borlase Warren's and Edward Pellew's frigate squadrons. She put to sea on 4 September, but before leaving, Moore had a memorable encounter:

> *I saw the brave Rear Admiral Nelson on his return, with the loss of his right arm, from the unfortunate attempt upon Sancta Cruz. He is in perfect health and spirits; his wound with that of Freemantle, the death of the Gallant and able Captain Richard Bowen of the* Terpsichore *and many valuable officers, seamen and marines would have been by far too dear a price for the success of the expedition. I think, from all that I have heard, that the attempt was a rash one, and altho' unsuccessful, yet honourable to the British Navy, much daring enterprise, courage and perseverance having been displayed in the execution. I believe their intelligence has been very erroneous.*

The *Melampus* beat her way along the south coast in thick weather, for the autumn rains had set in early. Nevertheless, Moore was in good mood, for he was about to join Warren whom he considered '. . . *a very active, dashing and brave officer*' and he was anticipating a future where he would

> . . . *possess £800 a year for myself and the lass I love, with whom I wish to settle in the country within 30 miles of London and there occupy*

myself with the study of human Nature, my friends and my family.
Occasionally visiting those parts of England and Scotland that are most
interesting.

It was a happy vision – and one which had been fed on the reputation
of the Falmouth Squadrons for taking prizes.

Then, three days after reporting to Warren at Falmouth, Moore's
hopes were cruelly crushed. The two independent frigate squadrons
were to be returned to the close control of the widely disliked Admiral
Lord Bridport;

This is both disagreeable and prejudicial to the Captains composing the
above squadrons as it takes away one third of their Prize Money, and
cramps them in their operations.

The move was quite probably equally unwelcome to the seamen
also. The *Melampus* herself was also to be placed under Bridport's
command.

For nearly two weeks, the frigates waited for orders to see how they
were to be redeployed. Finally, Moore received orders to join the
frigate *Phoebe*, commanded by the extremely capable and experienced Captain Robert Barlow, to cruise west of Scilly for the
protection of several homeward-bound West Indiamen, which were
thought to have become separated from their convoy. Moore was
now in the best position he had ever been of obtaining his heart's
desire. There was no other

. . . chance of becoming independent than by Prize Money, this station
may produce in the course of a few months enough to double my
stock[57]; I should then be rich enough in my own eyes, to try the affec-
tions of the woman I love; if she considered the mediocrity of my
fortune as an obstacle to her consenting to marry, I would give up all
thoughts of her, convinced that she did not love me and that I had
mistaken her character. My wishes are now for retirement, not
completely so, but living in the country, with a small society of old
friends; married to the woman I am sure I love, and meeting
occasionally the men I love, admire and esteem; ready at the call of the
Country to come forth and serve it with zeal and vigour; having
enough to leave my family in decent and moderate circumstances,
becoming their rank and situation in life, while I am absent or in case
of my death.

The cruise nearly ended prematurely in disaster when the two frigates were twenty-two leagues south-west of Scilly. At 5am on the 26 September, they were ploughing through a very heavy cross sea, lashed by squalling rain, when

> . . . by the ignorance of the Officer of the Watch, we had very nigh pitched all the masts away, he brought her up against the sea when we were going 7 knots. The fore sail was filled with water and split to pieces, one of the Bumpkins snapt short off and the step of the other tore up; An hour afterwards we split the main top sail in the act of taking it in. The Phoebe split her fore and main top sails.

Two days later they fell in with the battered West India convoy, and their almost disabled escort, the *Janus*. Bad weather continued as the convoy made its way towards the Lizard, and the conditions were beginning to have their effect on the morale of their crew. Provisions were running low and Moore had been obliged to reduce the grog ration, serving small beer instead. He was aware that this had caused some discontent and grumbling, but he also detected the long-term effects of the mutiny. Whilst he had always encouraged the men to express any grievances, rather than bottle them up, he felt '. . . *they are too apt now to come up with frivolous and ill founded complaints'*. Off the Lizard, the *Phoebe* disappeared to the south-west, leaving the *Melampus* to struggle on up the channel with the convoy. Off Portland the weather improved, but the whole gathering became becalmed and Moore surveyed his charges gloomily: '*I fear we shall not get rid of these lads tomorrow.*' Nevertheless, the wind soon picked up, and by 3 October he was heading back towards Falmouth.

Relieved of his charges, Moore had time to review the performance of his crew during this latest cruise. He had to admit that the *Melampus* was now better manned than she had ever been. But he still could not overcome the shortcomings of his officers;

> One of the lieutenants is a mere boy: some of the midshipmen are pretty good men and might be trusted on occasion . . . I hope we shall soon sail on a cruise where we may meet a rouser, or else that we may have a speedy peace to set us all about our business.

The *Melampus* passed Portland Bill at about midnight and was heading towards Start Point when a lugger was sighted acting suspiciously. Moore gave chase and brought her to about five leagues from the Caskett Lights, having fired two shots at her, the second of which tore through her main topsail. This ship proved to be a privateer,

A very fine Lugger mounting 14 small guns of 2 and 3 pounders and manned with 54 men, from Cherbourg which she only left last evening at 6 o'clock. She is called le Rayon . . . *during the chase she threw all her guns, spare sails and lumber that was upon her deck overboard.*

The French crew was transferred across to the *Melampus* and replaced by a mate and fourteen seamen. Moore then took the prize in tow and set off for Falmouth where he found the *Phoebe* at anchor. Once again orders arrived for the two frigates to head west, this time to join the homeward-bound Jamaica convoy which was being escorted by the frigate *Sheerness*, see them past the Isle of Wight and then return to Falmouth. Before departing, garbled news arrived that there had been an engagement in the North Sea between Admiral Duncan's fleet and the Dutch.*

On 17 October, south of Scilly, the two frigates ran into the *Stag* with a recaptured Portuguese packet ship. The four ships hove to, to exchange the usual news and Moore went on board the *Stag* to visit his old acquaintance, Captain Joseph Sidney Yorke. There was the usual naval gossip. Both Warren and Pellew were being wastefully detained by Bridport, whilst a squadron under the command of Robert Stopford, in the frigate *Phaeton*, had taken eight prizes between Quiberon and the mouth of the Garonne;

The ground that they have been on is at present by far the best on any part of the home station for cruising, as there are a number of large privateers from Rochfort, Nantes and Bordeaux that go as far as the Western Islands looking for our merchant ships, they generally bring their Prizes to the Port they belong to, so they have a very good chance of intercepting them. Where we now are the French privateers are in generally small vessels from Cherbourg, St. Malo, Morlaix and sometimes from Brest. We have a tolerable chance of meeting something of this kind, but I am afraid we are not far enough to the Westward to meet any thing considerable.

Barlow and Moore set about patrolling in the western approaches to the Channel, a particularly busy area at this time. Within days they had encountered homebound English convoys from both Quebec and the East Indies, but not the Jamaica convoy. Moore also gave chase on two occasions to French privateer cutters but, inexplicably, Barlow

* The Battle of Camperdown, 11th October 1797. Duncan's fleet defeated the Dutch after a severe engagement.

recalled him on each occasion as dusk fell. A frustrated Moore recorded angrily in his journal,

> I am sick of the Phoebe. I respect Barlow but I never wish to cruise with him again. I have no idea of leaving off chase of a vessel, evidently an enemy, while there is even a possibility of coming up with her; in this instance I really believe we should have taken a very mischievous French Cutter had we thought fit . . . It is a cursed damper to me.

On the following day, the *Melampus'* carpenter reported

> . . . the fore topmast and fore top gallant mast sprung . . . Shifting the top mast proved to be a very tedious job, as the Mast had never been [properly] fitted, a circumstance with which I was unacquainted.

At the end of October, they turned back for Falmouth, where Moore busied his crew in overhauling the frigate's rigging. Although the crew worked hard at this for seven days, Moore knew that he could not complete the job properly without help from the dockyard – besides, the crew were also long overdue their pay. He submitted a request to both Barlow and the Admiralty, and was immediately ordered round to Plymouth. On 23 November, he sailed in a hurry to get the work carried out, but that evening while sailing at five knots, the *Melampus* ran aground on a rocky shoal off Penlee Point, striking with alarming force. Fortunately, the tide was flowing and twenty minutes later the frigate lifted off the rocks, and continued to Hamoaze;

> We were hauled into a Dock with everything in except the guns and powder the day after we got into harbour. We found the false keel as far aft as the Main mast from forward, beat off, and part of the lower part of the Gripe shattered. The ship was lifted in this state about an inch, her damages repaired, and she hauled out the night after she went in. We got out into the Sound in seven days after our coming into Hamoaze. This was quick work. Since we came into the Sound there has been an almost continual gale of wind, blowing very hard and directly in. We have sustained some damage by the gale but nothing very material.

Although the *Melampus* had now had her hull repaired and rigging overhauled, she lay idly for a month awaiting orders. This was particularly galling because, in the *Melampus'* absence, on 21 December, Barlow had captured the 36-gun French frigate *La Nereide* and carried her triumphantly into Plymouth.[58] Happily, Moore had re-

1. Graham Moore, as painted by Sir Thomas Lawrence in either 1791 or 1792. The uniform suggests that this was intended to record Moore's promotion to the rank of Master and Commander. *(By courtesy of the National Portrait Gallery, London)*

2. Captain Alan Gardner. Son of an admiral and promoted earlier than Moore, the two men became firm friends and remained so until Gardner's early death in 1815.

(Author's Collection)

3. Liverpool, in around 1790. Moore, who would have seen this view often as a Lieutenant, was impressed by the city's commercial energy.

4. Dynevor (Dinefwr) Castle. The romantic ruins of Dynevor Castle, in the grounds of Newton House, Carmarthenshire, probably as they would have been seen by the dinner party when leaving the house.

5. Captain Sidney Smith: controversial, charismatic, heroic and often downright infuriating

6. Model of the frigate HMS *Melampus*. This model was commissioned possibly by her builders, J M Hillhouse of Bristol, and has been dated to 1793.

(Bristol Museums & Art Gallery)

7. Cork Harbour, around 1809, after a drawing by Nicholas Pocock.

Published May 31 1809, by J. Gold, 103, Shoe Lane, Fleet Street.

8. Warren's action off Ireland. This convincing contemporary sketch of Warren's frigates engaging Bompart's fleet off Ireland, by Nicholas Pocock, reflects the artist's concern for accuracy. *(National Maritime Museum, Greenwich)*

9. This chart of Brest Harbour, from the Naval Chronicle, would have been highly familiar to all the commanders of British frigates blockading the French coast.

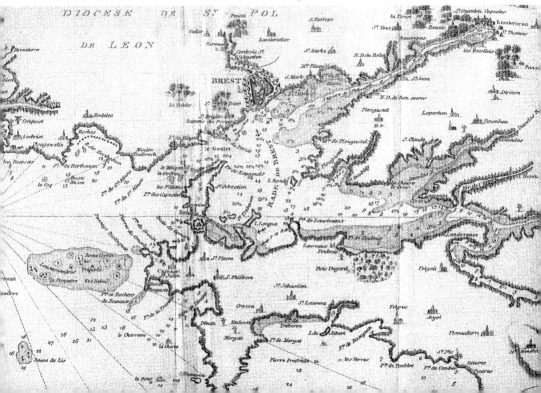

10. Every frigate captain's dream - Moore's encounter with the Spanish treasure convoy in 1804. This aquatint was produced by Thomas Whitcombe and Daniel Havell.
(National Maritime Museum, Greenwich)

11. The *Mercedez* explodes. An aquatint after a painting by Sir John Gore.
(National Maritime Museum, Greenwich)

12. Brooke Farm, Cobham, Surrey, painted by J Hassell in 1822, when Graham Moore owned the property.   *(The British Library)*

13. Graham Moore's grave in the mediæval churchyard, Cobham, Surrey.
                                                             (Author's own collection)

covered from his fit of irritability, and was able to share in Barlow's jubilation: *'I am very happy at his success, he well deserves it, being a worthy man and a very able officer.'* Less happily, ten of the *Melampus'* seamen had deserted, breaking their trust when Moore allowed them leave on shore; *'. . . this I attribute in a great measure to my indulgence, it is a circumstance that frets me extremely.'* It was extremely frustrating for an officer who was determined to show his crew every humanity that he reasonably could. Finally, on the last day of 1797, he was ordered to take the frigate *Seahorse*, Captain Foote, under his orders, and cruise about 400 miles west of Scilly, an area through which all incoming transatlantic trade would have to pass for the entrance to the Channel. Moore was well pleased because he liked Foote, whom he considered

> *. . . a very intelligent man in his profession, and has established a consid-*
> *erable reputation for activity, zeal and ability; we are on very good*
> *terms with each other and have agreed to share for the cruise. I hope*
> *fortune will give us an opportunity of trying our metal.*

Despite the number of frigates already cruising to the westwards, this was potentially good hunting ground and Moore was optimistic in spite of the battering weather. The only downside lay in the state of the *Melampus'* sails. On the frigate's first day out, the main and fore topsails both split, partly due to the stress of the weather, but more on account of the fact that wet and stormy weather, while they were lying in the Sound, had made it impossible to dry the sails, leaving them rotting with mildew. On 11 January they sighted a privateer brig but lost her during the night. Then, on the 16th, they sighted another ship which gave all the appearance of being a privateer of eighteen to twenty guns. They set off in close pursuit with the *Seahorse* dropping to leeward in case their quarry should attempt to escape by going away large. The privateer, meanwhile, could be seen heaving her guns overboard. Just before noon, Moore opened with his bow chasers, whilst Foote turned to bring his broadside to bear – and the privateer brought to and struck her colours. Moore sent a boarding party across and learned that she was *La Belliqueuse* from St Malo with a complement of 120 men. She had originally been a French navy corvette, but had been sold off to a private speculator for privateering.

The task of transferring the French prisoners to the frigates had barely been completed when the wind started to blow up, and the seas became rough. The prize hastily headed eastwards under the command of a Master's Mate and by the following morning the two frigates were caught in

> *... the hardest gale that I have ever known on this side of the Atlantic. This hurricane, I may almost call it, lasted for 12 hours, during the greatest part of which time we could only shew a storm mizzen stay sail to it and that was blown to pieces at last.*

On the afternoon of the 18th, the gale abated but was replaced by fog. In spite of this, amazingly, the two frigates never separated – '*... greatly owing to the attention of Captain Foote who is certainly a very diligent and able officer*'. Moore's orders authorized him to cruise until 22 January, and on the 20th Moore decided that they should head as far to the west of their cruising ground as possible. By being at the westernmost limit on the 22nd, he would therefore need extra days to get back to Plymouth. This was, apparently, a common method of stretching the limits of authority without undue impropriety.

The following day, as they headed westwards, they sighted a strange ship which, having seen them approaching, immediately made all sail to escape. By 8pm the weather had turned very squally and Moore had lost sight of both the chase and the *Seahorse*. He burned blue lights in the hope that Foote would see them, but there was no signal in reply. In spite of this, he continued westwards in the hope of again making contact with the chase. Before daybreak the next day, he decided on a ruse, and busied the crew of the *Melampus* in disguising the frigate by striking her fore and mizzen topgallant masts. They could barely have completed this task when, at 9am, a lookout reported a ship to the north. The stranger, a large corvette flying no colours, made sail to escape and the *Melampus* immediately set off in chase. By noon, Moore was able to open with his bow chasers. The stranger appeared to have no heavy stern chasers, and by keeping the *Melampus* tight on her quarters, the ship was forced to yaw regularly to bring her sternmost guns to bear. However, the continual yawing put her top hamper under strain, and not long after she began firing back, her main topmast went by the board. Moore approached cautiously, unsure of whether the corvette had struck, as any flag which she might have used to signal her surrender could have become entangled in the wreck of the mast. The *Melampus*' gun crews were ready at their stations, but he was unwilling to give the order to fire, so he shot up alongside intending to hail her. As the *Melampus* drew up under the lee of the corvette, her crew cleared the wreckage

. . . and bearing up, as if to run us on board, gave us their Broadside and a very smart fire of Musketry; we returned their Broadside and wore round along with them to prevent them from boarding us and from getting to Leeward of us; she passed under our stern and as we came to the wind on the other tack we carried away the Mizzen top sail yard in the slings and had a good deal of our running rigging cut away: I saw she had hoisted her colours to the Mizzen top mast head just before she fired into us. When on the other side of us she tried to cross our fore foot but we filled and shot close up to her and I believe should have sunk her had she not after one more Broadside struck. I had ordered the men at the Main deck guns to raise the breeches of their metal, seeing that most of our shot went over her, and they seemed well pointed for doing their business when they struck. She proved to be the Volage, Corvette, *lent to, and fitted by the Merchants of Nantes, mounting 20 nine pounders and 2 long 18 pounders, with a crew of 195 men; 2 of my best men were killed in this affair and 3 dangerously wounded. One of the men killed was Joseph Wyat, my Coxswain, a very brave fellow, who had been with me these six years. He fell close to me, but I did not see him, being so much engaged with the working of the ship, I am glad I did not see him fall, for I loved him; he was a fellow of infinite* sang froid, *and no ceremony. A true English sailor. I understand that we only killed two of the enemy and wounded eight or ten of them. It was late on the night of the 23rd before we had all the prisoners exchanged from the Prize and her in a state to make sail, but as soon as that was effected I made the best of my way in company with her to the eastward; as I have now about 50 men out of the ship and about 240 prisoners I intend getting into Plymouth as soon as I can . . .*

The *Melampus*, carefully shepherding her valuable prize, arrived in Cawsand Bay on the evening of 27 January. There they found their other prize, the *La Belliqueuse*, which happily had arrived just a few days earlier. The frigate's mainmast had been damaged during the action, but the dockyard officials decided it could be fished, and Moore was ordered to return to Falmouth. Happily, before they sailed, the crew of the *Melampus* learned that both the *La Belliqueuse* and the *Volage* were to be purchased by the Navy Board for re-use as men-of-war.

Moore returned to Falmouth and, while anchored there, a cartel arrived carrying men released from imprisonment in France. Among them were a number of seamen from the *Amazon*, the ship wrecked on the coast of France during the action with the *Droits de L'Homme* in January 1797. Moore had every sympathy for them, but this did not stop him pressing them for service in the *Melampus*;

> *These poor fellows have suffered much from bad and short provisions and long imprisonment, they will soon come round again I hope, and God send they may gain as much credit in the* Melampus *as they earned in their old ship.*

On 22 March, orders arrived for the *Melampus* to cruise for a month off the Isle de Bas (north of Ushant), to intercept vessels sailing between St Malo and Granville, for Brest. In London there was great alarm about political unrest in Ireland and Moore was aware that there was every possibility that the French might try to seize upon this opportunity by landing an army there. If they did, then the *Melampus* might be in a good position to get involved. However, he was also aware that he was cruising in the area which had been patrolled by Pellew's and Warren's squadrons, and he could not help lamenting their demise:

> *The squadron that used to be under the command of Sir John Warren seems now to be knocked up, and that under Sir Edward Pellew instead of having the range to the Westward that they had some time ago are now limited to the entrance of the Channel or the neighbourhood of Scilly. This change is generally attributed to the Jealousy and avarice of Lord Bridport who it is said remonstrated against these Squadrons of Frigates cruising in the Channel and the Bay of Biscay independent of him; it is further said that Warren laid himself open to his Lordship by running away from him at one time in spite of the signals to call him in. However this may be, Warren was put by the Admiralty under the orders of the Commander in Chief of the Channel Fleet, and soon afterwards got the command of the* Canada *of 74 guns. A squadron of frigates, some of them the same ships that Warren had with him before, have since been employed under Lord Bridport's orders, but commanded by the Honourable Captain Stopford of the* Phaeton, *on the same ground that Warren used to be. This squadron has been very successful against the enemies privateers, and has retaken property to a very great amount belonging to the British, American and Danish merchants. Warren at present commands this squadron but under the orders of Lord Bridport in London or Bath, instead of the Admiralty.*

On the last day of the month, the *Melampus* chased a lugger 100 miles, only to find out that she was a French Royalist lugger commanded by an extremely nervous English lieutenant. Moore turned back for the Isle de Bas, struggling for a week against worsening weather. When he arrived back on station he found the seas deserted and was convinced they would have no success. After a week, he noted gloomily in his diary,

> I am heartily sick of this station where there appears, really nothing to be done especially without a pilot for the coast.

The only people who seemed to have any luck on this station were the infuriating Jersey privateers, who were shallow enough to operate close inshore – indeed, Moore had to watch while a number of these sailed past with their prizes in tow. Another week dragged by and Moore became increasingly despondent. At least the weather had been kind;

> I hope it will continue so for the remainder of our uninteresting, flat cruise. I have no spirit to write. I have nothing to say. Is it worth while to write such stuff? . . . This has been a dull cruise . . . [but] the men have behaved, on the whole, well. The great body of them are well disposed although there are some Ruffians among them. I shall be extremely happy if we sail from Plymouth as strong as we go in.

It was not just the lack of activity or prizes that depressed him. A poor cruise had its effect on the crew and if they felt their commander was either unlucky or unskilled in finding prizes, they would take the next opportunity to leave the ship and find a better commander. Some commanders might try to prevent this by refusing the men leave, but Moore could not, in all conscience, deny his men the leave they deserved, and once they got their pay, they would be off. Technically it was desertion, but Moore understood the process that was going on in the men's minds. The *Melampus* was better equipped with seamen than she had been for a long time, and Moore was dreading the return to Plymouth. On the 23rd, a cutter arrived with orders for Moore to report to Falmouth, where he was to escort the *Canada* westwards of Cape Clear. On arrival there, however, he learned that the *Canada* had sailed over a week before. Again, the *Melampus* was held up awaiting new orders, and Moore fumed quietly about the inefficiency of keeping his frigate bound in port without making use of her. Then on 31 May, urgent orders arrived. There was trouble brewing in Ireland, and he was to set sail immediately for Cork.

10

Ireland
(May 1798 – November 1798)

Moore's orders were to patrol between Dublin Bay and the Tuskar Rock off the south-east corner of Ireland, to intercept any vessels attempting to land arms and supplies to rebel forces. Although he liked to keep up with politics – especially where they bore some relevance to the war – he had to admit that he was ill equipped to judge what was happening in Ireland;

> *There are so many extraordinary stories abroad of the designs and force of the Men called United Irish, that I can form no fixed opinion on Irish politics.*

As he, and certainly the Admiralty saw it, the gravest danger lay in the French taking advantage of the situation. He was convinced that, once again, the French would attempt to land a force in Ireland but he believed they would be taking a terrible risk. An invasion force would have to be carried in a number of transports, and if a frigate or small squadron fell in with them, the only way of 'securing' the troops, would be to sink the transports. As a frigate commander, Moore shuddered at what he called *'a dreadful dilemma'*, that is, being forced to choose between drowning the men by sinking the transports or letting them reach the shore.

They were off Dublin Bay on 3 June, when an Irish sloop informed them that civil war[59] had begun. Several days later the *Melampus* was joined by the frigate *Glenmore*, which had been sent by Admiral Kingsmill at Cork, also to intercept arms shipments. George Duff of the *Glenmore* was the senior Captain, and he suggested the two frigates should cruise together. The *Glenmore* was a frigate of the same class as the *Melampus* and Moore thought that she sailed *'very well indeed'*. Duff also passed on a copy of a Dublin newspaper which

146

carried accounts of horrific atrocities committed by the rebel Irish armies. Moore was aghast, for their actions seemed more like

> . . . the furious and abominable excesses of a horde of Indians than the prepared and digested plans of a conspiracy to overset the government.

Perhaps predictably, he viewed the rebellion as an attempt to undermine the real task of defeating the French and, as a consequence, he had no sympathy for its leaders. On 5 June, the men on the two frigates saw heavy smoke inland, which could only come from a large-scale engagement. Two days later the *Ramillies* (74) joined them, commanded by Captain Bartholomew Rowley, who took them under his orders. From Rowley they learned that the smoke they had seen came from the action at New Ross where a rebel force under the Protestant, Bagenal Harvey, fought bravely but was defeated with great loss. Moore was coming to the conclusion that the loyalists would overcome this rebellion, and if the militia held true, they would also defeat any French invasion force. But it would be a hard fight, for '. . . *their* [i.e. the rebels'] *numbers are very alarming*'. Within hours, Thomas Williams arrived in the frigate *Endymion*. He had orders to take the frigates *Melampus*, *Unicorn* and *Phoenix* under his command and patrol the coast with the direct purpose of preventing any assistance arriving for the succour of the rebel forces. It was clearly understood by the officers of the squadron that this meant a French invasion force. Moore was confident in Williams' leadership, believing him to be

> . . . an active, brave and judicious officer and I think will conduct us well if we have any thing to do. I believe on this service he would attack five or even six frigates with the three ships* under his orders.

As things stood on 10 June though, the wind was against anything reaching Ireland from France. Moore had become more pessimistic about the rebellion. His confidence in the ability of the militia had evaporated and he thought the government now needed to act quickly to crush the rebels before the French arrived. Ireland was clearly in widespread revolt and if experienced French troops were landed now, they would receive much better local support than they had on the previous attempt at Bantry Bay. Still, there was some optimism, for Moore had learned that his brother John had been sent to

---

* *Phoenix* had not arrived at this point.

take command in the area nearby. By the 12th, the squadron was drifting on a windless sea, in thick fog. Moore could see none of the other frigates, but felt that they could not be far off. In such poor visibility it would not be possible to see a French force either, but Moore knew that Strachan's squadron was guarding the French ports between Brest and Le Havre, and he thought it improbable any French frigates would evade them. The next day the fog lifted and,

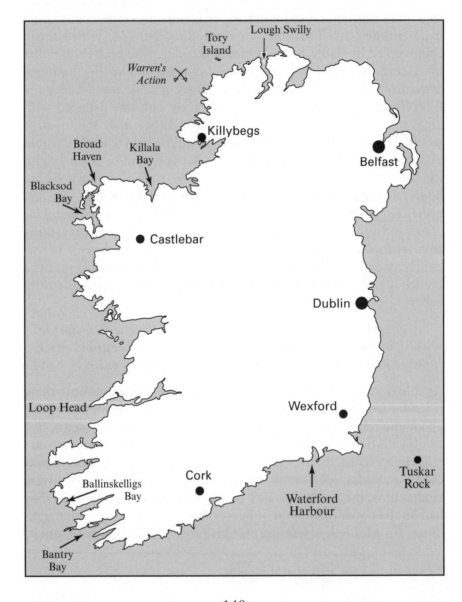

sure enough, the *Endymion* and *Unicorn* were on their station, close by. Also to be seen were English transports, hurriedly carrying more troops to Dublin[60] and over the next few days there came the sound of heavy guns from the direction of Wexford. There was no news of what was happening on land – but there was naval news. The French fleet had broken out of Toulon and Admiral Curtis' squadron, which had been stationed off Bantry Bay on the south-west tip of Ireland, had been diverted to join St Vincent's fleet off Cadiz in case the French should manage to join up with the Spanish fleet there. Rear Admiral Nelson was said to have sailed eastwards up the Mediterranean in the hope of meeting the French, but Moore thought that if the Toulon fleet was engaged on any expedition, it must be against Ireland. But, as yet, the wind still stood against an expeditionary force sailing from the south.

The next day the wind shifted to the south, bringing with it beautiful weather and the expected frigate *Phoenix*. The four ships hastily took up positions off the Tuskar Rock, where they were joined by the cutter *Fox*. She reported that a major battle had taken place at Vinegar Hill and loyalist forces under the command of Sir James Duff had defeated a rebel army, killing upwards of 2,000 of them. Moore noted grimly that the commander of the *Fox* had reported that '. . . *neither side took prisoners'*. Moore could not understand the strategy of the rebels; *'Is it choice or necessity that confined the Rebels to this part of the Country? Have they no retreat?'* Or was it because they hoped the French would land between Waterford and Wexford. Moore had to concede that in spite of *'our zeal and vigilance'* it would still be possible for the French to throw a party of men on shore along that stretch of coast. Wishing to understand more about the rebellion, Moore borrowed some newspapers and read them carefully;

> *This Irish Rebellion is a most serious affair, it is difficult at this moment, to form a clear notion of it, but I am of opinion that the leaders and Promoters of it have been forced to precipitate the general rising by the late rigorous measures Government have adopted.*

Yet this gave him no cause to sympathize with the rebels, for he believed that the revolutionary views of their leaders, combined with the strength of disaffection in Ireland, would make any compromise the English government offered unacceptable. Moore's conclusion was typically pragmatic. If the rebels had to be dealt with, it was better to do it now than leave it till the winter when it would be harder for the navy to guard the coast. With equal interest he learned that his

149

brother John had marched with part of his division against the rebels in Wexford;

> *Notwithstanding the danger . . . [to] my brother and my dearest and noblest friend, I rejoice that he is here, in the Vanguard, where the cries of their Country call her bravest sons. This is the post of the Fate of Britain.*

New orders arrived with the frigate *Glenmore* on 19 June. The frigates were to move closer to Wexford to prevent any rebels escaping from there by sea. However,

> *. . . owing to the incorrectness of our best Charts and the ignorance of the Pilots, we were under the necessity of anchoring 8 or 9 miles from the entrance of the River of Wexford.*

The problem was overcome by sending the squadron's boats closer inshore, armed with carronades and under the direction of the *Endymion*'s First Lieutenant.

By the 22nd, news came that Wexford had been taken by General Moore, and it was arranged for the squadron's captains to be taken up to the town in the *Endymion*'s barge. The town itself was full of soldiers and Moore soon heard about the engagement. After their defeat at Vinegar Hill, the rebels had thought that they might have to abandon Wexford, so they

> *. . . took the abominable resolution of murdering all their Prisoners, accordingly they were dragged out in groups of 15 or 20 and massacred with pikes on the bridge [at Wexford] and their bodies tossed into the River to the number of near 100.*

While this was going on, General Moore's force had arrived. The rebels sent out a flag of truce, offering to surrender and mentioning, by way of an incentive, that they had Lord Kingsborrow as prisoner. Moore had refused to accept the surrender terms offered and ordered his force to advance. The nervous rebel force, hearing the approach of the loyalist drums, panicked and fled, leaving their prisoners behind. It was a comparatively bloodless victory, but not without its share of brutality. Wandering the streets, Moore had found his brother and managed to spend an hour with him until the General was suddenly called away. A rebel officer by the name of Hay had been captured, and within the space of an hour he was tried by court martial and hanged.

I saw this miserable scene, he was led off by some Dragoons and taken to the Bridge at Wexford, the planks and rails of which were drenched and clotted with the blood of those who had been cut to pieces on it in cold blood by the rebels the day before. A halter was thrown over a lamp iron at the end of the bridge, some of Williams's Barge's crew[61] made the knot and assisted. Hay was led under it on horseback and as soon as the halter was adjusted the horse was whipt from under him, the rope broke and the wretched man fell, his eyes staring wildly and quite alive, he was lifted up, the broken part knotted again and he suspended as before. I was very much shocked, some of the Wexford people crying, 'many a life has he to answer for'. Others saying 'what a pity that Jemmy (or Willy) Hay should bring himself to this'. He was a stout middle sized man with rather good countenance, about 35 years of age, with a landed estate to a very considerable amount in the County and heir to more than double at the death of his Father. He never appeared to me to be affected either with rage, fear or sorrow from the time I saw him taken before the Court martial until he was hanged. Not the slightest degree of pity or concern was shown him at his death, he seemed unwilling to die, as a man might appear rather unwilling to set off on a long journey, but no symptom of violent agitation. After he was dead, he was stript and thrown into the River among the murdered loyalists without any kind of ceremony.

On the following day, the squadron's launches intercepted a sloop sailing from Wexford and its Master was arrested and sent in to Wexford, under suspicion. He was immediately court-martialled, convicted of being 'a very active rebel' and handed back to the navy for execution. Moore, seeing the man hanged from the yardarm of a gunboat, commented with helpless despair, 'Dismal work! But what remedy?'

By 25 June it seemed as though the rebel forces had been crushed in the Wexford area, and the squadron weighed anchor to resume their patrol of the coast. From the town itself, boats delivered a gift of a cow and a pipe of cider to each of the frigates. On the *Melampus*, Moore ordered that this be given to the crew and warrant officers. Sailing south, Williams ordered the *Unicorn* to keep position off the Tuskar, while the rest of the squadron carried on westwards towards the Hook lighthouse. Off Waterford Harbour, everything seemed quiet so the squadron's captains (incredibly) decided to go on shore in search of refreshments. However, once landed they became nervous and were clearly unhappy about moving too far from the beach. Even so, they attempted to purchase some provisions but found, 'Everything was extravagantly dear, and the Country people endeavoured to impose upon us as much as they possibly could', and with suspicion beginning to break through his naïveté, Moore noted in his journal, 'I do not like their looks.'

There was still no firm news about the whereabouts of the French Toulon fleet. It was said that St Vincent also had gone up the Mediterranean looking for them, and a packet reported that he had met the French and captured thirty transports – but nothing was certain. While they waited, Moore had the opportunity of casting a professional and critical eye over Williams' frigate;

> The Endymion appears to me to sail faster than any ship we have ever been in company with, with the wind large, but in a chace to windward I think we beat her, if it does not overblow; for she could certainly outcarry any of us. Upon the whole I think her the finest frigate I have ever sailed with, and in excellent order.

On 1 July, Williams' impatience drove him to a decision. He divided the squadron up so that the individual frigates could patrol in different sectors of the coast for two days. Privately, Moore thought this imprudent because if the French did arrive, a single frigate would be useless against them. On the other hand, he was increasingly doubtful of the value of keeping such a powerful frigate squadron on its present station;

> I hope that we shall be removed from this station in consequence of the suppression of the Rebellion; it would be a great thing for the French if they could force us to employ so great a force as is now on the coast of Ireland merely to prevent their threatened invasion instead of hunting down their Cruisers and protecting our Foreign Trade.

One advantage of the station was that they seemed to get newspapers reasonably quickly. By 4 July, Moore was conscious that public attention in England had turned to focus on Admiral Nelson's search for the Toulon fleet, which was now known to be conveying an expedition under the command of Bonaparte. He sincerely hoped that Admiral St Vincent

> ... is gone himself on that important service. The extraordinary courage and activity of Nelson is well established, but I wish to see the judgement and clear headed conduct of the Admiral employed on so great an occasion.

152

Despite his misgivings he had no doubt that Nelson's squadron would deal with Bonaparte's expedition and that the French would be *'roughly handled'*. But he simply could not understand how it was that nobody knew of Bonaparte's destination;

> *I cannot for a moment believe the Egyptian story, and it appears to me that it cannot be destined for so long and dangerous a voyage as Ireland.*

Wherever the French were bound, the Admiralty seemed to be taking no chances, for Sir Charles Thompson's squadron at Cork had been withdrawn to reinforce Admiral Bridport's fleet off Brest. Moore was less pleased to read the parliamentary news, where opposition MPs were making speeches which could only give succour to the rebels. As this could only serve to undermine the general war effort, he could not understand how such criticisms of government policy were allowed. He was particularly incredulous and incensed about one opposition MP who had asked in the house, *'As we have no authentic documents laid before us, how do we know that the Irish are not making use of a justifiable resistance'*. To Moore's mind, this was as seditious as the rebellion itself.

Operating so close to the theatre of the rebellion was, however, beginning to generate problems on board the *Melampus* itself. From one of his officers Moore learned that one of the seamen, who had been sent in the frigate's launch to assist at Wexford, had been abused by other members of the crew on his return. Moore sent for the man and questioned him on the subject but

> *... he either did not know or would not tell me who had reproached him, but he said he had been railed at. Being under the necessity of punishing a seaman this day for drunkenness and disobedience of orders, I took the opportunity of speaking to the ship's company on the other business. I told them I could no other way account for the conversation that had been held on that occasion, although the authors were unknown to me, than by supposing that we had some villains in the ship who wished well to the cause of these Rebels and Murderers; that I had but an indifferent opinion of the man himself, that the words had been used to, for not coming openly and manfully to me and telling me of the circumstance, for I could not believe that he did not know their names[62]. That I had long known we had a set of villains in the ship, but at the same time I was convinced that the great body of the Ship's Company were good men and good subjects, and it particularly became the duty of every good English man or good Irish man, to bring forward any Rascal whom they should*

ever hear making use of any language of that nature, which was most disgraceful to the ship and injurious to our Country. That for my own part I was determined to bring any man to a most severe account that I ever knew in word or deed to favour the cause of the Rebels, whom we were employed against, and I expected the ship's company would do the same. – The man who occasioned all this is himself an Irish man, and I am convinced that the fellows who abuse him are some of the Irish whom we received 13 or 14 months ago at Portsmouth from the Puisant; *however, I was not anxious to bring it home to them, that they may have it in their power to try back and endeavour to wipe off the impressions I may have conceived against them. I am not at all afraid of them, they are few in number and not at all leading men.*

The issue was an additionally sensitive one, for there had been rumours that Irish dissidents among the crews of ships on the Cork station might make an attempt to seize their ships. Moore refused to believe the rumour, pointing out that the proportion of Irishmen on board the ships was too small to make the attempt. He did think that some of them might have taken the Oath of the United Irishmen before they joined their ships and, indeed, many might join a mutiny, but he did not think they were motivated enough to lead such an attempt and risk the gallows. He also strongly disputed any suggestion that other seamen might be encouraged in any way to join them:

The British Seaman will not be easily induced to join the cause of the Irish Rebels, which is avowedly that of the French. Besides, I hope and trust it is a lost cause.

Although this may sound naïve, one has to remember that, fresh in all naval officers' memories was the experience of the Spithead mutiny where the seamen had dutifully sworn to put to sea to attack the French if need arose. The officers of the squadron had heard just before this that the Americans had finally declared war on the French. Moore was glad for, as he had previously noted, they had suffered provocation for some time;

The French are very foolish in driving their friends the Yankees to the wall, they will not easily forgive the outrages that have been committed upon them, and the insolent and contemptuous treatment their Envoys received at Paris.[63]

The squadron lay at anchor until 6 July when a fresh wind blew up from the west-south-west, '. . . *and a considerable swell was tumbling in to the bay'.*[64] Williams ordered the squadron to weigh anchor, but the *Endymion* could not bring home their anchor before the tide turned and the frigate was forced to remain in position until the tide slackened. The *Unicorn* was ordered to remain in company to give her some support if an enemy vessel appeared on the scene before she could sail. The other frigates managed to put to sea, but as the weather became boisterous during the night, Moore was concerned that *Endymion* and *Unicorn* would be having a difficult time and would find it even harder to get to sea the next day.

The squadron reformed three days later, and on the evening of 9 July the *Unicorn* was sent to stand guard off the Tuskar. Despite the urgency of their situation, Moore's fixation with Miss M was beginning to haunt him with greater frequency. He sat and drafted a letter declaring his feelings for her, but having finished it, he knew he could not send it; yet at the same time, he could not bring himself to destroy it. Instead he took the unusual step of sending it to his mother. Although, in the journal, he attempted to reduce the significance of this by stating that she might find it amusing, and then either keep it safe or destroy it, there can be little doubt that he secretly hoped she would forward it to Miss M. Such a move would remove him from the immediate responsibility for what happened when Miss M received it;

> *To say the truth I feel very ridiculous with this love of mine; the only thing that can do away the ridicule is success, this is very precarious . . .*
> *I am dog sick of this cruise, would it were over, or would lead to some end. No society. With the high minded old Ossian, I talk very little with men. O how I feel the melancholy enthusiasm of the old blind Warrior . . . but how dreadful it must be to die of a broken heart which often occurs in his sublime tales!*

At this point several pages were cut from the journal, but where it resumes, we learn that Moore finally dispatched the letter to his mother with a request that she forward his declaration to Miss M if she thought fit. Moore's agonizing was becoming too embarrassing even for himself.

Over the next few days, Moore tried to distract himself with thoughts about his professional duties and the potential for the current cruise. He decided that he would very much like to cruise in company with the *Endymion* and Captain Thomas Williams, whom he described as '. . . *an intelligent clever fellow in his business, with a good deal of ambition, without which few men rise to any eminence'*. But inevitably his thoughts returned to Miss M and now he was doubly anxious that the letter, which had by this time been dispatched, would represent him very feebly. He began to wish that he hadn't sent it after all. More pages had to be cut from the journal;

> *What am I distrest about? Why, if she is indifferent about me she may show my letter to her father and the family; I shall be laughed at by them, and they will have some cause to be offended. The part of a rejected lover, whose vanity led him to think a pretty woman had some love for him, when the utmost she felt was a friendship founded on long acquaintance from her childhood. This is the mortifying side of the picture. It is humiliating.*

On the other hand, he also rationalized that if she did feel love for him, the letter might tip the balance in his favour. But then, there was a third possibility:

> *After all, my Mother will be so astonished that she will never venture to send the letter, nor will she ever have an opportunity of giving it to her, for her mother is always with her. I wish she had the letter at this moment in her own room, by herself, and let me know the worst.*

By the 16th, Williams had sent the *Melampus* to cruise further west and to call in to Cork for provisions and water. At Cork there were a number of ships in port and Moore had the opportunity of catching up with some old friends and acquaintances, spending an agreeable time with *'men that I like'*. He also learned that his brother, John, had been promoted to the rank of Major General;

> *This brother of mine is a rising man in the service; he possess[es] some of the best qualities of a soldier in an eminent degree, prudence, enter-prise, great activity, cool and determined courage, with great presence of mind and a clear and sound head. With all this he is one of the most amiable fellows living, although, from his infancy, rather reserved until he knows his men. He is very firm and decided, and has the gift of being beloved by his men at the same time that they are kept in very strict discipline . . . I love him, and he well deserves all our loves, he is a very noble fellow.*

Having completed her stores, the *Melampus* received new orders to head for Lough Swilly to join a squadron under the command of Captain Jonathan Faulknor in the frigate *Diana*. Faulknor was in search of several Dutch men-of-war which were reported to be

156

waiting off Shetland for the homeward-bound Dutch Greenland trade. One of the Dutch ships was thought to carry fifty guns, while the rest were frigates. However, there were some doubts about the veracity of these reports – as there were also claims that the ships were Russian.

Moore set sail on 22 July, resolving secretly to stretch out to the westwards on his way round the west coast of Ireland, as this would put him in the track in which he had captured the *Volage*. Even so, he was pessimistic about taking any prizes this time. He was also a little surprised to find himself sent to the opposite end of the country, but decided that this was a ploy by the Commander-in-Chief to keep the *Melampus* on the Irish station. By sending her so far away from Cork it would be difficult for Kingsmill to issue any recall orders from the Admiralty. Moore was not displeased with this, for even though he thought there was little chance of prizes, he believed that if he were going to '*do something*', it was more likely to be on the Irish station than anywhere else. He was certainly glad to be further offshore, for six men had deserted within the last three months;

> *... this is very distressing to me, as I do not believe any Officer treats the men under his command with more kindness than I have always done, and those men in particular have been more indulged than any others. I have come to a determination never to forgive any man who leaves a boat, and on no account to pardon Desertion, which has prevailed to a very great degree in the* Melampus *ever since I have commanded her.*

The recent desertions may have been due to another factor which he had previously mentioned; some of the crew may have been either United Irishmen, or at least in sympathy with them.

As they sailed past the north-west coast of Ireland, Moore was struck by the large number of well armed and well appointed letters-of-marque he encountered bound from Liverpool to the West Indies. He saw this as a consequence of the commercial health of that port, but in particular of the entrepreneurial spirit of its merchants. On the 28th, Moore turned the *Melampus* southwards towards Lough Swilly, conscious of the fact that neither he nor the ship's Master were acquainted with this part of the Irish coast. Had he known his destination before he left England, he would have purchased the appropriate charts, because '*The French Charts I have of these seas are very incorrect*'.

Two days later they entered Lough Swilly to find that Faulknor's squadron had sailed the previous day to search off Shetland, the Orkneys and the Faeroe Islands. As night was falling, Moore anchored, but was appalled when the ship was surrounded by boat-loads of common people who crowded on board to try and exchange their fowls and eggs for old clothes. These impoverished people were reluctant to accept money for their goods, and were indeed mostly half naked or covered in rags. In spite of the high level of disaffection which was said to exist in the vicinity, Moore was both shocked and moved by their plight;

> *I hope when Government have succeeded in completely disarming the Rebels, that some wise and healing measures will be adopted in this Kingdom; I am quite ignorant on the subject, but I have no doubt that much reform is required.*

Moore determined to sail after Faulknor the next morning, mortified with the thought that the squadron might fall in with the Dutch before he could join him. However, south of the Hebrides the wind dropped, and as they slowly drifted northwards, Moore could not help reflecting on the degradation of his native highlanders. In a romantic mood he concluded that the introduction of commerce had changed the character of the Scottish Highlander from

> *. . . hardy, high-minded, warlike shepherds and husbandmen*

to

> *. . . knavish merchants, Pedlars, and wicked, debauched manu-facturers . . . I never went through the narrow dirty streets In London where old iron is sold in one shop, candles and pickled salmon in the adjoining, old rags in a third, a retail butcher's shop with the liver and lights hanging up opposite, without having my spirits sunk. Poverty in a large city is a thousand times more disgusting than in the country, and I think the poor of a city, independent of the effect of being bred in a crowd, more likely to be mean and vicious than the country labourers, who live sub jove in the expanse, and familiarized with the grandeur and beauty of Nature. This idea I have entertained for many years.*

Off St Kilda the wind dropped again for twelve hours, and as they passed the Orkneys on the following day, Moore gazed dreamily at the passing mountains and thought of his beloved Ossian;

> *I cannot believe the Poems ascribed to Ossian are of modern com-position, and I am sorry that Macpherson, instead of challenging*

Johnson to meet him in the field, did not furnish the world with better proofs of his being only the compiler and translator of these noble compositions.[65]

He was prepared to concede however, that if Macpherson's work was fraudulent,

I do think it the most masterly trick that I have ever heard of in that way. But I believe Mr Macpherson to have acted perfectly fair in this business, and I certainly owe him much for the pleasure his researches have procured me . . .

Moore's continued faith in the authenticity of the works of Ossian was in fact bolstered because he had learned that Napoleon had claimed Ossian as his favourite author. This, in turn, simply confirmed Moore's belief that Napoleon was *'the hero of the age'*. Another heroic figure also occupied his thoughts at this time: Admiral Nelson, whose fleet was now thought to be far up the Mediterranean where there were no friendly ports to provide aid in case of trouble;

. . . They are liable to many accidents, especially when led by so daring a character as Nelson. No great action was ever achieved without great risk, but I wish he were possessed of more prudence than he has the reputation of. His second, Trowbridge, I believe to be one of our first sea Officers; I am glad he is so well backed.[66]

After cruising for several days without seeing any sign of Faulknor's squadron, Moore decided to turn back towards Lough Swilly. The following day, between Faeroe and Shetland, Faulknor's ships appeared. Moore reported on board the *Diana* and Faulknor informed him the Dutch squadron had really been Swedish. There were new orders for Moore. He was to sail under the command of Lord Ranelagh[67], commander of the 18-pounder frigate *Doris*. Moore was pleased to have Ranelagh as his senior officer because he

. . . may not be so religious in keeping within the limits of his station as I have always been. I know he is a brave fellow, and not over rich – Good qualifications for a Cruiser.

The two frigates headed south through fog and drizzle; weather which Moore thought *'the most dreary and uncomfortable at sea'*. Competing on different courses, Moore was glad to find that his *Melampus* beat the *Doris* close-hauled[68], but fell behind when sailing with the wind free[69]. After some consideration he thought the

Melampus was down by the stern, so set the crew to shifting stores forward in the hold, and after that she sailed as well as the *Doris*.

On 15 August they entered Lough Swilly to find orders to proceed to Belfast. It was also reported that two French frigates were on their way to land arms on the coast. Meanwhile, in the Lough, the *Melampus* was again surrounded by local people wishing to exchange produce for clothes. Moore had to forbid their coming on board and it becomes apparent that there were two reasons for this, both of which related to the welfare of the crew:

> *Most of our people would by degrees have parted with all their clothes for a few fowls, potatoes and the itch, which few of the Irish peasantry, that we have seen, are clear of.*

The two frigates entered Belfast Lough on 25 August, with a hard gale in their teeth. There they learned that three French frigates had landed between 700 and 1,000 troops at Killala in County Mayo on 22 August, together with a great quantity of arms and ammunition.[70] Faulknor, with the rest of his squadron, had already departed to make his way there. Moore cursed his ill luck, for Killala was on the north-west coast, some 100 miles south-west of Lough Swilly. If he and Ranelagh had heard the news while they were at Swilly, they would have fallen on the French frigates by now. While he was preparing to sail, a new report arrived that gave him greater cause for hope. A much larger force was said to be ready to sail from Brest under the command of Commodore Bompart, consisting of a 74-gun ship and eight frigates.[71] The eagerness of the two frigate commanders to get back to sea was now hampered by a north-easterly which pinned them in Belfast. While they chafed, waiting for the wind to change, Moore received letters from home. To his sudden relief, he read that his mother had decided not to forward his letter to Miss M. With something of a weight lifted from his shoulders, he opened a letter from his brother John who was now in Dublin, having just completed a campaign to disperse the rebels in the Wicklow Hills; *'This he tells me he effected as much by kindness as by force.'*

On the 28th, the two frigates sailed from Belfast in the evening, heading north-west between Fair Head and the Mull of Kintyre. There, Moore spoke to the Master of a Liverpool ship who said that he had encountered twelve ships sailing west-south-west, five leagues from Barra Head, and that two of them chased him. He was convinced they were not English, even though it was common for English frigates to chase their own merchantmen on suspicion. Moore went on board the *Doris* to discuss this information with Ranelagh and both became convinced that these were Bompart's ships and that, as a consequence, the situation was very serious. Reaching Lough Swilly on the 31st, the two frigates called in to obtain the latest intelligence. The people of Mayo had risen in support of the French force landed on 22 August and there were now 4,000 under arms, they having inflicted a heavy defeat on Major General Hutchinson's force at Castlebar[72]. A heavy cannonading had also been heard off the coast, which was thought to have been Faulknor's squadron engaging the first French squadron[73]. At this critical moment, Moore had to act promptly to deal with one of his officers:

> *I am badly off for officers, and to mend the matter one of the principal of them has behaved in a late instance with such brutality that he is now under an arrest and I believe must be brought to a Court Martial; if so, I shall be deprived of any assistance that he might be of for some time.*

A few days later, he noted in his journal,

> *I have settled the dispute with my Officer to my satisfaction, there is to be no Court Martial, but I am to get rid of him quietly.*[74]

The *Melampus* and the *Doris* began to patrol between Lough Swilly and Tory Island, where they were joined by a Revenue ship under the command of a naval lieutenant. There was no sign of Faulknor and his squadron, and Moore had concluded that the cannonading could not be attributed to him. Despite a very hard gale the two frigates maintained this station for several days, while Moore filled his spare moments reading Sir George Staunton's account of Lord McCartney's Embassy to China[75]. Moore did not enjoy the book though, as he didn't like Staunton's prose, and thought the narrative *'forced and pedantic'*. On 5 September, Moore managed to get his hands on some London newspapers in which it was strongly rumoured that Admiral Nelson had defeated the French fleet in the Mediterranean, but there was no confirmation of this. On the 11th, the *Melampus* and the *Doris* put back into Lough Swilly where Ranelagh and Moore dined with General Cavan, who gave them an account of how General Lake had completely defeated the Franco-Rebel force at Ballinamuck on 8 September.[76]

The *Melampus* being short of provisions, the Purser and one of the officers were dispatched to Londonderry to purchase more. This brief stay in the Lough was not without incident:

One of our best seamen died suddenly in his hammock the day we went into Lough Swilly, and another whom I had given leave to assist at his funeral, deserted.

On the evening of the 17th, Moore arranged a dinner on board the *Melampus* for Ranelagh and some army officers. They were sitting in the middle of this repast when an excited messenger arrived with intelligence that two days earlier a brig had moored south-west of the Lough to land arms on the coast. Ranelagh immediately leapt from the table and returned to his ship, ordering Moore to lose no time in putting to sea. Moore sailed with the naval cutter *Cygnet*, in company, but he had to leave behind his two officers together with the provisions which they had been sent to purchase. Once outside the shelter of the Lough, the three ships began to encounter a heavy sea and strong winds. Continuing along the coast of Donegal they learned that the brig they were searching for was the *Anacreon*, carrying the rebel leader Napper Tandy, who had landed with arms and a small body of men, to support the rising. Tandy had departed again on the 17th, having learned both of Humbert's surrender and the lack of local popular support for the rising. Moore was not surprised about the latter. Even the rebels in Wexford, he believed, were not inspired by

. . . the Hum Bugs of the Rights of Man etc, but they all could feel the hardship of paying tithes to the Clergy of a Religion they hated, and they were stupid enough to be easily persuaded that the Orange men intended to extirpate them.

Ranelagh decided they should continue cruising off Tory Island, partly in the hope of falling in with the *Anacreon* – though in all seriousness they had little faith in this – but also because the frigates cruising to the west had been lucky taking prizes. The *Melampus* had not been on a really good cruising ground for the best part of eight months, and Moore knew that time was running out, for the *Melampus* was short of provisions and in need of a refit. As the two frigates searched to the westward in the vain hope of taking a prize, Moore turned once again to self-deprecation:

This month I am 34. No Chicken – but certainly a man who has not made the most of his talent. Except in the faculties and affections given him by Nature and Education, but an ordinary fellow. Shall I ever rouse myself to exertion. I say (the head being the dupe of the heart) yes, when I have finished this romance which now occupies me . . .

The frigates returned to Lough Swilly on 25 September, but they were beset by heavy gales and unable to send boats ashore to collect their provisions.

Nevertheless, they were able to collect the latest intelligence regarding the French squadron, and it was now confirmed that Bompart's squadron of nine ships had left Brest and were somewhere at sea, bound for Ireland. On the 28th the gale worsened and even though the two frigates were in the comparative shelter of the Lough, they were obliged to strike their upper masts and yards. Moore could not help wondering how Bompart was faring in this storm;

The French ships crammed with troops must be in a shocking pickle. I fear they have put back, for if at sea this gale will do their business . . .

Even so, within a couple of days Ranelagh received orders to sail immediately to reinforce Faulknor in the frigate *Doris*, at Killala Bay. Faulknor had been ordered to intercept Bompart and he seems to have positioned himself at Killala because this was the place that Humbert had landed. However, both *Melampus* and *Doris* were still pinned in Lough Swilly by the winds, and neither frigate had yet been able to complete her provisions because of the gales.

At last, on 3 October, the wind changed and the two ships weighed anchor at around noon. Just as they were standing towards the mouth of the Lough, the battery there started to signal to them. Unable to distinguish the signals, but believing it might be something important, the frigates hove to while the pilot cutter went ashore. Four impatient hours passed until the cutter returned with what indeed seemed to be important news. The French squadron had been sighted on the 22nd and was now being shadowed by three English frigates. Ten ships had been sighted off Telling Head the previous day. Telling Head lay en route to Killala Bay, but Ranelagh seemed to be hesitant about the course of action he should take. To Moore's exasperated mind, it seemed obvious; head west to Telling Head and then south-west to Killala. Finally, Ranelagh ordered their departure, and the two frigates crept westwards during the night. At daylight, Moore's impatience overcame him and he pressed ahead in the hope of seeing something;

I hope this lingering and loitering may have no worse consequences than the mortal disgust and fretting it has occasioned in me, but if it should prove the cause of our missing an opportunity of being employed against the Enemy, I shall curse the cause of it with all my soul.

On 5 October the two frigates stood in to Killala Bay, but there was no sign of either the French or Faulknor. The two captains were already aware that, several weeks before, a dispatch from Humbert had been intercepted recommending Black Sod Bay as a good landing place and Moore believed that this was where they should now find Faulknor, so they set off towards the west once more. The following day, the two frigates were off Broad Haven in fine weather. The wind had come round to the south, and Moore firmly believed this would bring the French very shortly. Here they received another intelligence dispatch, which confirmed that the French were being shadowed by the frigates *Ethalion*, *Amelia* and *Anson*. Indeed, it was Captain George Countess in the *Ethalion* who had first intercepted the French, and he had clung doggedly to their heels ever since.

Ranelagh proposed that they should patrol on a line west by north of Broad Haven for, if the French came this far north, they would have to pass through this zone. Moore agreed, though he seems not to have been entirely happy with the plan, as it was hardly consistent with their orders to reinforce Faulknor. By the time they had reached a point some fifty miles from the coast, the weather had turned thick with misty rain. Visibility fell sharply, so they turned back towards Broad Haven but on the following evening, 9 October, the two frigates became enshrouded in thick fog, and Moore lost all contact with Ranelagh. The wind was still from the south, and just before daybreak the *Melampus*' lookouts sighted a frigate to the south. Moore decided that this must be Faulknor in the *Doris* so he bore up to close with her. As the day brightened, and the weather cleared, they suddenly saw that they were heading for a line comprising a battle-ship accompanied by three other large ships. They were already within shot of the battleship and Moore immediately wore away from them, and spread all sail as quickly as he could. The ships began signalling in response, and to Moore's relief, he found that he had run not into the French but into Sir John Borlase Warren's squadron, consisting of the 74-gun ships *Canada* and *Robust*, the 84-gun *Foudroyant*, and the heavy frigate *Magnanime*. When Ranelagh arrived in the *Doris*, Warren immediately took them both under his command, giving them orders to patrol on a line from the squadron. Before they could depart, the *Amelia* hove into view bringing news that six days earlier she had left the *Ethalion* and *Anson* still shadowing the French squadron. Moore decided to delay his departure from Warren's squadron until the next day, hoping that the French would put in an appearance before he had sailed too far away to get into any engagement.

Two days later, although the *Melampus* was off Eagle Island, Warren's squadron was still in sight. During the course of the morning the wind became so violent that, rather conveniently, Moore was obliged to return to the squadron. Then, at around noon, the frigates *Ethalion* and *Anson* appeared in the south, and not far behind them, the top masts of Bompart's squadron appeared over the horizon. On board the *Canada*, signals were hoisted ordering a general chase, and the ships of the English squadron immediately began making more sail after Bompart, whose squadron, it could be seen, had now turned to the south-west. Through the afternoon and night the English ships pressed on with all possible sail, regardless of frequent heavy squalls of rain and hail. This was not without consequences, for the *Anson* carried away her mizzenmast and was forced to bear up to clear the wreckage, and several other ships split sails. Moore was ordered to take the *Melampus* to leeward of both the *Canada* and *Foudroyant*, to discourage the French from attempting to drop to leeward of the squadron. On the morning of the 12 October, with the wind at west-north-west but now much lighter, the French squadron was still visible close to windward, with *Canada*, *Foudroyant* and *Melampus* to leeward (i.e. to the south-east) of them. Warren closed and wore the *Canada* round the sternmost of the ships and crossed to windward of them, while the *Robust* and the frigate *Magnanime*, commanded by Captain Michael de Courcy, brought the rearmost ships to action;

Finding myself alone with the French between me and the Canada, *I bore down to join the* Foudroyant *to leeward. I expected at that time that Sir Thomas Bayard, the Captain of that ship, would have stood on towards the French van to have stopt them, but he tacked, as I suppose for the purpose of joining the* Robust *and* Magnanime, *who had just begun to fire upon the French Rear; Sir John Warren had made the signal for the ships to engage and to form as best they could for mutual support. I tacked along with the* Foudroyant, *but seeing that this manoeuvre would throw us out I wore immediately and made all sail towards the Body of the Enemy's squadron. The* Foudroyant *doing the same. At this time the French Commodore's ship* Le Hoche *which had lost her main top mast in the chase the day before, was engaged with the* Magnanime *and* Robust, *being supported by some of his heavy*

165

frigates. The rest of the French ships drew out in good order, apparently with the design of receiving the Foudroyant *and* Melampus. *The light winds and the swell retarded us a good deal, and we were a good deal exposed to the Enemy's fire before I would open, being afraid of firing into the* Robust *and* Magnanime. *When we got a clear place between these two, we began a very well directed fire on* Le Hoche *and then passing the* Robust *we continued to fire at her antagonist until she struck, the* Robust *being at that time on her beam and cutting her up. As soon as* Le Hoche *struck we pressed on after the rest, we being the leading ship, the* Foudroyant *on our lee bow about six points; the next ship* La Coquille *struck on receiving a few distant shot from the* Foudroyant *and on seeing us all ready to give her a close fire, being well up on her quarter. I determined to engage the frigates successively as we came up with them and to leave them to be taken possession of by the ships astern viz the* Robust *and* Magnanime *which had both suffered considerably in their Rigging. At this time the* Canada *was the nearest ship to us astern, a French frigate* L'Embuscade *which had suffered nothing apparently was on our bow firing her stern chase guns at us. We shot up alongside, but not so near as I wished, and opened such a fire upon her, at about a cable's length distance, as brought down her colours in about ten minutes, we passed on. The next was* La Bellone; *the wind was so light that we gained very little upon her, she hauled close to the wind to separate from the remaining five frigates and to endeavour to get off to windward, I hauled up after her, being the weather most and nearest to her. The* Ethalion, *which prior to this had only fired distant shot, being favoured by the breeze, passed to windward of us in chase of* La Bellone, *upon which I determined not to lose any more time after her as the* Ethalion *was sure of closing with her first, and was quite enough for her, I therefore bore up for the remainder of the Enemy, firing two or three distant broadsides at the* Bellone *as we passed on. The* Ethalion *soon after shot up abreast* La Bellone *and, after a spirited resistance, took her. The remaining five frigates were now making off, with all possible sail set. The* Canada, Foudroyant, Amelia *and us in pursuit, the* Amelia *was sent by Sir John to assist the* Robust *and* Magnanime *in securing the prizes. We were the weathermost ship and kept to the northward for the purpose of hemming them in with the land. At this time we saw the* Anson *directly to leeward and in the track of the flying enemy, without her mizenmast; she stood for the headmost of the five ships in the handsomest manner and endeavoured to close with her, but the enemy's ship, which we have since found was* La Loire *not being at all disabled, by carrying a great press of sail passed the* Anson, *the two ships engaging as they passed but apparently at too great a distance. The* Anson *then stood for the van of the four other French ships and engaged them in the handsomest manner, keeping up a tremendous fire. The sternmost of the four hauled up athwart the stern of the* Anson *and passed her to windward, firing at her as she passed; the three others were engaged with the* Anson *until some time after dark, but from the disabled state of that ship she could not close with any one of them and they at length all passed her. A little before dark the* Canada *made our signal to observe the enemy's motions during the night. Soon after the four French ships had passed the* Anson, *the* Canada *and* Foudroyant *likewise passed her in chase, we were on their weather bow, the wind being at this time NW and the four French ships nearly abreast of Tillen Head. My design was to pass on to the headmost one, leaving the others to the* Canada *and* Foudroyant; *as it was impossible for them to weather the land of Broadhaven or even to fetch Killala, as the wind then was. I had no fear of more than the headmost of all escaping. At 11 at night the weather became more hazy and the wind took us aback from the Southward, this brought the enemy's ships on our weather quarter, we being on the larboard T[ack]. I lost sight of them, but as I was perfectly sure where they were, I made the signal for their being in sight and kept a light at the mizzen top mast head all night to lead the* Canada *and* Foudroyant. *My design was to carry a press of sail all night so as to be able to weather the enemy on the other tack, if they stood off, and if they stood on the other tack they must either run on shore or be taken. At daylight we tacked but the wind still balked us, backing to the southward so as to enable both the* Canada *and* Foudroyant *to weather us: two only of the enemy's ships appearing in sight a long way to windward I was convinced that three or at least two of them must be in shore of us either in Sligo or Donegal Bay. I made the signal for the two ships, and the* Foudroyant's *signal was made to chase and our signal to pass within hail. Sir John Warren informed me that the* Anson *had chased a ship at three o'clock in the morning and he thought it probable she might be gone into Killybegs; I told him that we had not lost sight of the ships until just before the shift of wind, that I had no doubt of the two ships to windward being the headmost of the enemy, and of there being at least two, but I believed three in shore of us. Sir John said 'I believe there may be one in Killybegs, you will go in and see; if there is but one you will take her, if there are two or three you will make the signal to me and I will come to your assistance.' I answered that I was very happy to have the*

167

prospect of meeting the enemy and that I had no doubt of there being more than one. That I would not lose an instant.

The wind by this time was blowing fresh, directly off shore, we stood in and passed the Anson, *a good way to windward of her; she seemed to have suffered very much less than I should have suspected, considering the heavy fire she had had on her the evening before. The* Foudroyant *and* Canada *continued on the opposite tack, as I believed in chase of the two ships to windward, one of which had no mizzen top sail set, and we soon lost sight of them and the* Anson. *At sun set we were in sight of the entrance of Killybegs, but not near enough to see what was there. I declared my intention, if there was one frigate to go and anchor alongside of her, and if there were two or three to block them up until Sir John Warren should rejoin us, and to fight them at all events if they came out. We continued during the night to stand across and across the Bay keeping a very sharp lookout. At midnight we saw a large ship coming down upon us, as soon as she drew near she hauled up on the opposite tack, and we saw another at a little distance to windward of her. Being convinced that they were two of the Enemy's frigates endeavouring to get off the coast in the night, I thought it became me instantly to attack the nearest and endeavour to secure at least one of them. We tacked and gave chase, the wind blowing as much as we could show close reefed topsails and courses to. We shot up alongside of the nearest one, going at least ten knots, hailed and received no intelligible answer, but seeing her to be a large frigate and that she wanted to cross our stern and get to leeward of us, I fired one shot into her and repeatedly ordered her to bring to. No answer – a broadside – hailed again, ordered her in French to bring to – no answer. Saw the other ship make a signal – fired two more broadsides into her without receiving a shot in return. We heard them cry out and they hoisted a light and hauled it down again. I supposed at the time that that was meant as token of having surrendered, but as she did not heave to and the two ships at no time were going less than five knots, I told them in French and English that I would sink them if they did not put their helm a starboard and heave to. This, however, although she never fired at us, she did not do until she had received five or six broadsides and been cut to pieces in her sails and rigging, when she threw up in the wind, and we sent the second lieutenant and 20 men on board of her, at a very considerable risk, as the wind had increased to a hard gale at SE. We saw no more of the other ship, but lay to in a very great anxiety close to the Prize until daylight, when we ran down under her stern and found her to be a 36 gun frigate, and that her sails were cut into ribbands. I had ordered the Lieutenant, if possible, to send the French Officers on board, but the Gale had increased so much that one of the boats was stove along-side and the wreck of the mizzen mast on the morning of the 14th October carried away the tow rope of the other boat (my eight oared cutter) and broke her adrift. It was two days before we could get the Officers out of her and increase the number of our men on board of her to 50. We found her to be* La Resolue *of 36 long guns, 12 pounders on the Main deck, and four 36 pounder Carronades making 40 in all, with 500 men, of whom 265 were the Quadre of the Regiment de Lee, that is to say L'Etat major and the rest Grenadiers. The Regiment to be filled up with Rebels. The other ship which left us so civilly was* L'Immortalite *of 40 guns, 24 pounders on the Main deck. I think it was the third day after we took her that we towed her abreast of Lough Swilly where we saw two ships beating in, which I have no doubt were the* Canada *and* Foudroyant. *We made the private signal and our own particular signal to show what ship we were, they did not bear up for us but continued to beat into the Lough.*

In the action, although we had our share of it we had not a single man killed or wounded by the enemy's shot. One man lost his arm in ramming home one of the carronades that hung fire, and was otherwise dreadfully burnt by the explosion he is however likely to do well. Our men behaved most admirably throughout the whole affair, and it is my opinion that not one of the French frigates could have lain alongside of the Melampus *half an hour.*[77]

Moore, with the *Resolue* in tow, headed for Lough Swilly, but the weather became too bad and, casting off the tow rope the two ships headed across to Greenock instead. The arrival of the two frigates there on 19 October brought the first intimation of Warren's victory over the French squadron and, arriving just days after news of Nelson's victory at the Nile, prompted exultant celebrations in the town. Moore was welcomed in a *'highly flattering'* manner and at night the town was illuminated with transparencies displayed at the windows with Warren's name alongside those of Howe, Jervis, Duncan and Nelson. A few days later, Moore travelled to Glasgow, to revisit the scenes of his boyhood, and whilst he was there the town awarded him the Freedom of the City.

The *Amelia* arrived several days later carrying 450 French prisoners of war and news about the rest of the squadron. The *Immortalite* had been captured by Captain Byam Martin in the frigate *Fisgard* on 20 October; the frigate *Mermaid*, commanded by Captain James

Newman, had attacked the much heavier frigate *Loire* on 17 October and had fought stubbornly until the gale intervened preventing a conclusion to the action. The *Loire* was taken on the following day by Captain Philip Durham in the *Anson*.

At Greenock, Moore was able to land his own prisoners of war, but he also lost thirteen seamen who took this opportunity to desert;

> *I was exceedingly chagrined at the desertion, indeed I cannot account for the desertion that has prevailed in this ship where they certainly are treated with very great lenity and indulgence.*

Certainly, desertion at this point seems a little odd, for the crew of the *Melampus* stood to profit a good deal from their prize. On the other hand, it is possible that there were those on board the frigate who, having gone through the experience of one engagement, really could not cope with the thought of more. Moore simply pressed eleven men at Greenock to make up for the loss, and then proceeded with the *Resolue* to Plymouth, where he had been ordered to refit. Arriving in Plymouth Sound on 12 November, he waited anxiously while the dockyard surveyors inspected the *Melampus*. Hearing that she could be made good in three weeks, he immediately applied for leave to travel to London, for there was business there which he could delay no longer.

11

Love's Labours
(November 1798 – November 1799)

Moore's main intention now was to see the woman he described as *'my goddess'*, Miss M. Her family received him with the greatest kindness and hospitality – not surprising since he had just been 'gazetted' following his capture of *La Resolue*. Nevertheless, whenever he was in the presence of the lady herself, he could not be certain about her affection;

> *I could not find a favourable opportunity of convincing myself on the subject most interesting to me, but I was treated by the Damsel with the apparent cordiality of a sister.*

Confused, he decided that the only recourse was to write an open declaration of his love for her. He then retreated to his parents' house, while he waited with considerable anxiety for the response.

The answer came on 15 December, but it was not exactly the answer he had been hoping for. Miss M wrote expressing both '. . . *the highest esteem, the warmest friendship'* but could not give any indication that she loved him. She continued, explaining that she was persuaded that *'Peace and a connexion with a Person of my* [i.e. Moore's] *profession is incompatible.'* This last was explained further when she added that the fact that neither of them possessed wealth could only render them both miserable. Although this may seem a little harsh to us today, it has to be remembered that a naval officer in peacetime was often a very poor animal indeed. Many officers simply refused to serve because unless they had the chance of commanding a ship of the line with a regular income, the inability to make prize money meant that their profession could cost more than it paid.[78] On shore, the officer and his wife would be expected to maintain a certain standard of living, without which they might

171

find themselves ostracized within a socially over-conscious society. Moore's only hope was to make more prize money. He was dismayed at Miss M's response, but at the same time he found her response to his letter admirably sensible. Paradoxically, her letter '. . . *increased my esteem for her, and cut me to the soul*' and he found himself worshipping her more as a result of it. The problem, he concluded, was not that she did not love him, but that they had no money.

With that form of insanity that naturally afflicts those so obsessed, Moore responded to this rejection by spending yet more time with the Ms who, perhaps unconsciously, continued to entertain him in their '*highly prosperous state*'. He applied for, and was granted, two more weeks leave by the Admiralty, and then he received more news which he could have done without. The *Coquille*, one of the prizes taken on the *Melampus*' last cruise, had been

> . . . *burnt to ashes in the harbour of Hamoaze; this accident was occasioned by the carelessness and bad conduct of those who had her in charge, which I believe were part of the crews of the* Amelia *and* Magnanime. *I look upon her destruction as £300 . . . out of my pocket. I am low in spirit.*

Just as Moore had been hoping to make enough money to win Miss M, he had lost the equivalent of nearly £10,000 (at modern-day prices) – it was hardly surprising that he was depressed.

Seeking diversion, Moore visited his acquaintance Fuseli , but now found the painter's company of little relief and a day or two after Boxing Day, 1798, Moore returned to Plymouth in a gloomy state of mind. Although the *Melampus* was ready for sea by 10 January, no orders arrived. Moore's financial prospects seemed to be getting worse. He had submitted a request that the *Melampus* should alone receive the prize money for *La Resolue*, but this had been declined. The money was to be shared with the entire squadron. He had also lodged a claim to share with the *Anson*, the prize money for *La Loire*, but he didn't seriously think that this would be granted, though he did believe that they had a right to it.

> *I think I shall not touch above £2000* [79] *for the Irish cruise, we did expect three or four thousand, and, certainly, if the business had been well managed we might have secured more ships. Two capital blunders were made on the day of the action, the first, in not engaging in the morning to leeward with the* Canada, Foudroyant *and* Melampus,

leaving the rest of the squadron to get into the action according to circumstances, the next blunder was after the Canada *had got ahead and to windward of the French van that she did not bring them to close action, instead of taking a long sweep to get at* La Hoche *in the rear which was already fully occupied by the* Robust *and* Magnanime *and could not escape. It has been an excellent letter* [i.e. lesson] *to me which I could not have got either by book or precept.*

As if things could not get worse, he received a letter informing him that two of the *Melampus'* prizes, *La Bellone* and *La Resolue* had been surveyed by the Officers of the Dockyard at Plymouth and had been undervalued because of their poor condition; '*Both together have been valued under the sum which the* Volage *alone produced.*' The value placed on the ships had, he knew, been influenced by their age and condition; but there was a more suspect influence, whereby the value was reduced

. . . very considerably by a schism that has taken place among the officers of the yard who are at present jealous and afraid of each other. At one time, ships, that were captured and purchased by the Government, were valued here even too highly, but now, owing to this jealousy, they do not even do us bare justice.

Eventually, Moore could wait no longer for a resolution to his obsession. Ignoring his mother's entreaties to wait, he wrote directly to Miss M for a final decision on his marriage proposal. The letter was agony to write, but he had to bring his mental turmoil to an end, because it was again distracting him from his duties;

God knows how it will end, but I am sick of suspense which torments and unhinges me . . . I am good for nothing in this state of mind.

Miss M's reply brought no end to Moore's heartache, for she simply reiterated her previous letter. Moore decided that his only recourse now was to make a direct approach to the young woman's father. He wrote a detailed letter, outlining his financial prospects in the hope that this would appeal to the paternal interest and received what appeared to be an inconclusive but not discouraging response.

Meanwhile his professional responsibilities imposed themselves on his attention. The *Melampus* had been waiting for stores and new sails, and these were all stowed on board by 8 February. Moore decided to take the frigate out into Cawsand Bay while waiting for orders, probably because this would move the crew a little further from temptation. However, this time he was not sorry to have been in port for so long, for there had been severe weather in the Channel. This continued, and on the 11th

> . . . *we had one of the most violent storms that I have ever seen in this country, we drove on board of the* Cambrian *in the afternoon, but fortunately neither of the ships sustained any damage of consequence.* Days later he recorded: *The ship is now ready for sea. We received six months pay this day and are at this moment in a complete state of drunkenness. The* Phoenix *came in this morning with a very fine privateer of 20 guns, which she has taken. I wish we were out* . . .

A week later, he was still waiting as the frigates *Cambrian* and *Fisgard* sailed on a cruise. Grumbling inwardly, Moore tried to distract himself with reading books and papers. News spread quickly through the port of a very extensive promotion of Post Captains to flag rank, including Sir John Borlase Warren. Moore had a naturally professional interest, for

> . . . *by this measure a considerable number of good officers are put on the shelf by getting their flags, for certainly not one half of them can be employed. However I am glad to see that very few are passed over, indeed I do not think any man that goes through the service fairly and honourably ever should be passed over.*

At last, on the 22nd, the *Melampus* received orders to return to Cork, and the Irish Station. Moore set sail on the 25th, passing the battered *Cambrian* and *Fisgard*, who had been forced to return from their cruise prematurely because of bad weather. Moore headed in a wide sweep to the south towards Ushant in the hope of meeting something worth taking. The following morning, in mid-Channel, a stranger hove into sight and he immediately gave chase. The two ships were in sight of Ushant when

> . . . *we were very sorry to see two English frigates standing out from the land which proved to be the* Nymphe *and the* Melpomene, *they had the pleasure of seeing us fire a few rounds at the Enemy's ship and force her to strike*[80]. *She proved to be* Le Mercure *of St Malo pierced for 20 guns mounting 16 and 103 men; she had been out near a month and had taken 3 or 4 prizes, one of them, the schooner, was in sight when we gave chase to the ship. She struck at 5 o'clock in the afternoon we had prisoners exchanged in about two hours, and having spoken to the* Melpomene *and* Nymphe *we are now steering over for Cape Clear with*

the Prize . . ., a . . . very pretty little ship and certainly sails well, but she is not coppered.

Moore put one of his lieutenants and thirty men on board her and the two ships headed northwards for Cork. Unable to weather the Scillies, they proceeded cautiously in thick fog. Moore found himself happier with the *Melampus'* sailing qualities than he had been before. Whilst at Plymouth he had persuaded the Navy Board to let him change twenty-four of his main deck guns for a lighter type of 18-pounder,

> *. . . which has made a difference of near five tons on our deck, and the new light guns appear to me to carry the shot as far as the old heavy ones.*

On 1 March, the *Melampus* arrived at Cork to find three frigates and a West Indies convoy waiting there. Moore hoped to be ordered to accompany the convoy for some distance, because it would cross good cruising ground. Besides which, he had a number of new hands on board and the crew were generally in need of shaking down;

> *. . . the ship is by no means in good kilter yet. The remains of the drunkenness and debauchery of Plymouth still continues its baleful effects.*

At dinner one night in Cork, Moore found himself in the company of an older officer who was now employed by the Transport Board. The man urged him to continue in active service at sea as long as he could, while he was still young, because in that way

> *. . . we are continually adding to our professional skill by experience, whereas by remaining on shore, by degrees we lost much of what we had already acquired and besides gradually became more and more unwilling to return to the business. This is all very true, but I do not intend, when our Country's service does not call upon us, to spend the remainder of my best days at sea, where I die by inches with ennui and want of society. I cannot think of sacrificing the comfort and happiness of my life to the idea of keeping up my nautical skill. As long as we are called for – here I am – but in Peace, when it requires considerable interest to get a ship and when so many young men are eager to be employed, I shall stay at home and cultivate cabbages. I go to sea now merely from a sense of duty and with the hope of adding to my wealth and reputation. My heart is in England.*

It was obvious why Moore's heart lay elsewhere, but the group around the table also had more sombre matters to discuss, as he noted afterwards in the journal:

> There is a most melancholy account of the loss of the Proserpine *frigate in the ice in the mouth of the Elbe, which, I hope in God, will prove to be false. Mr Grenville[81] was embarked on board of her, it is supposed on a mission to the Emperor. Every soul on board is supposed to have perished. There are but too strong reasons to fear that this dismal tale is well founded.*[82]

Moore's wishes regarding the convoy were soon granted. He noted rather cynically that this was probably because Admiral Kingsmill was hungry for more money, and therefore wanted his cruisers out taking prizes[83]. His orders were to escort the convoy to Madeira, from whence it would continue under the escort of the 22-gun *Volage* (which Moore had taken as a prize the previous January), and then cruise for a fortnight. For most of the voyage the *Melampus* would be accompanied by the frigates *Glenmore* and *Galatea*. As the convoy of some seventy ships left Cork on 7 March, Moore was in a buoyant mood. The *Volage* led the way with the other two frigates on the wings, and the *Melampus* in the rear. Moore noted happily in his journal: '*I like this job very well, we have a very good chance of meeting something either going or coming.*' The crew too seemed in good morale; '*We are all in high spirits this cruise, we have strong hopes of success . . .*' and capturing a Spanish West Indiaman '*. . . would nearly do my business*'. Indeed the beneficial effects of the return to sea-routine was evident everywhere on board;

> We begin to get into rather better order now that we have got to sea again. We are best at sea in every respect; the idleness, dirt and debauchery of the harbour ruins both officers and seamen. Things now begin to find their places again.

When the *Glenmore* and *Galatea* parted company, Moore became the senior officer and he found himself increasingly dissatisfied with the behaviour of the *Volage*. Her commander, Captain the Hon. Philip Wodehouse[84], had a tendency to run too fast at the head of the convoy, instead of setting a pace to suit the slowest merchantmen. As a result the convoy was becoming strung out, and thus would be vulnerable to attack, especially from fast privateers who could slip in and cut one of the ships out with speed. However, even though he was the senior officer, Moore didn't want to undermine Wodehouse's authority:

I do not like to interfere with the management of them [i.e. the convoy] *as he is to take them out and we are merely to escort them a certain distance.*

It was always difficult for the escort to keep back. Moore even tried an experiment with the *Melampus*, having every sail on the frigate furled, all the yards braced round, and the topgallant masts struck – and she still trod on the tail of the slowest vessel. While he was doing this, the *Volage* was some seven or eight miles ahead of him. It was no wonder that the Admiralty received so many complaints about the escorts that were provided for convoys.

Meanwhile, Moore dreamed about his hopes for the future and how he would achieve it:

My favourite visionary plan at present depends upon our taking a French frigate, which I intend to carry into Portsmouth, where while the ship is repairing the damages sustained in the action, I have a project for leaving her, to attend to what is far more interesting to me . . . O! that we may meet something to try our stuff with, or at least a rich Spaniard on our return.

On 19 March, Moore parted company with the convoy and headed north for Latitude 49N, which was thought to be the best parallel for meeting enemy cruisers. As they ran northwards however, Moore's hopes, and no doubt that of his crew, began to sink, for there were no ships to be seen. Four days passed, and there were still no other ships;

If we meet nothing this cruise we shall all feel mortified; this is the favourite service that Admiral Kingsmill's cruisers are liable to be sent upon and it is by far the most promising cruise that I have had all the war; yet it may very well happen that we may see nothing.

On the morning of the 25th, he sent the crew to their quarters and put his gun crews through their paces, at the same time calling boarders to defend different parts of the ship[85]. On this occasion, the exercise enabled him to make an interesting assessment of his crew's performance, and to compare it with an incident which clearly troubled him;

I am thoroughly persuaded that this ship could not be carried by boarding as the Ambuscade was, unless the men were panic struck and ran from their quarters. That unfortunate affair[86] is the only action of the kind that has happened this war, and I think is to be attributed in the first place to the extraordinary gallantry of the attempt by the enemy, and in the next place to a panic which I think must have seized the crew of the Ambuscade. *The circumstance of the* Ambuscade *being upward of fifty men short of Complement will not account for it, as there must have remained more men than were sufficient to have repulsed the boarders, especially from a ship lower than the* Ambuscade. *The death of the Lieutenant and Master and the absence of the Captain who, I understand, was carried below badly wounded, must have thrown the ship into confusion, and I daresay the ship must have been very ill appointed with inferior officers, otherwise I should imagine the Seamen and marines might have been rallied. The* Melampus *is at present much better furnished with officers of all kinds than she has ever before been in my time, and I think no frigate of the enemy could resist us for any length of time, unless some very untoward accident happened.*

There was a good reason why Moore should have been troubled about the defeat of the *Ambuscade*, for he was a conscientious commander who often doubted his own abilities. The commander of the *Ambuscade*, Captain Henry Jenkins, had, through serious misjudgement and poor management, caused deep divisions within his crew, with the result that their morale collapsed very quickly in action. The case provided an important lesson for all those frigate captains who chose to notice it.

Two days later, the *Melampus* at last sighted a ship and gave chase, but she proved to be an American brig bound for Madeira. The Master of this ship gleefully reported that the American frigate *Constellation* had captured the French frigate *L'Insurgente*, after a severe action.[87] Later that day, they reached their cruising ground. As before, Moore disguised the *Melampus* by altering her sails to make her look more like a merchantman, hoping in doing so to tempt any French cruiser close enough to bring her to action. But, as always at sea, everything depended on the weather. The following day Moore had to abandon the ruse, as a north-westerly gale set in, accompanied by squalls of rain and hail. The sea continued to increase and more and more sail had to be taken off as the gale grew more violent.

In the privacy of his cabin, Moore pondered the progress of the war. He had hopes that the defeat of French ambition in Egypt might undermine enemy morale and result in a negotiated peace. However, the danger in this was that, if peace was declared, English seamen would become restless and demand to be allowed home. Any delay could cause another mutiny, though he also thought that the experience of the Nore mutiny might make them more cautious about repeating the strike;

> ... indeed I verily believe that the great body of them are very averse to a renewal of these fatal disorders, which they see when once begun lead them irresistibly much farther than they had any inclination to go. I think my people are very well disposed; I believe they will not easily be brought over to anything of that kind, but I could not confide at all in their actively resisting others in practices of that nature.

A brief encounter with the frigate *Flora* on 2 April did nothing to lighten Moore's mood. Her commander, Robert Gambier Middleton (who was junior to Moore) came aboard the *Melampus* and caused offence with his opinion that French cruisers were seldom to be found this far south. In fact, during the course of their conversation it became apparent that Middleton had deliberately strayed some way west of his appointed station. Frigate commanders were often jealous of their own cruising ground, and this explains why, when Middleton finally explained that he was short of stores and begged anything that could be spared, Moore decided he 'would spare them very little'.

Following the departure of the *Flora*, the weather deteriorated considerably and despite his irritation with Middleton, Moore decided to extend both the duration and area of his own cruise. At the same time the discomfort caused by the weather drew out his empathy with his men;

> The gale has increased, with rain and excessive hard squalls. We are lying to under a reefed fore sail, rolling about in a miserable way. It must be owned if sailors are wild and licentious when ashore, their dreary and fatiguing functions call for some relaxation, some solace, some joy.

The gale lasted the better part of three days, and when it subsided, Moore took stock of the effects it had on his crew and their performance:

> The natural suites of a gale and the consequent exertion it calls forth, with the exposure to wet and broken rest, is a degree of lassitude in the crew. As I think this a relaxation of nature I do not love much to spur them up for a while in that state unless circumstances demand it, but go on with what is to be done in the jog trot style. We require something now to rouse us, disappointed as we are with seeing nothing for

so long a time. It will be very grievous to us all to return into Port empty handed.

He knew all too well that a poor cruise would result in a dispirited crew, and if they lost faith in their commander some of them would simply desert on return to port – especially if there was the opportunity of finding a luckier frigate;

> *A Frigate, or even a stout privateer would infuse life spirit and confidence to our Rogues, and the good effects of it would be felt for a long time . . . The business of the ship has gone on very quietly since we left Cork, I have not been under the necessity of punishing a man, a ceremony I avoid as much as possible. We have not been very brisk but I can look over trivial neglect when there is no immediate call for great exertion. This is inconsistent with strict discipline but I never was a disciplinarian. I do not despise discipline, but I do not practise it strictly, it so often cuts across my feelings, and sometimes even my judgement opposes its details.*

This goes a long way to explaining why Moore's credit remained high with his men. However, he continued to be thwarted by the weather. Gales blew up again, and when they subsided on 10 April, the ship's carpenter reported that the frigate's foremast was badly sprung. After discussion, it was agreed that they would try to secure the mast and thereby avoid going into port, but it was also clear the ship had been strained by the heavy seas; and perhaps worst of all, he feared the continual bad weather would have driven all the enemy privateers into port. Moore was becoming increasingly despondent:

> *We are all in the dumps. We pay for a few hours of exultation, in this occupation of ours, by months of fatigue or languor. We have, thank heaven, always the chances of the Lottery in our favour: the scene may be quite changed tomorrow, and in the course of 24 hours we may be masters of a very good prize. We may in a shorter time be in the hands of the enemy or have met our death, but these numbers are not looked for in the Wheel.*

There was some excitement on 13 April when the *Melampus* came upon a schooner from Poole in some distress. Moore discovered that she had been cut out from a Newfoundland convoy by the French privateer *La Nantoise*, five days earlier. Unable to put a prize crew on board, the privateer Captain had left just two of her original crew on board as he took the ship in tow. They had escaped by cutting the towrope during the storms. The Mate of the schooner reported that *La Nantoise* was accompanied by another privateer, and, realizing that the privateers were probably still shadowing the convoy, Moore set off to the westwards in pursuit. As he did so, the news spread through the frigate and everyone was suddenly much more cheerful. He was also confident that Kingsmill would approve of his actions;

> *I have no doubt of his approving my conduct if we bring in a prize or two . . . The reception I meet with on my return from the Admiral will greatly depend on our success. We must take a little on ourselves and risk something when an opportunity offers on an occasion when all depends upon myself, as those who could order me on this service could not be acquainted with the circumstances.*

Once again, Moore reminds us that a frigate commander was often 'the man on the spot' – having to make decisions without the ability to consult higher authority, having to adapt to meet different situations and ultimately bearing the consequences.

On the morning of 17 April, the *Melampus* spotted a brig, which was clearly alarmed at the appearance of the frigate. Moore gave chase and, at 2pm, opened with his bow chasers. The brig though, had the advantage of the wind, and soon began to draw away. By nightfall she was five to six miles ahead, and Moore kept the deck throughout the night, watching the brig with his night glasses and giving directions to the helmsmen. At daylight she was still in sight and the *Melampus* began to close. Twenty-five hours after first sighting the brig, the *Melampus* closed to broadside range and the brig brought to and struck. She proved to be *Le Papillon*, a privateer from Nantes, carrying fourteen guns and manned by 123 men. Moore believed her a good prize for she was comparatively new and only on her second cruise. As the prisoners were being transferred, another suspicious vessel was seen in the distance. The *Melampus'* Second Lieutenant, De Busk, together with two midshipmen and twenty-five seamen were ordered to take the prize back to Cork, and the *Melampus* set off in chase once again. As night fell, a hard gale set in with gusts of snow, hail and rain. With such poor visibility, night glasses were useless; the chase simply disappeared into the darkness.

As day broke on the following morning, Moore and his crew could not have believed their luck. For a ship was sighted running down towards them and Moore was convinced that she was a French privateer and that she had, incredibly, mistaken the *Melampus* for *Le Papillon*. Moore waited, without making any more sail, so as to avoid creating any alarm. The approaching vessel then hauled onto the same tack as the frigate, and hoisted a number of different signal flags. The *Melampus* could obviously not respond to these '. . . *and seeing she began to smoke us we gave chase to her*'. The French prisoners on board the *Melampus* were consulted about the vessel and confirmed she was indeed *La Nantoise*;

> She endeavoured to cross us to get to leeward of us and in doing it she got under our guns. The sea was so high and it blew so very hard that I would not take the half ports off the main deck guns, but yawing to bring our broadside to bear we fired some of the quarterdeck and fore castle guns at her. She would not bring to but made all possible sail from us and much more than I thought he ought to have done in such a sea with so much wind; Being forced to carry sail after her to the imminent danger of our own masts we carried away our studding sail Booms.

Moore found that the *Melampus* could do just as well without the studding sails, and did not want to risk his masts, especially as the foremast was already badly sprung. So he

> . . . continued to pelt her with a chase gun, and determined to shoot up close under her lee and settle the business with our quarterdeck guns and Musketry. We were within ½ gun shot of her when on our firing a gun at her, she gave a yaw up in the wind, overset, and in two minutes went down, and not a vestige of her was to be seen. On seeing this dismal catastrophe, we hove to as soon as the sails could be taken in as near the spot where she had been as possible, but not an atom was to be seen on the water.

The crew of the *Melampus* was shocked by this sudden turn of events. *La Nantoise* had 150 men on board plus the crew of the Poole schooner. Moore also was affected, describing it as a *'melancholy spectacle'*; but despite his feelings for the fate of the seamen on board, he attributed this disaster completely to the obstinacy and misjudgement of the French Master.

On the morning following, the *Melampus*' carpenter reported that now the frigate's main topmast had sprung. The crew set about trying to shift it but then, as bad weather set in again, Moore decided they would have to return to port. He was disappointed that they would have little chance now of taking another prize, but he was cheerful:

> My spirits have been raised wonderfully by the little success we have had, and I can plainly see the good effect of it on all on board. We shall

go to sea next time as sanguine as ever. It appears to me that the destruc-
tion of French Commerce and the diminution of their Navy has had the
effect to throw into their Privateers a more respectable set of Officers
than formerly used to command them.

. . . The Captain and officers of this Privateer Le Papillon *are very*
decent, well behaved men. The Captain is Captain of a Frigate in the
service of the Republick, a man about my age and an active intelligent
fellow in his business . . . he has been very successful in making captures
and I believe has realized a tolerable fortune.

Moore was particularly interested to learn that a number of the
privateer's crew had volunteered to serve in order to avoid conscription.

Off Cape Clear, on the 21st, the crew of the *Melampus* learned from
the frigate *Shannon* that the *Papillon* had arrived safely in Cork, and
they joined her there on the following day. Unfortunately, Moore was
unable to get rid of his French prisoners until 3 May, on which day
an urgent dispatch arrived from Lord Bridport reporting that the
French fleet had broken out of Brest on 26 April, with nineteen ships
of the line and eighteen frigates. It was thought that they might be
attempting another descent upon Ireland and the *Melampus* and the
Shannon were hastily ordered to prepare to sail under the command
of Captain Lumsdaine in the 64-gun *Polyphemus*;

Lumsdaine is an excellent seaman and a brave officer, we are very
good friends. He possess[es] much of the sagacity, mother wit and
shrewdness of the Scotch and is really a manly, honorable and clever
fellow.

But he thought the *Polyphemus* in poor condition, even though she
was well manned.

Although the ships were prepared quickly, Moore knew that south-
easterly winds had been prevalent since the 26th. These would have
blown the French out to the westwards and, at the same time, would
have brought the ships from Portsmouth down to guard the entrance
of the Channel. Ironically, Lumsdaine's ships were unable to get
out of Cork harbour, and Moore was growing anxious about missing
any engagement. While they lay in Cork, news came that a fleet had
appeared off Bantry Bay, but Moore was convinced that this would
be Bridport's fleet. While waiting for an opportunity to leave the
harbour, Moore received several letters, including one from Miss M's
brother confirming that his sister was not indifferent towards him.
This set Moore's hopes soaring once more and he again dispatched a

proposal of marriage via his mother. There had also been news of an old acquaintance:

> *I see by the News Papers that Sidney Smith is off St. John D'Acre with his ship the* Tygre *[74]. He will cut out some work for himself there with Buonoparte, I wish he may not by his extraordinary valor and enterprise venture too far and get into some fatal scrape.*[88]

The three ships finally managed to escape Cork harbour on 6 April and headed towards Bantry Bay where Bridport eventually joined them. The assembled fleet now consisted of twenty ships of the line, one 64-gun ship and nine or ten frigates. The captains of the fleet were all summoned on board Bridport's flagship, the *Royal George* (100), for a meeting where it was generally agreed that the French must be heading for Ireland. However, it was also deduced that any landing would be attempted on the north coast, and the fleet headed in that direction with the weather closing around them and visibility declining. Back in the privacy of his own cabin, Moore confided in his journal that he had

> *. . . no very high idea of the abilities of the Commander in Chief or his principal adviser, but I have the firmest reliance on his courage and perseverance,*

which would enable him to destroy the Brest fleet if they met them.

On 15 April, Bridport dispatched the *Melampus*, the fastest frigate in the fleet, to scout ahead and look into Black Sod Bay on the coast of Mayo. There Moore landed with a boat full of armed seamen and learned that nothing had been seen of the French. He sailed on to Killala, where again nothing had been seen, before returning to join Bridport off Achil Head. Reporting on board the *Royal George*, Moore was informed that it was now thought the French had sailed southwards but, given the recent alarm about Ireland, Bridport decided on the advisability on leaving a screen of frigates around the Irish coast,[89] while he remained in Bantry Bay, Moore and the *Shannon* were sent back to watch off Black Sod Bay. However, the whole exercise was jeopardized because bad weather drove Bridport's line of battleships out to sea. Off Erris Head, Moore had become convinced anyway that the French had gone elsewhere and thought that they were all wasting both their time and the health of their ships and men: '*The* Melampus *begins to complain now a good deal, she has run a long time and been much at sea and in the worst weather.*' The *Shannon* too was suffering, having sprung the knee of her head and Charles Pater, her Commander, reported that she was in danger of losing her bowsprit. At such a critical time, Moore was infuriated to learn that Bridport had withdrawn to Beer Haven, from where he could give little protection to the Irish coast. The French could attack the north coast of Ireland long before Bridport would get anywhere near them. With his small squadron off Black Rock, Moore inscribed angrily into his journal, '*This is the place for the Grand Fleet for that purpose, I say it and say it again*'. By the last day of May, Moore and his crew were heartily tired of their current cruise. Moore was even more convinced that the French would not come, and he bemoaned the fact that they were daily wearing out their sails and rigging. To a large degree, he blamed Bridport:

> *Our Fleets are too often commanded by men of no talents, but the great excellence of the English Marine in general renders the faults of those who happen to command less fatal.*

With the *Shannon* sheltering in Black Sod Bay while she tried to repair her bowsprit, Moore received a report from the Carpenter of the *Melampus* that the frigate's foremast was sprung. The crew struck the foretopgallant mast and shortened the jib boom, but that same night the ship was suddenly taken aback by a violent squall. An anxious few hours followed, with the frigate embayed near a lee shore, and all hopes resting on a reefed foresail on the damaged mast. Happily, the temporary repair held and next day Moore received orders to rejoin Bridport. Arriving at Cork on 9 June, the frigate was ordered to proceed to Spithead for repair. At Spithead he was told the frigate would not be ready for sea again for three weeks so, as planned, he travelled to London. He called at the M house at the first opportunity and spent some time with Miss M; however, for the first time, he sensed a certain coldness on the part of her mother and he could not ignore the fact that she seemed to be trying to keep him at a distance. Nevertheless, he resolved to press ahead with his proposal of marriage and made the necessary arrangement to call upon Mr M. When they met, Moore outlined his feelings towards Miss M, detailed his financial position and prospects, and then asked that he might be granted permission to propose marriage. M's response appeared to be kind and encouraging, and with regard to his daughter,

> *. . . he believed her to be perfectly disengaged, that he knew she had a high opinion of me and a very great regard for me, but whether it went*

so far as to make her willing to quit her family or not he did not know. It was agreed that I should see her the next morning.

In a buoyant mood, Moore returned to his parents' house and acquainted them with the situation. The very next morning he would return to the Ms' house and ask the woman he had dreamed about for so long, to become his wife. His reverie was shattered when, but a few hours later, a letter from Mr M was delivered by hand. Opening the letter, Moore read that M had

> *. . . found he had undertaken more than he could perform, that his daughter had begged of him to spare her the pain of saying what she could not bear even to write again. That she hoped I would forgive her when she acknowledged that with the highest respect for me she was yet unacquainted with any thing that could reconcile her to a separation from her family. This came like a thunderbolt upon me. I instantly went to her father and there had a scene which I can never forget. He told me that when she heard that he had appointed me to see her next morning she was so agitated and distressed that he found it was impossible.*

In considerable distress himself, Moore begged M to let him see his daughter. M promised that he would ask his daughter if she would speak to him, and requested that Moore return a little later – but when Moore returned it was to find that she still *'could not bear to see me'*. She had, however, written him a letter in which she explained that she wished to spare them both the pain of a meeting, and that what she had said was both final and decisive; *'I read this like a man stupefied: my mortification was extreme . . . I can say no more.'* In fact, he was so broken that he burst into tears. M was kindness and understanding itself, but nothing could lessen the pain. Shattered, Moore returned to his parents' house, where after a few days he attempted to commit his feelings to his journal:

> *I believe I shall never get over the misery of this bitter disappointment where I had set my heart. I feel myself to have been unworthily dealt with, but I am incapable of resentment. I love her as much as ever . . . I have been wretched ever since, and I am now fit for nothing that requires thought, for I cannot turn my mind from this subject.*

His heart was broken, and his confidence badly shaken. It was probably no coincidence that brother John appeared in London a few days later. He was being sent to the south coast to help train a brigade as part of the preparation for an unnamed expedition. Graham could only envy John's self-possession and single-mindedness: '. . . *he has his whole heart, soul and faculties turned to his profession. Would it were so with me!'* The older brother clearly attempted to console his younger sibling over the next few days, and almost certainly in an attempt to distract him from his pain, the two had discussed plans to live together in the country within a few hours of London. Moore was inexorably drawn towards Surrey because of its *'naturally beautiful and luxuriant scenery'*.

On 17 July, the *Melampus* sailed from Spithead once again, but her commander was deeply unhappy, noting emptily in his journal, *'I am heavy and low'*. An old friend[90] had decided to accompany him on this cruise, almost certainly out of concern for his welfare, and although the man tried to be entertaining, Moore's state of dejection was too intense. His spirits were lightened somewhat when, three days out of Spithead, they sighted and gave chase to a strange brig but just after they had set the royals, the main topmast was found to be badly sprung. The officers and crew of the *Melampus* could have been forgiven if they had, at this point, succumbed to despair at what appeared to be a resumption of their bad luck with topmasts. But, instead,

. . . in three hours and 25 minutes the mast was shifted and the Royals set again. This without any previous preparation, was the smartest job I have ever seen done by the crew of the Melampus. *I applauded them heartily and ordered them an allowance of grog besides their beer as a proof of my satisfaction at their good conduct. The Brig is still in sight, I believe her to be an English cruiser. I have painted the* Melampus all Black *which will certainly render her more deceitful at sea than ever, we have more than once succeeded by deceiving the Enemy's cruisers.*

Arriving at Cork on 22 July, Moore reported to a surprised Admiral Kingsmill who had been led to believe that the *Melampus* was no longer under his orders. However, he knew better than to fail to take advantage of a plum dropped into his lap. He agreed to speedily supply the frigate with a new topmast, and gave Moore orders to cruise northwards with the frigate *Galatea*, commanded by Captain George Byng[91], under his command. They were to search for a privateer that had been causing some trouble off Tory Island, and then cruise to the west of Cape Clear to protect any convoys – especially an expected East Indies convoy. Moore was particularly pleased with these orders because, whilst in London, it had been intimated to him by Earl Spencer that the *Melampus* might be appointed to a new expedition. Moore's brother, John, was being sent to Holland, and Moore thought that was no station for the *Melampus*.[92]

The *Galatea* and the *Melampus* sailed northwards from Cork at what seems an easy pace;

> *Captain Byng proposed to me to share Prize Money together for the cruise which I declined as I think in case of separation we have a better chance of making captures than the Galatea. Besides I do not yet know what kind of a cruiser she is.*

From experience, Moore knew that two frigates sailing together would instantly alarm any French privateer which saw them approaching. There would be no chance of taking a privateer by deception – a tactic that Moore had found to be effective in the past. Any chances they had were further reduced by the arrival of the frigate *Naiad*, commanded by William Pierrepont. She was also waiting for the East Indies convoy and seemed reluctant to leave the area. Moore knew that her presence meant that his chances of surprising a privateer were practically nil.

Predictably it was difficult for Moore to avoid thinking about his recent personal disappointment which, as the weeks passed, he became increasingly bitter about. He became convinced that the deciding factor had been his lack of fortune:

> *If I can only make two or three more cruises as good as that in March and April last I shall be able to sit down very comfortable as to the affair of income. Indeed I could do very well at present as a Bachelor, but that is not the state that I can rest satisfied in. I can form no plan of happiness unconnected with this Jade that has torn my heart to pieces; she makes me wish for money which otherwise I should care very little about.*

In this state of mind he longed for the opportunity of bringing an enemy ship to action: *'Something to rouse and animate me, to divert my mind from despondency.'* At least he could find some joy in his ship, though to some degree he was probably venting his feelings on Martin, his First Lieutenant:

> *We exercised the great guns today, whenever this is the case the appearance of our men fills me with confidence and makes me long to bring them alongside of a French Ship. It is not that they are by any means in good order, but they are stout and confident. I am wretchedly off for*

a 1st Lieutenant, he wants activity, skill and zeal; all that is in his favour is good nature and I believe honesty with the manners of a gentleman and the dirty appearance and dress of a sloven. He is I believe some-what attached to me and I do not believe he is deficient in personal courage. I cannot hurt his feelings by shaking him off, but it is melan-choly to have such a second.

Moore was also unable to avoid slight pangs of guilt about deliber-ately trying to escape the expedition to Holland, after all his brother John was being sent there. With great perspicacity he observed:

If the attack is to be on Flushing and the Isle of Walcheren, I believe we are likely to lose a good many lives, as it is full of broad ditches and embankments which afford cover for troops acting on the defensive . . . I pray God my excellent friend and brother may survive the dash of the landing which I think will fall to his lot. [93]

Continuing northwards the two frigates found no signs of enemy ship-ping. As usual Moore wiled away the hours reading in his cabin, quickly devouring Diderot's *The Nun*, Thomas Matthias' *Pursuits of Literature*[94] and then, in desperation, borrowing *The Necromancer: Or The Tale of the Black Forest* [95] '*. . . a very indifferent novel*', which he read in a single day and then berated himself for his idleness. He was also poring over some newspapers for naval news and was pleased to learn that Admiral Keith had succeeded St Vincent as Commander-in-Chief of the Mediterranean fleet. Keith was '*. . . a man of spirit and I have no doubt will conduct them ably and gallantly*' and, of course, he was also a fellow Scot! Moore also read of a number of gallant cutting-out expeditions by frigates:

There is no service so hazardous as attacks by this nature, and I hardly ever have consented to risk any boats on attempts of a similar nature. In general on these occasions the men who compose the parties are all volunteers, and of course have prepared their minds for an action of vigour.

On 10 August the two frigates fell in with the *Dryad* and the *Revolutionnaire* who had been cruising on the ground to which Moore and Byng were heading. They reported not only that there had been no enemy vessels sighted in the last four to five weeks, but that they had also already escorted the East Indies convoy to safety. Reassured by this news, Moore felt at some liberty to extend his cruise, sweeping south and west before turning back towards the north coast of Ireland. He was well aware that once again he was over-stepping his orders, but if he was called to account for this, *'I shall plead guilty and urge only my good intentions as my excuse'*.

Three days later they reached Lat 46.57N and Long 23.51W, approximately 900 miles west of Ushant – and a considerable distance from his official station. With a gale blowing up, he decided to head north-west hoping that he would not run into any convoys, packets or English men-of-war who might report seeing him so far from his authorized position. Despite the activity, Moore found it difficult to avoid thinking of Miss M, and he found himself slipping into what he described as a *'morbid languor'* which was certainly not helped by the weather, for they were soon lying-to in foggy rain;

> *Rainy weather is the most uncomfortable of any on board of a ship, we have then no kind of resource; when the weather is fair even a Gale of wind affords some kind of amusement.*

A report from an American brig, of a French privateer with an English East Indiaman in tow, caused a brief flurry of excitement but this dissipated when the only suspicious sail they found disappeared during the night. By noon on 23 August the *Melampus* and *Galatea* were just seventy-eight leagues from Cape Ortegal on the north coast of Spain, when they should have been off the north coast of Ireland. Moore could only pray that they didn't run into any other English men-of-war who might report their position. Two days later they recaptured an English brig which had been taken by a letter-of-marque from Bordeaux. Moore put a midshipman and ten men on board and sent her to Cork, gleefully recording in his journal, *'I believe this to be a very valuable vessel, she is laden with Salt Petre, Gum, Almonds, and skins.'*

Then, unbelievably, on the last day of August, the *Melampus'* carpenter reported that the main topmast was badly sprung. As this was already the spare mast, the crew had to sway up the spare fore topmast in its place, but because this was smaller, it meant the *Melampus* would not be able to carry as much sail. Moore was perplexed:

> *I am at a loss to account for the frequency of these accidents to our Main top masts, this being the fourth that we have carried away since we sailed from Plymouth in the beginning of March.*

His suspicion was that when the ship was last refitted, the futtock plates on the new main top had been fitted further aft than they should have been and this was putting undue stress on the topmast.

The next day Moore retired to his cabin to bury himself in an English translation of Saint Pierre's *The Studies of Nature*[96], but his attention was called sharply to his duties next day when what appeared to be a large French frigate was sighted. In fact, the ship was a very fine 30-gun letter-of-marque from London, bound for Martinique. She had been a French frigate and was as large as the *Melampus*. Moore took his revenge upon her for causing some alarm, by pressing three of her seamen, even though her Master, *'a fine old sailor'* tried his best to have one of them returned. Later that day one of the *Melampus'* men fell from the mizzen topsail yard while reefing the sail;

> *He fell on a netting about 8 feet from the Quarterdeck, from thence he tumbled down on the deck. He is a good deal bruised, but has received no permanent injury. It is a wonderful escape that he was not killed on the spot. He was half drunk, and had been punished three days before for that fault.*

A few days later they came across a London ship bound for Jamaica. From her Master, Moore learned that she and the sloop-of-war *Serpent* had become separated from a West India convoy of forty-nine ships in foggy weather. Moore decided that he had better go in search of the convoy to offer his protection and later the same day they fell in with them. The *Serpent* reported she was desperately short of provisions and Moore gave her what he could spare, and decided that he had better continue to escort the convoy, even though

> *Thus ends our cruise, as it is impossible for me, consistent with my duty, to avoid escorting the convoy, which is very valuable, into safety.*

He ordered Byng to escort the London-bound vessels as far as the Isle of Wight, whilst the *Melampus* would escort the Liverpool-bound vessels into the St George's Channel. He then set about running past the different ships in the convoy to inform their masters of the arrangements. Behind the dutiful benevolence, however, Moore had his own additional motives, for he planned to press some good men out of the Liverpool and Bristol ships before taking his leave.

> *September 9th: I was obliged to punish a Marine today for impertinence to the Sergeant – cursed disgusting – the French Prisoners stare at an exhibition of this kind, they punish only thieves with stripes, for the generality of other crimes they confine and sometimes diminish their rations. This would not do with our people, although confinement is in*

fact a severe punishment it is not at all exemplary. Stopping any part of the provisions . . . [is] the same and is liable to other objections. A Punishment is nothing if it does not terrify the guilty.

Falling in with an American brig, Moore spoke to the Master and managed to acquire a relatively recent newspaper. The naval news contained a letter from Admiral Rainier, the Commander-in-Chief of the East Indies station,

. . . giving an account of a very gallant action between the English frigate La Sybille *Captain Edward Cook and the French frigate,* La Forte, *in which the brave Cook was so desperately wounded that there were no hopes of his recovery; after an action of one hour and forty minutes* La Forte *was taken. Captain Cook was well known to me, he was a fine, gallant, young fellow, we served together on the coast of France with Sidney Smith. I sincerely regret his loss.*[97]

There was also news of the British expedition to the Walcheren, where 300 men had been killed:

I have a strong idea my brother was busy when the landing was made. The Americans said none of our Generals had been killed or wounded.[98]

The following morning the *Melampus* sighted what seemed to be a privateer with a larger prize. Moore signalled to Byng to give chase, but no-one on the *Galatea* seems to have seen the signal. Moore tacked in pursuit, which he thought must have been noticed by the *Galatea*, and even fired a gun although this would also have alerted the privateer, but still the *Galatea* made no move to increase sail. Moore soon lost sight of both the convoy and the *Galatea*. When the two quarry separated, Moore gave chase to the larger, which turned out to be an American ship from Bristol. He put a prize crew on board and sent her into Cork before turning after the privateer. That ship however, had disappeared. Moore could not pursue further, for he had lost the convoy and he was seriously short of water. The crew of the *Melampus* was already down to a quart of water per day per man and, because they had used up so much of their provisions, Moore had the empty water casks filled with seawater to restore the frigate's trim. The following day was 14 September; Moore's birthday. In his journal, he noted dispassionately that he was thirty-five years old, as if that was all he needed to say on the subject.

The *Melampus* arrived back in Cork on 21 September, where the brig they had captured earlier had been placed in quarantine by an officer of the Customs. Moore was more concerned about his latest prize, the American ship, fearing that she might have been recaptured on her way to Cork. Admiral Kingsmill had gone to England, and Moore found himself the senior officer at the port. Waiting at Cork for him was a package of letters including some from his family, and one from Mr M. The contents of the latter were a particular blow, for he had written to tell Moore that his daughter had accepted a proposal of marriage from another. Moore knew the man concerned, for they had both been acquainted with Miss M for the same length of time. He

> ... is a very good natured, honest fellow, and heir to <u>immense wealth</u>, <u>that</u> is the charm ... it levels her in my opinion with the common run of women who are capable of the legal prostitution of an interested marriage ...

There was also news about brother John, who had been wounded 'slightly' in the hand. He also learned that the day after he had left Cork, orders had come for him to sail to the Downs, to join the expedition to the Walcheren. Moore was greatly relieved that he had not been around to follow those orders, especially as '. . . *the* Melampus *is ill calculated for the shoal water there'*.

There was still no sign of the prize – and Moore was most regretful at the possible loss of the prize crew, which included an excellent quartermaster and some very good seamen. His feelings could only have been exacerbated as he watched other frigates bringing in fine prizes. On 14 October, the frigate *Revolutionnaire* arrived with

> ... the Bordelais *of 24 guns, her prize, the finest French privateer I ever saw, which she took after a chase of 9 hours, in which they ran 120 miles, a proof of the extraordinary good sailing of both ships.*

Then on the following day Captain Robert Barlow arrived in the *Phoebe*, with a prize privateer carrying sixteen guns. Moore had also been reading the latest newspaper reports about the Walcheren expedition, and had learned of the more serious wound received by his brother. Perhaps because of its potentially dreadful nature (a wound from a bullet that exited below his left eye), he made no comment about it in the journal until several days later, when he unrolled his sea charts to study the disposition of the forces at Walcheren;

> I suppose the wounds my brother has received will lay him up for some time, thank God there are now Quarters for the wounded. We have lost many brave men. Such is the inevitable consequence of war.

With Barlow's arrival, Moore was superseded as senior officer. When Moore reported that the *Melampus* was ready for sea, Barlow gave him orders to cruise for six to seven weeks between Lat 48–51 N and Long 20 – 25 W, a box that straddled the latitudes from south of Cape Clear to Ushant. This was the sort of ideal cruise that only a frigate commander could devise. It was just as well that Barlow had ordered him out on such a promising cruise, for the latest London papers carried an announcement of the engagement of Miss M. Moore was extremely bitter:

> The reluctance at leaving her Father and Mother may be construed into the attachment of a cat, which is to the house more than to its in- habitants. She could not bear the privation of the ease, comforts and luxuries to which she had been accustomed; but as soon as an honest, good natured, dull Homo appeared, holding these things out to her in still greater abundance, she instantly, simpering, closed with his snug proposal and proved herself to be a worthy help mate to this son of the earth.

By 22 October Moore was well on his way to his cruising ground when, in the early morning, three ships were sighted to leeward, sailing on a south-easterly course. Seeing that they were men-of-war, Moore guessed them to be three of Bridport's frigates

> . . . but took care to keep the weather gage in approaching them. We crossed the weathermost one on different tacks at the distance of about 2 gun shots, it was not until she was directly abreast of us that I perceived she was not an English frigate; they all three gave chase to us, we made the private signal which they did not answer, but one of them hoisted a yellow flag at the Mizen top mast head. I now plainly saw they were enemies, but could not be sure whether they were French or Spaniards. The wind blew a fresh gale from the Westward and we stood to the southward close to the wind, we could with difficulty carry single reefed topsails, we weathered upon them all.

Moore's caution had paid off; keeping the weather gauge had enabled him to keep control of the situation. At 8pm, it being dark, Moore tacked to throw the frigates off his tail, but the wind baulked him and the *Melampus* lost ground down towards the enemy. With what must have been bated breath, they watched as one of the frigates loomed out of the darkness close behind them. From the quarterdeck Moore could see her plainly, but she gave no sign of seeing the *Melampus*. As soon as she had disappeared he ordered all sail set, and the

Melampus sailed hard all night even though a violent squall in the middle watch split the jib. In the morning, there was no sign of the enemy frigates – but the *Melampus* had, once again, sprung her main topmast.

It is possible that the *Melampus'* failure to complete her tack on the night of the 22nd was the fault of poor seamanship for, a little unusually, Moore began to find fault with his crew:

> *I am less satisfied with the stuff of which our crew is now composed than ever I was, we have too few seamen. We have been greatly diminished of late by accidents and by the Hospital, I have by no means the confidence in the Ship's Company that I had. I do not mean that they are ill disposed, on the contrary I believe they are in general very well disposed, but they are not brisk nor in my opinion very effective.*

If his crew was less than normally efficient, he may have felt that his chances against the French were reduced;

> *The French within these three years have brought the construction of their Privateers to a pitch of excellence which they never before attained. They often escape from our Frigates by fairly outsailing them, being of a very great length, armed with brass guns (for the sake of lightness) and having very little top hamper. From the account Captain Twysden of* La Revolutionnaire *gave me of his chase after* Le Bordelais, *I doubt very much if the* Melampus *could have caught her. I trust greatly to deceiving them by our appearance, the consequence will probably be that they will fire into us, taking us for a sloop of war; this is an inconvenience but it is not so bad as their escaping from us.*

He was not to get the chance even of trying this. On the evening of 30 October, with a hard wind blowing, the *Melampus* sprang her mainmast. It was fished in the hope that this would enable them to continue their cruise, but they then discovered a second spring higher up the mast. The heel of the topmast now had to be lowered below the spring to act as a form of splint, and the head of the lower mast had to be secured by lashing the topmast to it above and below the spring. As Moore explained, this was called 'reefing the topmast', and it would enable it to carry the double reefed topsail. However, to the crew's disappointment, the damage meant that they would have to abandon their cruise and head for Plymouth immediately. As if the elements were now also against them, they were buffeted by a series of hard gales. Moore recorded that '. . . *the sea was very high and the ship strained and worked very much making a great deal of water in at her upper works.'* The rough conditions continued for over a week and water from the deck found its way into the after magazine, damaging forty to fifty made-up cannon cartridges. Moore had the ammunition and powder shifted, and scuttles were cut in the platform to release the water. Once it had dried as best it might, the powder was replaced. There were a few days' relief until 9 November, when the storm set in again,

> . . . *blowing and raining with excessive hard squalls; the ship made a great deal of water, not a man in the ship had a dry hammock from the leaky state of the decks and upper works, and the labour at the pumps had become serious.*

On the 20th, the *Melampus* anchored in Plymouth Sound, and Moore requested new orders. His belief was that he would be sent to Spithead for a major refit, and indeed this was the case, though with a slight twist. The *Melampus* was to carry 160,000 dollars in bullion taken from two Spanish galleons by the frigates *Naiad*, *Ethalion* and *Alcmene*. The government had purchased the bullion from the very happy captors and Moore had to deliver it to the Collector of Customs. His views on the success of his fellow frigate captains on this occasion were not recorded – but it would be surprising indeed if he were not both a little envious and bitter about his own hard luck. Reporting to the dockyard at Portsmouth, the *Melampus* was surveyed, and found to be in need of '. . . *very considerable refit'* before she would be able to put to sea again. And Moore too needed a break. He obtained leave and set off to his parents' new home, Marshgate House at Richmond.

12

The West Indies
(January 1800 – September 1801)

After a fortnight in London, Moore rejoined the *Melampus* and, at the early part of February, he was instructed to prepare the ship for foreign service. Within a few days he received orders to proceed to Cork to join a convoy bound for Jamaica and the Leeward Islands. Once there, he was to put himself under the orders of Admiral Sir Hyde Parker. Before leaving, he received a blow, when Lieutenant Martin was promoted to the rank of Commander and given the armed ship *Xenophon*. Moore applied for his Second, Lieutenant Busk, to be promoted in Martin's place but the Admiralty had their own candidate, Lieutenant Edward Moore.[99] The new Lieutenant made a good first impression:

> *The Lieutenant whom they have appointed has conducted himself exceedingly well as yet and I hope will continue to do so. He seems to have much method and detail.*

The *Melampus* left Cork with a convoy of eighty-four vessels. Accompanying them was Captain Lord Garlies in the frigate *Hussar*, which was to accompany them only as far as the North East Trades near Madeira. Moore was in two minds about his new station. He was not overjoyed about the prospect of Jamaica, with all the health problems which came with it, but on the other hand some of the station's cruisers had been very successful over the previous six months. He had hopes, therefore, of some success himself,

> *. . . which . . . will probably render me tolerably easy for the rest of my life as to money matters. As to reputation I do not expect to acquire any on the Jamaica station for any thing but activity. Although the most brilliant* Coup de main *has been lately performed there of this or the*

preceding war, in the boarding and cutting out the Hermione *from under the batteries of Porto Cavallo by Captain Edward Hamilton of the* Surprise[100]. *I shall be very curious to learn the particulars of this heroic exploit from this gallant officer himself.*

The passage was not without incident; on the night of 22 February, one of the more valuable ships, the *Clarendon* of Bristol, collided with the London vessel *Beaufoy*, striking her violently amidships. The *Clarendon* was badly damaged, as her stem was forced in considerably and her bowsprit broken off. When day broke, the *Beaufoy* had disappeared. Twice the frigates gave chase to vessels which they thought might be privateers, without catching them. Then on 27 February the weather deteriorated and the convoy began to scatter involuntarily. Moore struggled to gather them all together again into at least the semblance of a manageable group, but he was beginning to suffer the perennial stress of all convoy escorts;

> *We are retarded considerably by the inattention of the generality of the Convoy to our signals which occasions our frequently heaving to to collect them . . .*

though

> *. . . a few of them, among which is a beautiful Greenock ship called the* Harmony, *are very correct and never out of their stations.*

On the last day of the month they sighted Madeira and Garlies took his departure. Moore was sorry to see him go;

> *I felt a little at the* Hussar *leaving us, Lord Garlies has made up a good deal to me and I think him a very fine fellow. He knows his business well and is certainly very sharp and intelligent, he is an amiable fellow too, and a very agreeable companion.[101] His ship is in exceedingly good order and will always continue so while he commands her, he however does not give me the idea of a keen cruiser, but then we have had very little opportunity of judging.*

As they headed off across the Atlantic, Moore found himself satisfied with the *Melampus* which was now in reasonably good condition, and Moore had her painted once again to help disguise her nature. However, some of the crew had deserted and the ship was no longer so well manned;

> *I can safely say that there are not 50 good seamen in the ship and about as many Ordinary seamen, the rest are not fit to be in a man of war's*

top. I cannot account for the very great desertion that has constantly prevailed on board the Melampus *whenever she has been in a place where there was much opportunity for it or temptation.*

At least, for the present, the crew were all healthy and as they moved into the warmer latitudes he could only hope that they remained so;

Our men find a very great difference between this and the severe cold and wet they have been accustomed to; a Frock and trousers is now as much cloathes as a man wishes to wear, it is therefore a very easy matter for people to keep themselves clean and comfortable. If we can only keep clear of the cursed Fever, I am convinced our men will prefer the Jamaica station to Channel service.

There was, though, another change he noticed: as the days became warmer, a small number of the men complained of headaches, and some suffered spasms of some form or other. Moore too was beginning to suffer from the change in climate:

I am not sure that my practice of wearing a flannel waistcoat under my shirt may not exhaust me too much and some think that bathing so often as once a day debilitates, I hope not, it is such a luxury.

Reaching Barbados on 23 April, Moore detached the ships for that island pressing seven of their seamen. On 1 May the remainder entered Port Royal and he pressed another eight tolerably good hands.

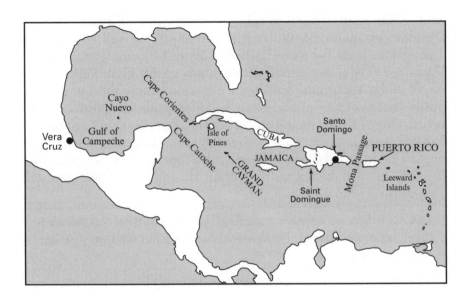

Having reported to the Commander-in- Chief, Moore had the opportunity to meet some of his fellow captains and catch up with news and gossip. He quickly realized that he was going to find the West Indies station difficult. His romantic tendencies encouraged him to believe that he was fighting in a just cause against an ignoble Republican tyranny. He was therefore shaken by his first real encounter with slavery in Jamaica, for the '. . . *sight of so many mortals deprived of liberty has a gloomy effect on my mind'*. He was also perturbed to find that the ordinary rules of war, to which he had become accustomed on the European seaboard, no longer applied. His colleagues warned him that neutral vessels were not to be trusted and should all be treated as potential hostiles. Moore was used to adopting ruses to lure enemy shipping under his guns – but this was a practice with which he felt distinctly uncomfortable:

This is a business I am quite unexperienced in and do not at all like. Harsh measures are absolutely necessary to procure the real papers of the vessels, and this is vile and disgusting to people you are at peace with.

He may also have been a little taken aback by his visit to Admiral Hyde Parker, who

. . . lives in great comfort, and there is the appearance of expense to profusion, but the cruisers have realized to him a very ample fortune, and he seems inclined to enjoy it.

Moore was soon ordered to take the frigate *Juno*, Captain George Dundas commanding, under his command and sail to the Dry Tortugas to hunt for three Spanish frigates carrying treasure from Vera Cruz. The cruise started with a handicap, for Hyde Parker took off all of the *Melampus'* Midshipmen leaving Moore short of men to put in charge of any prizes. Fever had also made its appearance on board. One of the stoutest members of the crew, the ship's armourer, had been struck down and was now delirious. He was soon joined by one of the ship's lads, struck down with a *'putrid fever'*. The surgeon had little hope of the former recovering, though Moore was sceptical about the surgeon's abilities:

I do not believe we have much medical skill on board; but this subject I do not at all understand. I believe for everything but the scurvy we are better here than in port.

On 10 May, the armourer, a handsome, strongly built Irishman, died;

He was always rather a favourite of mine. I used to go and talk to him very often and see that he wanted nothing but I never could cheer the fellow up, he was from being a daring licentious wild Irishman, become a poor chicken hearted creature. I am of opinion that the Irish, although brave and impetuous are much inferior in fortitude to the English and Scotch. They sink under adversity and are deficient in passive courage and firmness.

On 16 May, the *Melampus* and the *Juno* encountered an American ship which informed them that a Spanish convoy had recently sailed from Vera Cruz, but warned that it was heavily escorted. The two frigates set off once again to hunt for it, but Moore was having difficulty with navigation. Although he had a copy of Hamilton Moore's *Practical Navigator*[102] with him, he was unfamiliar with the West Indies and its currents, and his timekeeper was proving unreliable. Even so, they scored an early success, capturing a Spanish brig from New Orleans, which was loaded with case wood for making sugar crates. The vessel and her cargo were of only limited value, but Moore decided it was worth sending her in, and requested that Captain Dundas put a prize crew on board and send her back to Port Royal.

By now, two more of the *Melampus*' crew were dangerously ill with fever and one of these died on the following day. He had been taken ill, complaining of dizziness whilst working in the top. Within a few hours he was delirious, and five days later he died. The seaman had complained constantly of dizziness and pains in his legs and thighs. The ship's doctor had identified it as *'putrid fever'*, and treated his ailment by purging, vomiting, and then keeping him on a diet of sago and bark. Moore observed this treatment with contempt, for he had little time for the medical man's opinion, believing that he knew as much as the Doctor when it came to treatment. His friend Dr Currie had long been an advocate of cold baths as a treatment for the fever, and so Moore had applied this remedy to the other patient – to the obvious consternation of the rest of the crew;

I believe it had a very good effect on the other man who is ill and by no means out of danger, but the seamen stare at it.

Three days later the second seaman, a twenty-one-year old from Devon, died; and the Doctor himself was struck down with violent spasms. Fortunately, within a week he had recovered and the ship was free from fever. Even the sick lists were shorter than usual – though whether this was due to the threat of Moore's personal remedy can only be guessed.

Moore liked what he had seen of Captain George Dundas[103] of the *Juno*. He was not a young man, in fact he was older than Moore, and had reached the rank of Post Captain late, in October 1795. He seems to have had little command experience until appointed to the *Juno* in September 1798. Nevertheless, Moore recorded in his journal,

> *I am well pleased with what I see of the* Juno, *she seems to me an active and effective ship, commanded by a shrewd and steady man.*

The two frigates had now been several weeks out from Port Royal and the only enemy ship they had seen was the one they had taken. There had been plenty of neutral vessels, many of which might have been carrying enemy trade, but Moore had

> *. . . no inclination to speculate upon the Neutrals as many of my brethren have done, and some with great success, it is a species of gambling that I am not disposed to enter into.*

However, their luck was about to change.

On 2 June the two frigates captured a Spanish Felucca from Vera Cruz laden with sugar and cochineal. Then the *Juno* captured a 12-gun letter-of-marque brig laden with indigo and sugar. Three days later, they had more success, capturing what Moore described as a '*beautiful*' copper-bottomed Spanish schooner laden with yet more cochineal, indigo and sugar. The crew of the schooner, when examined, were found to be carrying 2,000 dollars about their bodies. Moore was deeply suspicious that this was really part of the cargo of the ship and that they had pocketed it when they realized that they were not going to escape. The men were questioned closely and, perhaps surprisingly, Moore decided to give them the benefit of the doubt and let them keep the money.

The two frigates were now burdened with nearly a hundred Spanish prisoners, who were consuming water at an alarming rate. Moore was also worried that they might introduce some form of contagion, especially as the ships were now free of fever. In reality though, Moore was also losing men through accidents. On 13 June, a young seaman who had volunteered from an English Fencible Regiment at Cork, fell from the mizzen topsail yard and was killed. It was their fourth fatality through accident or disease since leaving Port Royal.

Moore's next encounter was not with the Spanish, but with an American frigate, the *General Greene*, armed with thirty-two

12-pounder guns. The American commander hove to at Moore's request, and the Lieutenant sent on board was – perhaps surprisingly under the circumstances – received with '. . . *much civility by the American Captain'*. From the American ship, Moore learned that a Spanish convoy had sailed from Pensacola, escorted by a large frigate. The two frigates had not long parted when the *Melampus* sighted a brigantine flying what appeared to be an unrecognized American provincial flag. Moore was suspicious and fired several shots in an attempt to bring her to, but before this could be achieved, the American frigate intervened, placing herself between the *Melampus* and the stranger. Furious, Moore had another shot fired at the brigantine

> . . . *to show that I was not to be led from my purpose by such an unofficer like conduct, and finding their frigate still kept close to the Brigantine, I prepared for action and in passing the Frigate on our way to our object, hailed and asked if they knew what vessel that was which we had fired so many shot at. I was answered from the frigate that she was an American from New Orleans bound to Salem, and under her convoy . . . I then said, I mean to send an officer on board to examine her papers, and if she is under your convoy I will be obliged to you if you will direct her to bring to for that purpose. I was answered that they had no objection to our examining her papers and that they would direct her to bring to. The frigate then hailed the brigantine and told them to shorten sail and bring to while we examined her.*

Moore sent a boarding part over to check her papers. The brigantine was carrying cotton, and seemed innocent so Moore let her go, though it is questionable what he would have done if he had found grounds for suspicion;

> *I certainly was not pleased with the conduct of the American frigate on this occasion, it appeared to me to be neither discreet nor dignified, as it is certainly to be presumed that the Brigantine making sail after speaking the frigate was in pursuance of her directions, she therefore suffered with a bad grace what could have been no discredit to her if she had made no shew at first of contesting.*

It obviously has to be seriously doubted that the Americans saw it in the same light – and indeed, the incident might be seen as a precursor to the tensions between the two nations that were to explode a decade later. The incident amply illustrates the care that Moore had to take, for not only was he on unfamiliar ground, but there were large numbers of American ships in the area, including many privateers.

The *Melampus'* bad luck seemed to continue a few days later when a seaman fell from the foremast rigging, hit one of the guns and dropped into the sea. Moore's Coxswain leapt over the side to try and save him, but found only his hat. A boat was lowered, but the man was nowhere to be seen; '*A sad accident happened,*' on the following day,

> when we were reefing the topsails, one of our best Top men, a fine young Welch sailor fell from the Main top sail yard and was killed on the spot. This is the Third sailor we have lost by accident this cruise, besides the three men who were swept off by the cursed fever.

On 29 June, Moore fell in with a licenced Spanish vessel and put forty-six of his prisoners on board with a generous one-week's supply of water and provisions. Dundas in the *Juno* was soon reporting a shortage of water and, reluctantly, Moore had to order him back to port. This was a blow because it was unlikely that the *Melampus* on her own would be able to engage three Spanish frigates. Moore continued westwards past Cuba where he fell in with the frigate *Quebec*, commanded by Captain Henry Bayntun. The two frigates cruised together for several days until they were separated during a violent storm. Moore was at his most poetic when describing it in his journal:

> Between 9 & 10 at night we had a sudden squall with a tremendous clap of thunder which obliged us to put before the wind and clew up everything. This continued about 20 minutes with the most violent rain and the lightning as it were streaming from the clouds close to us and all around, while we could scarce hear or see for the dreadful explosions of the thunder and the continuous flashes of blue forked lightning darting down and across us. I expected some fatal calamity every instant either to the ship or the crew, but we escaped completely, and the heavy laden clouds, pregnant with the thunder, passed away to leeward, the air cooled and the sky became clear and serene. I have never before seen lightning so terrible, and I think we were in very great danger. One of the ships on the Jamaica Station has been struck repeatedly when cruising in the Gulph and has lost several men, besides having on one occasion her main top mast shivered to pieces.

On 12 July, the *Melampus* was about twelve leagues WSW of the Isle of Pines and Moore calculated that, with twenty tons of water remaining and the crew consuming more than a ton per day even in rationed amounts, he only had enough left for twelve days. It was time to turn back for Port Royal. The crew had already been on salt provisions for some time, but so far they were still healthy and seemed in good humour and spirits. The situation made Moore aware of the real disadvantage of his current station for his cruising ground was so far from Port Royal that he could spend little time there once he arrived. He decided to stop at Grand Cayman where the frigate's purser purchased a small supply of vegetables and other refreshments, including turtle, but the island could only supply them with sufficient water for three days. They set off again for Jamaica but progress was painfully slow, and on 20 July Moore had to ignore a strange sail to leeward, even though it might be a valuable prize, because he could not afford to lose a minute in getting back to port. However, when a privateer felucca fell into his lap on the 22nd, he did not hesitate to deviate slightly to take her as a prize. With their water running out, the *Melampus* finally reached Port Royal on 28 July, where she found the *Juno* safely in harbour with their prizes.

Back in port, Moore found that Lord Hugh Seymour had replaced Hyde Parker as Commander-In-Chief, and there was naval gossip and news from Europe to catch up with. There were rumours that the Austrians might soon make peace with the French and Moore found himself speculating how long it would be before Britain and France made peace. He believed that the French had made no military impression on England at all, '... *but our expenses must in the end ruin us*'. Moore strongly desired peace now: '*I long to enjoy society, ease and Liberty, Liberty, Liberty.*'

The *Melampus* was caulked and fitted with new main course and topsail yards, but the stay in harbour saw a resumption of the dreaded fever and one of the Midshipmen,

> ... *a very fine boy*, died; *From perfect health he was carried off in the course of five days. He was nephew to Sir William Grant the Solicitor General, and was really a most promising youth. I have left another young Gentleman in a very dangerous way at the Naval hospital, and I fear his health is destroyed for ever.*

On 21 August, the *Melampus* and the *Juno* were ordered to cruise between Cape Corrientes and Cape Catouche (Cabo Catoche) the southernmost point of the Gulf of Mexico. Moore was also given permission to leave the *Juno* there while he entered the Gulf to search for a privateer off Yallaks Point. The general opinion was that the new station was a good one for intercepting Spanish ships sailing between Old Spain and Vera Cruz. Moore and Dundas agreed to share prize money until 15 October, which was when Moore planned to separate for the Gulf. The two frigates called briefly at Grand Cayman for turtle but were unable to obtain any. Instead they purchased fowl and plantains, much cheaper than could be purchased at Jamaica,

> . . . but dear enough of all conscience . . . if we did not get some Prize Money the Sea Officers on this station must ruin themselves as every article they purchase costs about four times the price they do in England. This last cruise will pay me better than any one I ever made on the home station but I shall not be able to remit a sixpence to England, it will all go here, I hope it will cover my expenses while on the station, that is all I expect of it.

On 30 August they stopped and seized a Spanish merchantman carrying thirty cases of 'Lady's Sigarrs', 500 dollars and a small parcel of indigo. She was of only little value, and Moore doubted that her sale would even cover the expenses involved. After some hesitation, he put a quartermaster and five men on board and sent her in to Jamaica, but could not help remarking that, 'I wish we had not seen her'. As they were now on the edge of their cruising ground, Moore was reminded once again of the long distance between their position and their base. This was going to be problematic when it came to sending in prizes, as he was already very short of Midshipmen. There was little chance of getting them back from Port Royal before the end of the cruise and, on top of this, there was always the danger that the prize and crew could be lost through shipwreck or recapture, which '. . . cuts up our ship's company terribly'. The Juno had already lost twelve men in a prize which had disappeared after they had sent her in.

Another problem was fever, which had broken out on both ships. The Juno had already lost seven men since leaving Port Royal and within less than two weeks she lost six more. Although Moore had been able to supplement her crew with three of seven men he pressed out of an American privateer, he was becoming anxious about the effect the Juno's losses were having on the morale of her crew: 'A great despondency pervades the ship's company, as soon as a man is taken ill he gives himself up.' It was almost with some apology that Moore recorded an ailment of his own:

> I have been grievously tormented by a whitlow on my fore finger, which by the unskilful treatment of the Surgeon's Mate (the Surgeon being ill)

206

I was afraid I should have lost, it is, however, now in a fair way and I hope soon to have the entire use of it.

By 26 September the two frigates had been on station for two weeks without seeing another vessel, but at least the fever seemed to be abating. Although the *Juno* had lost another man, the *Melampus* had lost no men and Moore wondered if this was because

> . . . *the Surgeon of the* Melampus *gives them great quantities of Calomel, which in general brings on salivation, after the fever is over.*

When at last the two frigates did sight a strange sail, it turned out, after a chase, to be an American vessel. Although disappointed, Moore was pleased to hear from the American Master that the English frigate *Seine*, commanded by Captain David Milne, had captured the French frigate *Vengeance* in the Mona Passage off St Domingo,

> . . . *after a handsome action, in which the* Seine *had one Lieutenant and 12 men killed and 29 men wounded. She had carried the* Vengeance *into Jamaica.*[104]

The next day, Moore's luck changed, but not without difficulty and cost. On the morning of 30 August, the two frigates sighted another English frigate in chase of a schooner. The frigate was identified as the *Retribution* (formerly the infamous frigate *Hermione*)[105], and Moore and Dundas joined in the chase. The *Melampus*, being the best sailor of the three, soon sped ahead and when the wind dropped,

> *I made the signal for the Boats manned and armed to chase her. Some hours after dark when the Schooner was within random shot of the* Melampus, *being the headmost of the three ships* [we] *ran aground and stuck fast, I instantly made the signal to the other ships to avoid the danger and ordered Captn Dundas to anchor the* Juno *in a convenient position for the* Melampus *to heave off by her. Almost at the same instant that the* Melampus *struck, the schooner ran aground and was attacked by the boats. The* Juno's *boat in which Mr Burns, the 1st Lieutenant was, not waiting for the other boats, ran on board the schooner in spite of a heavy fire of grape and musketry, he was almost instantly killed with 2 of the seamen and several others being wounded the boat was beat off in great confusion just as the* Melampus's *barge and cutter got along side, but on seeing the fate of the* Juno's *boat they hauled off along with her. Altho I saw by the firing that the boats were vigorously opposed yet I could not spare any more boats to assist them*

in a second attack until the Melampus *could be hove off, I therefore sent to Lieutenant Handfield[106] to desire him to watch her motions with the boats he had and not to run any risk unless she attempted to get off until I could send the Launches to his assistance. In the mean time by great exertion the* Melampus *was hove off the bank, but by this time it was near daylight and the schooner had got off and endeavoured to make off along shore to the Eastward* [of Cape Catouche]. *We made signals to the boats and they followed her along shore until after day light when they boarded her without meeting any further resistance. She proved to be a Government vessel called the* Aquila *from the Havana bound to* Campeachy *mounting 14 brass 10 pounders and manned with 100 men commanded by a Lieutenant de Frigate carrying the New Governor of the province of Yucatan and his suite. She had jettisoned all but three guns, had boarding netting all round and was completely fitted with small arms and pikes.*

Had lieutenant Burns made his attack jointly with the other boats, three in number, that were near him I am convinced they would have carried the schooner but hurried on by the impetuosity of his character he passed the other boats with his sail set and attempted to throw himself on board in spite of the boarding netting and the formidable opposition which he might have expected. He was a good seaman and a very daring gallant fellow. One of the Melampus's *Bargemen was wounded in the arm by a boarding pike, the schooner had one man killed and two or three wounded.*

Two days later they had more luck, capturing an armed brig called the *San Joseph* which was armed with ten 6-pounder guns, and carried fifty men. Although she was carrying a cargo, it was apparently not a very valuable one. Moore put one of the *Melampus'* lieutenants on board with ten seamen. The two frigates were now considerably burdened with prisoners who were, once again, making considerable inroads into the frigates' limited provisions. Moore decided to land most of these at Silan, retaining only those officers whose testimonies would be required for the Prize Court back at Port Royal.

Some nights later the *Melampus* gave chase to another schooner near the notorious Baio Nuevo shoal. Moore positioned men on both the fore yard and jib boom end, and with their help they were able to avoid running aground on the shoal, but they had several close shaves;

This bank . . . is I think as dangerous a one as I ever saw and we had a very narrow escape indeed of being lost upon it.

Despite these efforts the chase escaped. Moore was now once again faced with the inevitable shortage of provisions, and had only one month's supply of water left. To crown it all, and partly as a consequence, scurvy had made its appearance among the crew. Moore too was suffering, for through the incompetence of the frigate's surgeon's Mate, the surgery on the whitlow on his hand had become infected and he was now carrying one arm in a sling. Members of the crew had also begun to suffer from accidents. One of the ship's carpenters whilst using an adze, had managed to cut both an artery and his Achilles tendon. The surgeon

> . . . took up the artery and although he was in great fear of a locked jaw, or at least of the poor fellow losing his leg, he is now out of danger.

Also

> . . . a remarkable fine young fellow, a Forecastle man, the handsomest man in the ship, fell from the fore yard arm down upon deck, and although no bones were broke nor had he received much external injury, he was so terribly shook that after lying on his back in great pain for ten days he died.

By this time, Moore was leading his small squadron back towards Jamaica, which he expected to see on 2 November. The *Aquila* had to be taken in tow, having sprung both her main mast and the head of her foremast. Fortunately, the squadron reached Jamaica without further mishap or delay. After less than three weeks, Moore was ordered to return to the same station. The *Melampus* sailed in an unhappy condition, for the stay in port had resulted in considerable sickness on board. To make matters worse, the frigate's marines had been taken off by the Commander-in-Chief to help secure the island of Curacoa, which had surrendered to Captain Watkins in the frigate *Nereide*.[107] These had been replaced by an officer and ten men from the 20th Light Dragoons, who had all been ill and were considered to be in need of a sea voyage to aid their recovery.

Two days from port, the *Melampus* came upon a schooner which had been totally abandoned, and stripped of rudder, sails and anything which could be removed. The boarding party found that there had been an unsuccessful attempt to scuttle her, but she had obviously remained afloat. As she was of only limited value as a prize, Moore towed her to Grand Cayman where he quietly sold her to a Mr Bodden for £100 sterling. There also the crew of the *Melampus* was able to catch large quantities of fish, especially rock cod, which helped supplement their diet, and they were soon showing a general improvement in their health.

Moore cruised for ten days without seeing anything and then turned south towards Vera Cruz, where he fell in with the frigate *Cleopatra*, commanded by Captain Israel Pellew[108]. She had escorted a convoy from Halifax to Jamaica and Pellew had taken the chance of a quick cruise to the south in the hope of taking something before sailing back to Halifax. The two frigates parted the following day, but to Moore's annoyance, the *Cleopatra* kept appearing in the distance. He wished her gone because her presence was causing confusion and, if she ventured too near Vera Cruz, she would raise the alarm and prevent any vessels leaving that port.

Nevertheless, two days later, the *Melampus* sighted and gave chase to a brig. The pursuit continued throughout the night, as there was a bright moon, and Moore was able to watch the brig with his night glass from the frigate's maintop. Just before dawn, he ordered several shot fired from the bow chasers and the ship brought to and struck. She proved to be a letter-of-marque from Cadiz carrying a very valuable cargo of various merchandise to Vera Cruz. Moore took no chances, and put a prize crew of eighteen men, plus his Third Lieutenant and two midshipmen on board, and took off all of the Spanish crew. While the frigate's boats were busy shuttling back and forth with prisoners and provisions, another sail was seen to windward. Moore hastily recalled the boats and set off in chase. Before nightfall he had captured another letter-of-marque, this time from Corunna, carrying bar iron, paper and other cargo. She was named the *Falcon* and her crew had hove her guns and anchors overboard in their attempt to escape. Moore put his Second Lieutenant and eighteen men on board.

The *Melampus* now had 100 Spanish prisoners on board, and as usual they were causing Moore some concerns;

We suffer more inconvenience here from Prisoners than we used to on the home station, as I do not like to put them below and it is by no means so safe to keep them upon deck as we do.

With two valuable prizes, Moore decided to escort both ships back to Port Royal:

If these two Prizes arrive safe at Jamaica, I shall be as rich as I ought to be as I think I must share at least £8,000 sterling, which added to what I have in the funds will make at least £19,000.

210

This was the equivalent to 130 years' pay – or, at modern-day values, Moore was gleefully looking forward to a cool £573,420 – a very respectable sum indeed. By 15 January 1801, however, the three ships were still struggling back towards Port Royal and were making painfully slow progress. Moore had always had problems navigating in the Caribbean, where he was inexperienced in the effect of the various currents and tides. They were also beset by contrary winds, which made it very difficult to calculate their position, so Moore was delighted, when at 2pm on 22 January the lookouts sighted Grand Cayman, and he discovered that his calculations were only twenty miles out. On the following day they sighted Jamaica, having towed the Corunna ship 350 leagues against continual easterly winds and a strong lee current. That night, Moore celebrated, putting the crew back on their full allowance of food and drink – for they had been reduced to half rations, in spite of which they were in excellent health and spirits; Moore's only worry was the inevitable orgy of drunkenness at Port Royal.

The *Melampus* anchored at Port Royal on 31 January. The prizes were immediately dispatched to the Prize Agent at Kingston, and Moore collected what must have been a sizeable package of mail. There were letters from home and other news from England. Brother John was being sent with General Abercrombie's expedition to Egypt. The Russians had seized British ships in Russian ports, and it was widely expected that this would lead to hostilities with the northern powers.[109] Moore read the circumstances and was resolute:

We must never give up the right of searching Neutral vessels for Enemy's property, if we do we give up one of the most important advantages of our Naval superiority.

Moore also appears to have received a copy of his friend James Currie's four-volume edition of the works of Robert Burns.[110] Moore, of course, worshipped Burns' poetry and was full of praise for Currie's work:

I have not seen anything this long time to please me like his excellent performance. The accounts of the Scotch peasantry is to me quite an original work and the criticisms on the genius and writings of Burns are as honourable to the taste and judgement of Currie as they are just to the merits of that genuine and sublime Poet of Nature. Among the letters to and from Burns there are many well worth the pains which that friend to Genius and true Philanthropist has bestowed in culling

211

and bring them forth to view. I was particularly pleased with a letter from Tytler to Burns containing a very judicious criticism on Tam O' Shanter.

At Port Royal, Moore also found his fellow officers disenchanted with their new Commander-In-Chief:

I find that the Admiral has contrived to disgust every one of the Captains more or less by his manner of carrying on the duty; without enquiring into the state of preparation the ships may be in, he suddenly gives out an order which may and often does derange all the detail of arrangement, throws everything into confusion and jades and harasses the officers and Ships Companies so as even to endanger their health by the want of comfort which they experience amidst the inevitable dirt and lumber . . . The fact is that he wishes to be smart but does not seem to put the proper confidence in the Captains, whom it would be much better were he to consult before he ordered their ships to sail instantly.

Moore soon found himself the subject of the Admiral's hasty orders, but although he found it exceedingly irritating, he kept quiet. Perhaps this response was rewarded, for Seymour issued him with sealed orders to sail back to the Gulf of Mexico and, if he fell in with the frigates *Apollo*, *Acasta* and *Amphion*, to take them under his command and cruise as long as their provisions lasted. Moore sailed again with officers and men of the 20th Light Dragoons instead of his marines, but now his experience had given him a higher opinion of them. His cabin was also providing accommodation to a rather sickly Mr Cooke, a creole, whom Moore, much against his inclination, had been persuaded to take to sea for the benefit of his health. On 27 February, off Grand Cayman once again, the *Melampus* hove to when a boat put off from the island, which proved to be carrying Lieutenant Spence of the 74-gun ship *Thunderer*. The *Thunderer* had captured a slave ship bound for Havana, and had sent her with a prize crew to Jamaica. Unfortunately the prize ship[111] ran aground on the Grand Cayman and was wrecked. Spence had managed to get the crew and slaves ashore and now wanted to hire a ship to get them all back to Jamaica. The problem was that the shipowners of Cayman were demanding one third of the slaves in lieu of salvage, having brought them from the shipwreck. At Spence's request, Moore intervened, pointing out to the merchants at Cayman that the Lieutenant had no authority to make a decision about rights of salvage, and advised them to allow him to carry out his orders. However, he was clearly reluctant to jeopardize his own cruising prospects by doing much more than this to assist. Fortunately, several days later, Moore fell in with the frigate *Lowestofte*, which was making her way back to Jamaica, and her Captain, Robert Plampin, agreed to sail for Cayman to help Spence.

On 4 March, the *Melampus'* gunner, Alexander Downie, died from a bilious fever. Moore, always affected by the loss of members of his crew, was particularly saddened in this case:

He was a fine old seaman, a native of Dunbar and, most deservedly, a very great favourite of mine. He has left a widow and three children to be provided for, the rest of his family have been long married and off his hands, the two eldest boys are with me in the ship and the Mother has only one boy, the youngest of all, living with her near Plymouth. I think this hardy old seaman was as good a life as any in the ship. He was of a strong and active make, temperate and inured from his infancy to all the hardships of the Coasting trade and the Greenland Whale Fishery. He was about fifty years of age, had been prest on board the Edgar last war[112] when commanded by the present Admiral Elliot. He served as Captain of that ship's Fore Castle until the Peace when he returned to his wife at Dunbar, and continued in the Greenland trade from that port until his old ship-mate Captain Durham was appointed to the Hind frigate. He entered there and served as a Quarter Master until by Durham's recommendation he was made a Gunner. Durham afterwards recommended him to me. He was then in a sloop of war in Ordinary at Plymouth, on my application to the Admiralty he was appointed Gunner of the Melampus in the latter end of the year 1797 and has served ever since with zeal and fidelity, proving himself a brave and honest man and a thorough bred and complete seaman. He is a real loss to the ship.

The following day the frigate was becalmed off the Sisal Bank, and the crew occupied themselves catching groupers with great rapidity. Moore returned again to the subject of old Downie, and in doing so made some interesting observations about the crew generally:

My soul is sad for the loss of my worthy old Downie; of his two sons who are with me, one is only eleven years of age; the other is a fine lad about 16 and one of my best Midshipmen. Fortunately the old man had saved a handsome sum of his Prize Money, the interest of which with the Widow's Pension will I hope enable her to live comfortably with the youngest boy and keep him still at school. Alexander Downie was a specimen of the most respectable of the common Scotch Seamen, with

213

the disadvantage of having less education than many of them have, his did not extend much beyond reading his Bible in which he was well grounded. He was sober, temperate, handy as a Norwegian, active in mind and body, tenacious of reputation well earned as his was, most respectful to his officers, but although anxious to secure the esteem of his captain he was the reverse of a time server or an eye servant. I am not sure whether or not this description of Sailor is superior to the best of the English, but I am sure they are invaluable in a ship and may be depended upon in the hour of peril. I like to have a mixture of Scotch, English and Welch, nor do I object to a few young Irish, who give a turn for fun and a degree of mischief which when kept within due bounds has no bad effect, but gives a degree of life and jocularity that chases the Daemon of Ennui. I do not admire the Prussian discipline when applied to British seamen nor indeed to any men. Discipline is essential but a Discipline consistent with the local circumstances with National character with good sense and humanity. Let it always be remembered that we have Seamen ready made and that it is not in a Man of War that the best of them are formed. In this the navy and Army differ materially, you may make a good private soldier in six months but a sailor must have served five or six years in a merchant ship before he can be deemed an Able Seaman, and even then he has much to learn. There is something in the nature of a Seaman's profession which many men of superior endowments never acquire and which many comparatively dull men frequently excel in. This is what the French call gros Manoeuvre and what very few of the French Navy officers of the old regime knew anything at all about. They affected indeed to despise it, which men often wish to do when they find those whom they deem their inferiors more perfect in an art than themselves. The superior skill, however, in practical seamanship is one of the causes of the unrivalled eminence which the British Navy has attained, and I should be very sorry to see any more relaxation in the strictness of our young Midshipmen's time of probation.

By 8 March, Moore had fallen in with the frigate *Amphion*, and was cruising some twenty leagues from Vera Cruz. There had been no sign of either the *Apollo* or the *Acasta*, and he considered that they must have left the ground by this time. Moore was also becoming distinctly uncomfortable about his sickly guest for, far from showing any signs of recovery, the man was obviously getting worse:

. . . it is a most distressing spectacle to have constantly under my eye and what I will not expose myself to again unless I am closely connected

214

or deeply interested in the person. It is too much for any man to ask another to do.

Despite his frequent complaints about social isolation, Moore was the sort of romantic who actually enjoyed a degree of solitude. He was, therefore, far from happy to have this solace disturbed so upsettingly by a man of whom he knew little and with whom he could do less. In the privacy of his journal, Moore was brutally honest:

He is indeed in so truly pitiable a state that I most earnestly wish him dead, being almost constantly in a delirium and often apparently in a state of great pain.

By contrast, with one exception, the crew of the *Melampus* was all in good health.

Moore had formed a good opinion of Captain Richard Bennet of the *Amphion*, and the two Captains had written out an instrument stating their mutual agreement to share prizes until noon on 1 May.[113] As part of this admiration, Moore approved of the state of Bennet's frigate:

The Amphion *sails very well seems to be in excellent order and is a very good cruiser, she takes her station just where I would wish her to be in the day time and takes care to close at sun set to avoid the risk of separation. I have good hopes of doing something in such a favourable cruising ground and with so able a second.*

Nevertheless, the night after Moore wrote this appreciation, the *Amphion* went missing. Moore shone lights and fired a rocket to attract her attention, but at dawn the frigate was nowhere to be seen. This didn't inhibit the *Melampus* from capturing enemy vessels. On 15 March, Moore captured a Spanish snow, in ballast from Vera Cruz. As she was of little value and he didn't want to be lumbered with twenty-four prisoners of war, he decided to let her go. On the following day he captured the Spanish brig *Nostia Senora de la Conception* laden with sugar, flour and soap. This time, the prize was worth keeping and he sent her back to Jamaica with a mate and ten men on board. On 25 March, Moore sent boats in to cut out a felucca, which was taken without resistance. She proved to be from Cadiz carrying dry goods and wine, and Moore decided that she might prove to be a valuable prize because, according to the ship's papers, the cargo had cost more than 35,000 dollars in Cadiz. He put a mate and eight seamen on board and sent her back to Jamaica.

Moore's ailing guest finally expired towards the end of March. The surgeon was of the opinion that the man had suffered an abscess of the intestines,

> ... and he was so putrid before he breathed his last that we threw him overboard an hour afterwards for fear of infection. He has left a very fine black boy who was his slave, and who performed the duty of a Nurse to him most faithfully, as the Master frequently mentioned to me his wish that the Boy should be free after his death, I shall most certainly do all I can to procure his freedom for him.

Whilst his guest was failing so dreadfully, Moore had become increasingly troubled by an ailment of his own: rheumatism. On consulting the surgeon, he was surprised to be told that it was not at all rare on the West Indies Station, and that men were often invalided home with it.

Of the *Amphion* there was still no sign and Moore began to suspect that she might have taken a valuable prize which she thought best to escort back to Jamaica. Meanwhile, Moore's leisure reading led him to reflect on the fictional portrayal of the seaman. There is, he observed,

> ... a very common fault with writers of Romance but which I think Fielding, Smollett and my Father are free from. Trunnion, Jack Hatchway and Pipes are all English seamen, but they are described as different men and all their speeches and actions mark this difference. Tom Bowling is another seaman, perhaps the best portrait, he is as true to the character as the others and quite as original. It is a pity that Smollett allowed his humour to run wild, and to outré as he has done, Trunnion. The turning to windward is too ridiculous and perhaps the garrison is too highly coloured – but these are venial sins and his seamen are admirably drawn characters, and he is the only writer who has hit off to the life an English Sailor.

He turned from his critique of literary characters, to that of real contemporaries:

> The most interesting character at present in Europe is Bonaparte. I think his situation on the whole more out of the common track than any almost since the time of Julius Caesar, whose elevation is certainly less to be wondered at. He is a character that stands alone. I know not whether certain meannesses attributed to him early in his career are true, or if Sir Sidney Smith has as much reason to think ill of his moral

character as he supposes, but I own I am of opinion that, so inconsistent is man, he may have acted as a Rogue notwithstanding the splendid role he has since supported ... I believe Bonaparte is a far more uncommon character than Dumourier [was] yet I am not at all convinced that Fortune followed up by the most ardent ambition and daring courage may not, aided by peculiarly favourable circumstances have naturally led Bonaparte to his present situation. This to be sure may be said of Julius Caesar, Alexander and Cromwell ...

By chance, on 2 April, Moore received news of the missing *Amphion* when he spoke to a licensed Spanish brig, which reported that it had been boarded by a party from the *Amphion* on the previous day. At that time she had a prize in company, a brig laden with sugar. A week later, the *Melampus* sighted another vessel and had to fire a lot of shot at her before she brought to. The vessel proved to be another licenced schooner bound for Vera Cruz. On 9 April, the lookouts reported an English frigate approaching, and the *Melampus* was at last joined by one of her wayward squadron, the *Acasta*. Her Captain, Edward Fellowes, was rowed across to the *Melampus*, only to find Moore in some discomfort. His rheumatism had gradually become worse over the preceding weeks, preventing him from sleeping and generally making him feel wretched. Fellowes brought with him the latest news from Port Royal and Europe, where Admiral Hyde Parker had been appointed Commander-in-Chief of the North Sea and was to lead a force into the Baltic against the Armed Neutrality. There were also new orders for the commanders of British men-of-war to seize all Russian, Danish and Norwegian ships. Moore observed, ruefully, that by the time these orders had reached him, the English Channel ports would be well stocked with prize Danish and Norwegian vessels.

On 14 April, signals broke out on the *Acasta*'s signal halyard, reporting a strange sail in the WSW and she immediately dashed away in that direction, though Moore's lookouts could see nothing. Moore followed, slightly perplexed, in case Fellowes should need his support, but the *Acasta* had vanished. Two days later she reappeared with a prize brig in company. The *Melampus*' Third Lieutenant, Phillip Handfield was put in charge of her and Moore decided to turn back for Port Royal.

On the voyage back, however, the prize disappeared near the Isle of Pines,[114] just south of Cuba. The *Melampus* sailed into Port Royal on 18 May with Moore in considerable discomfort from rheumatism, and an inflammation of the eyes. Later the same day the prize arrived having beaten off an attack by a privateer after an action lasting two and a half hours. The privateer had been carrying three guns, which she fought on one side only, but was full of men;

This action I fear has cost us one good man dangerously wounded in the thigh; another of the Melampus's *was slightly wounded. Lieutenant Handfield has done himself great honor by the brave defence he made and when it is considered that he had only 13 men besides himself, a young midshipman and his servant, a mere boy, to fight his six guns, it is evident that a very gallant and firm conduct on his part could have alone enabled him to succeed against so great a disparity of strength. He speaks in the strongest terms of the spirit and determined valour of the seamen, five of whom belonged to the Acasta.*

The *Melampus* sailed again from Port Royal on 4 June, but her commander was now in poor health. His rheumatism was continual and what he described as *'a film'* was growing over his right eye. By the time they stopped at Grand Cayman to purchase fresh provisions on their way back to the Gulf of Mexico, he was describing himself as *'quite an invalid'*. He resolved that if his eye did not improve by the next time he returned to Port Royal, he would ask to be invalided home. But he was not the only person with troubles. On the 16th, they fell in with the 20-gun post ship *Tisiphone*, commanded by Acting Captain John Hayes.[115] Hayes had sent a boat in chase of a strange vessel and both had disappeared. He was now searching for the missing men, whom he thought might have been heading for Loggerhead Quay in the hope of meeting him. Unfortunately, strong currents had prevented him from getting there and he was concerned about their safety.

An even greater problem had befallen the British frigate *Meleager*, which was cruising in the Gulf or Bay of Campeche, just west of the Yucatan Peninsula. The first that Moore learned of this was when he fell in with a 28-gun Spanish frigate and a schooner, which were flying flags of truce. Moore approached to speak to the vessels and a boat from the Spanish frigate brought over an English Lieutenant and Midshipman from the *Meleager*. They explained that the Spanish ships were en route from Vera Cruz to the Triangles Shoal to rescue the remaining officers and crew of the British frigate. The *Meleager*, commanded by Captain The Honourable Thomas Bladen Capel, youngest son of the Earl of Essex, had run aground on the Shoal due to an error in the charts the ship was carrying. The ship bilged and Capel and his officers managed to transfer everyone to a nearby island before setting fire to the ship. The two officers had been sent to Vera Cruz to seek help and the Spanish ships were on their way to rescue them. Capel had already offered, on behalf of his officers and crew, to surrender themselves as prisoners of war. Arriving at the Triangles Shoal on 24 June, they found the island abandoned. Moore guessed that the people had been picked up several days earlier by the *Apollo*.[116] The wreck of the *Meleager* was still visible though:

> The wreck of the ship was burnt to the water's edge and the masts were still burning when our boat went on shore. They had built a large flat boat sufficient to have carried them all down to Vera Cruz which they left off the Key.

As the rest of the crew had gone, the Spanish Captain rather nobly acceded to Moore's suggestion that he might consider releasing the Lieutenant and Midshipman. Understandably, Moore was very impressed by this honourable gesture, and the two erstwhile enemy commanders parted amidst a shower of mutual compliments.

The incident, however, provided a lighter moment of relief to Moore. The problem with his eye seemed to be no worse, but he was in increasing pain from rheumatism which had spread around his shoulders and into his breast: '*It will be a most painful thing to me to be obliged to give up the* Melampus, *but I much fear this Rheumatism will force me to change the climate before I am too much reduced.*' His depression was not helped by an apparent lack of enemy shipping on the cruising ground:

> We begin to despond but certainly without reason. Whenever we take a prize it gives a fill up to all on board and they expect to take another every day. The only circumstance which really annoys me is my eternal Rheumatism, yet when I was in perfect health I always provided myself with some other paramount grievance. I have been reading the Mysteries of Udolpho[117], certainly an excellent novel, the work of a woman of genius, the great fault is, in my opinion, that she repeats the picturesque descriptions of Nature until she fairly satiates the reader with what at first delighted and would continue to delight him, if served out in moderation. . . . She often drew delicious tears from my eyes. But there is too much Mystery.

Despite the sublime delights of *Udolpho*, Moore's overall gloom was increasing. Three weeks passed and the only enemy vessel sighted was

219

a small schooner, which escaped. Moore began to feel like simply giving up:

> *I have been strongly tempted to make the best of my way to Port Royal and there give up the ship and return to England for the benefit of my health, but I still try to hold out.*

Officers and crew were somewhat cheered on 15 July when they stopped a brig from Liverpool which handed over newspapers carrying reports that Lord Nelson had attacked the Danish Fleet in Copenhagen roads,

> *... and after a very severe fight, had taken every ship that was there, amounting to upwards of 20 vessels or war including several ships of the line and a great many Frigates.*

Also

> *That the Emperor Paul had died of an apoplexy and has been succeeded by his son . . . that an ambassador was gone from England to Petersburgh to endeavour to conciliate the new Emperor and conclude a peace. That Sir Ralph Abercrombie had landed at Aboukir beaten the French and taken Alexandria.*

Moore surveyed these developments with near astonishment, adding,

> *If all this is true I think the Northern confederacy must be broken up, and that a general peace will be the result.*

The day after receiving this news, the *Melampus* gave chase to a schooner that took shelter in shallow water near Point Delgada. Moore sent in the ship's boats to cut her out, but before they could do so, she bilged. Denied of even this prize, Moore came to a decision. This would have to be his last cruise in the West Indies;

> *It is a painful prospect for me that of being forced to give up the Melampus in this country, we have been on the whole so healthy that, with the very little pressing that we have had, the ship is I think better manned than she has ever been since I have commanded her which is now five years. I think no enemy's frigate could stand us an hour's close action barring extraordinary accidents, but I must not trifle with my health, I hope to be useful to my friends and to my country and my wearing out my stamina here could serve neither. I do believe it will be a melancholy day among the crew if I am forced to leave them.*

By 19 August, the *Melampus* was very short of provisions, and Moore was in such pain that, to get any sleep, he was having to resort to opium

> *. . . a medicine which I have recourse to very unwillingly. Within these three weeks I have received some benefit from Bark and Chalybeate wine which the Surgeon has great faith in and which I think has been of service to my digestive faculties; but I am crippled with rheumatism in my breast, left arm, shoulder and neck. I must go to England by Hook or by Crook to save my shaken constitution. I give up a great deal if I give up the ship.*

On 1 September, the *Melampus* finally arrived at Port Royal, and a defeated Graham Moore made his painful way to the Admiral's office;

> *When I waited on the admiral and he saw the state of body I was reduced to, he asked what I intended to do, I told him if the* Melampus *did not go to England very soon or if I could not effect an exchange into some ship that was going I must request that he would order a survey to be held on me, as I was really incapable of doing my duty in the state I had been in for these last seven months. He said there was no intention of sending the* Melampus *to England, but he thought I would be very imprudent if I neglected the opportunity of going to England in the* Amphion, *Capt Bennet, which was to sail on the 7th. I was surveyed two days ago . . . and declared unserviceable in this country.*

He returned to the *Melampus* to pack his belongings and make his farewells;

> *I was so affected in taking leave of the* Melampus *ship's company which I had commanded for upwards of five years that I burst into tears while addressing them, and when I recovered myself I saw many of them as much affected as myself. One of the Admiral's Lieutenants has an Order to command the* Melampus *until the arrival of Captn Gossellin of the* Syren *now at sea, and whom the admiral has appointed to succeed me.*

That same day he boarded the *Amphion*, and on 7 September she sailed for England. The misery he felt at leaving his frigate was eased a little on the voyage home:

> *We have a very agreeable party in the* Amphion's *cabin of two captains of frigates who have lost their ships, besides a gentleman returning to*

England after many years residence in Jamaica where he has made a very handsome fortune. Since I have been relieved from all charge I find my situation more comfortable, I was before continually on the fret from having duties to perform which my bad health rendered me unequal to . . . I wish to God we may find peace on the eve of being concluded when we get to England; at all events I shall not be able to serve before the Spring.

13

Interregnum
(October 1801 – June 1803)

Moore's return journey to England was not altogether comfortable. The *Amphion* departed Port Royal some thirty tons short of water, and with 180 supernumeraries on board, so the cleanly-minded Moore found the need to economize '. . . *by no means agreeable*'. On passage they managed to speak to an American brig that gave them news of Lord Nelson's attack on the gunboats at Boulogne. Moore listened to the details and concluded that this action

> . . . *was, as far as I can judge with the imperfect information we have, rash, fool hardy, and if followed up, will prove a ruinous exposure of the lives of our invaluable seamen without an adequate object in the event of the fullest success, to justify the risk. If they had succeeded – What is the loss of 18 or 20 Gun Boats or Flats?*[118]

Six weeks from Port Royal, the *Amphion* entered the English Channel. Moore noticed the change in temperature, and although he was still tormented by rheumatism, he thought the change of climate was making him feel generally better. By the time that they anchored at Spithead on 21 October, they had heard the news that Preliminary Articles of Peace had been signed with the French. With very little delay, Moore set off for Richmond where he received attentive care from both his parents. The cooler English climate certainly seemed to be relieving his ailment; and his mental state was certainly raised on 10 November when his beloved brother John arrived from Egypt, with '. . . *the wound in his leg quite healed up and only requires a little time and exercise to become as strong as ever*'.

Whilst Moore's rheumatism seemed to be improving, he had developed another eye inflammation. Before this became so bad that he was unable to read, he had nearly been persuaded by James Currie to

223

purchase the estate of Craigieburn, just north-east of Moffat in Dumfries. The area appealed to Moore's romantic sensibilities as Robert Burns had stayed at Craigieburn House and the area was closely associated with him. Besides,

I am pleased with the idea of possessing a beautiful romantic spot where I may retire if I chuse, and that spot being in my native country and not more than 50 miles from where I was born.

However, he waited too long to put in his offer and the estate was bought by another.

Although technically 'on the beach', Moore was still keeping a close eye on naval matters. Just before Christmas 1801, the seamen in Admiral Mitchell's squadron at Bantry Bay mutinied. Moore was not surprised. He could well sympathize with the seamen, most of whom were pressed men. Now that the hostilities were over they wanted to go home, and they certainly wouldn't want to be sent to distant foreign stations. But Moore could also see the other side of the argument. There were still deep suspicions about Bonaparte's motives. The French were preparing to send a large force to St Domingo, and this necessitated sending precautionary reinforcements to the British colony at Jamaica, which would be difficult if naval manpower simply melted away. The problem was partly resolved when part of Saumarez's squadron was detached and sent to the West Indies. At home, the mutiny was suppressed and, in the middle of January 1802, thirteen of the mutineers were hanged after a trial at Spithead.

A month later, Moore was still at Richmond, suffering from his debilities. His brother John had been sent to train troops near Brighthelmstone (Brighton), and Graham planned to go with him '. . . *for a change of air as well as for the advantage of bathing*'. Unfortunately, the plans had to be abandoned as Dr Moore was suddenly taken very ill. Moore watched anxiously;

My Father's disease draws to a crisis, he has been two days confined to his bed. We have not a shadow of hope of his recovery and are now only anxious that he may not suffer.

It was nearly three weeks before Moore made the next, solemn entry in his journal:

On the 21st day of February in the morning my Father died. His disease is supposed to have been seated in the heart which occasioned a diffi-culty of breathing. He was apparently in a state of insensibility for the

last 20 hours before he expired, but while he was sensible he expressed himself in a calm and firm manner, convinced of the existence of an all ruling Providence, and in the hope of a future life. He was cheered in these awful moments by the reflections on his past life, the prosperity of his family and the love they bore each other. He has finished his course honourably and well.

With his father now buried, Moore was at liberty to join his brother at Brighthelmstone. He spent nearly a month there, taking warm salt water baths, but these did nothing to relieve his rheumatic symptoms. On the contrary, he began to feel that the rheumatism had got worse, causing him pains in the head, and by the end of April he decided that he would have to leave the town, for he was finding both the society and landscape of the area quite depressing:

The country is quite open, scarce a bush to be seen and the white chalky road is very distressing to the eyes. The sea is an agreeable object in fine weather and it is not unpleasant to gallop over the Downs, but the crowd of idle people . . . pacing over the same ground eternally, and the want of variety in the scenery is very tiresome.

Moore left Brighton on 3 May, stopping that night with the Lockes at Norbury Park in Surrey[119], and arriving back at Richmond on the following day. As Brighton had done little to relieve his ailment, friends now pressed him to try the waters at Cheltenham, '. . . *a place much resorted to by those whose constitutions have been injured by warm climates*'. However, he was sceptical that this would do anything to help.

Despite chronic headaches, and an eye infection that was exacerbated by reading or writing, Moore followed with close interest the ongoing parliamentary debates on the country's relationship with France. The opposition in parliament, led by Lord Grenville and Windham, persisted in calling for a renewal of the war against Jacobinism, and the restoration of the Bourbon monarchy. As far as Moore was concerned, a lot of energy was being expended in pointless arguing; the French were still a mighty power and energy in Britain would be better directed to restoring her own commercial and military strength. At the same time, he found himself, like many others, increasingly mesmerized by Bonaparte:

France seems to be rapidly sinking into Monarchy again with this difference that the Monarch instead of being the weak effeminate offspring of Hereditary dullness or imbecility, is the hardy production of

225

Temperance, nurtured by adversity, formed by education, excited by Genius and perfected by experience. Certainly the most extraordinary man of the age, the objects of whose ambition is quite unknown but whose history I believe is by no means near a close. He will rivet the attention of the World upon him while he lives and I believe his death will mark a new era in its history.

Moore resisted the pressure to try the cure at Cheltenham, but decided to go and visit his old and dear friend, James Currie, at Liverpool. Travelling by Post Chaise the journey took the best part of three days, and Moore arrived to find a changed city. His encounters at sea with Liverpool merchantmen had always impressed him with the commercial vitality of the place, but it had been fifteen years since he had last seen it, and he could not help remarking how much the city appeared to have flourished:

The society at Liverpool is not agreeable to me, but the picture which that great commercial town presents to a stranger is certainly very interesting. To a person who has no occupation there the residence of Liverpool cannot be very accommodating as all the inhabitants are busily engaged in their commercial affairs and an idle man is, of course, left entirely to himself for the whole day, but he may pass his evening better as the inhabitants are certainly very hospitable and much given to expensive entertainment.

Moore arrived in good spirits, feeling that in some way the journey had been beneficial for his constitution but he found his friend in poor health. Currie easily persuaded Moore to accompany him to Buxton where he wished to take the benefit of the mineral water baths. The next day the two men travelled to Buxton and took rooms at St Ann's Hotel in the Crescent. Frustratingly for Moore, the weather was bad and it rained incessantly for the first few days so that he was able to see little of the countryside. When at last the rain eased, Moore rode to Chee Tor,

. . . a perpendicular rock in a most beautiful valley clothed with trees and shrubs through which the Wye, a rivulet here, runs in a beautiful, picturesque, winding way, on its course to join the Derwent.

Although they had planned to stay for just three weeks, the visit extended into July, and then into August, for Moore's desire to leave the place had suddenly evaporated:

There is a person here who has given a charm to the place, and it will now require some resolution in me to leave it.

Nevertheless, on 16 August, the two men returned to Liverpool, though Moore was cursing himself all the way for leaving. He stayed a week at Liverpool, in emotional turmoil. He had fallen in love once more, and chided himself for being rash and imprudent. He had no wish to sacrifice his independence in a hurry or risk his future happiness on a whim. To prove to himself that he could escape this new attachment, he decided to travel north to Scotland. He rode to Moffat, the town nearest to Craigieburn, the property that he had nearly purchased and, while he was there, he impetuously purchased a property called Heathery Haugh

> *. . . a small place, . . . situated about a mile from the village of Moffat . . . Its situation is very pretty and may be made much of, if the improvements I propose making at it are directed by the eye of taste, I am building a cottage to replace the miserable Cabins which at present disgrace the place, and my present plan is to let it by the season when complete to any person frequenting the Well who may be allured by the situation and beauty of the place.*

However, within days he was beginning to have doubts. Moore was a social animal, and there was very little 'society' in this part of Scotland. The nearest town where he thought he might find entertaining company was Dumfries, twenty-one miles away.

By 5 September, heavy autumn rain had set in, and Heathery Haugh and Moffat began to feel dismal and depressing; the romantic idyll had dissolved. Moore's loneliness had exacerbated the situation, and he found himself thinking more and more about the young woman at Buxton. Within two weeks he was on horseback and riding south through heavy rain. His only regret was the rain which '. . . *prevented me from seeing to advantage the sublime scenery of the lakes*'. Arriving at Buxton with the same impetuosity that had persuaded him to purchase Heathery Haugh, he engaged himself to the young woman. Then within a few days, he was on horseback once more, riding to Richmond. He arrived in high spirits, partly because he had completed the entire journey on horseback, '. . . *a great proof of my improved health*', and partly because he had determined to follow through his affair with the young lady at Buxton.

By the end of October, Moore's rheumatism had returned. There was gloomy national news as well, as a downturn in negotiations with France over the future of the Island of Malta caused a panic in the City of London, sharply reducing the value of stocks. Moore believed that a resumption of war was inevitable:

. . . it would be better to go to war at once before we have given up all the important conquests that have cost the country so much blood and money. I sincerely wish for peace, as, independent of all other considerations, my health is in so precarious a state that the fatigue of professional employment would knock me up and in all probability completely ruin my constitution just as Nature seems to be struggling to restore it. And at the same time I could not bear to lie by when the Country was engaged in war. I hope we shall be able to avoid it with honour.

Moore had now been out of active service for just over twelve months. It was not unusual for officers who had not been at sea for many years to be given commands, but Moore was a conscientious officer and he was always worried that he might be losing touch with the skills and knowledge essential for command at sea:

I feel already as if I had forgotten the greatest part of the detail of my profession, and as if I should be at a loss how to act if I were immediately to proceed on service.

His hope was that once he was back on board a ship, it would all come back to him, like second nature, and he would restore his own confidence in his abilities

. . . as formerly when I was esteemed an efficient Officer and gained some degree of reputation . . . and trust to my zeal and experience that I shall be able to act as becomes me when the time for action arrives.

Towards the end of the year Moore moved from the comparative tranquillity of Richmond to London where

Professional men in the Army and navy, Literary characters, idlers distinguished for wit and humour, all may be met with at this time.

However, he was anxious not to be associated with the foppish urban set:

What is called fashionable society is extremely insipid and tiresome to me. I am sometimes amused as a spectator but never as an actor in it.

228

Although Moore had not seen his new love for some time, he received letters from her and was reassured about her feelings towards him, but he had also realized that marriage would mean giving up some of the freedom and pleasures of his bachelorhood. As 1802 closed, Moore found himself pondering the causes of the war with France, and the probability of renewed hostilities:

> The boldest experiment in Politics that has ever been tried is the French Revolution, and it does not appear to me that the People at large have benefited much by the destruction of their old vicious Government, and their old errors and Prejudices. If the existing inhabitants are much happier, I believe few people will think the increase of happiness was worth the price it cost of blood and misery . . . The medium seems to me to be the best in almost everything. We must work with the tools we have . . . I see many faults in this much vaunted form of mixed Government of ours, but I have no confidence in the good effect that may be produced by their removal, for the most enlightened men see not all the results that may be produced by a great change. I by no means approve of the system of no change, but they should be put in force gently and with great caution, only removing what is immediately and grievously felt by the great body of the Nation.

Considering the current state of the navy, he foresaw trouble ahead. The war had been over for a year and yet many of the frigates and ships of the line still in commission were manned by men who had been pressed;

> The consequence is that very great discontent prevails among the ships and many partial mutinies have taken place, and although they have been quelled and the Ringleaders punished, yet the disgust to the service is increased in the hearts of Seamen who have great reason to complain of being retained in the service so long after a peace in addition to the hardships of having been impressed during the War.

The only excuse the government could have for this state of affairs arose from the difficulty of finding enough men to serve on foreign stations;

> This is very true but it is not at all satisfactory and is calculated to increase the dislike of the service in the Seamen in general as well as in those who immediately suffer.

He could not understand why, now that the government's mind was not fully occupied with the war effort, it could not turn to analysing some of the lessons from the great mutinies at Spithead and the Nore. He found it supremely ironic that even on those two occasions, the country had been saved not by the government but

> ... by a fortunate concurrence of circumstances and by the general good disposition of the seamen themselves even in the midst of the excesses they had committed. It was not owing to a relaxation of discipline that the Seamen broke out into Mutiny, it was on board the best disciplined ships that it first appeared. No, it was owing to real grievances which they had long suffered, and it is real grievances which has again occasioned all the mutinies since the Peace.

Moore was not alone in this interpretation of the cause of the mutinies of 1797, and views such as these were helping to bring in new, more sympathetic ideas about the nature of command on board men-of-war.

By March 1803, Moore was convinced that a renewal of the war was imminent. Napoleon had been using aggressive language in his addresses to the French people and his diplomatic strategy seemed to be concentrating on isolating Britain from the other continental powers. On 12 March, Moore wrote in his journal:

> Three days ago the Armament commenced, I wrote an official letter to the Admiralty offering my services,

adding rather ambiguously,

> I hope I may not be appointed to a ship, which would put me to much inconvenience and involve me in expense.

But he firmly believed there was just cause for a new war:

> It is a miserable business for France and for Europe, that after all that country has suffered in the cause of Liberty, after all the struggles and crimes of the Revolution, the whole should end in an established Military Despotism in the person of Bonaparte – a man certainly of unrivalled talents, but of boundless and insatiable ambition . . . Public opinion cannot now be known in France. There is no liberty of the Press and the People dare not discuss Politics. They are controlled by an immense Army which Bonaparte has hitherto had the art to keep in allegiance to him. . . . he depends on the Army.

For many people, the real worry was that the British government – satirically known as 'The Ministry of all the Talents' – was simply not up to the task of managing a new war. Moore also wondered about this:

There seems to be a pretty general opinion of the want of talent and energy of character of the present Ministry. They appear to be generally regarded as well meaning men of middling ability. I do not know whether or not this opinion is true, I know of no part of their conduct which has yet evinced weakness, but I wonder at their bearing so quietly in Parliament the broad hints they frequently receive to that effect.

By the middle of April 1803, there was a growing feeling that hostilities might be avoided, but the re-armament continued nevertheless. The political situation also seemed to be unstable, and there were rumours that there might be a change of administration with Pitt, Melville and others returning to power, while Addington might remain as Chancellor of the Exchequer;

I would really be sorry to see Pitt again at the Helm after he had so pitifully abandoned it, while the Country was involved in a war of his own making, on a mere pretext, for if the Catholic question was a sufficient cause for his resigning, it certainly should operate with equal force against his returning.[120]

On a more personal level, Moore's romance came to a sudden end when both Moore and his fiancée realized how much her family was against the match. Meanwhile, a different issue caught the attention of London Society: the trial of Captain James Macnamara, commander of the frigate *Cerberus*, whom Moore had known for some years,

. . . a captain in the navy of acknowledged bravery who had distinguished himself in his profession, but who was little known in the circles of fashion.

On 6 April, Macnamara killed a Colonel Montgomery, '. . . *a very fashionable young man*', in a duel at Chalk Farm, to the north of London. The duel arose from an argument which took place in Hyde Park. Macnamara's Newfoundland dog[121] had become involved in a fight with another dog belonging to Montgomery. The two men exchanged angry words resulting in a duel that same evening. Both men were wounded, but the Colonel mortally so. The coroner found a verdict of manslaughter, and Macnamara was taken into custody. The trial attracted considerable attention in the navy because, in many ways, it became a trial between a representative of the navy on one side, and of fashionable society on the other. Moore attended to support Macnamara and provide him with a character reference. It was clear that in 'Society' Montgomery was considered with favour, whilst Macnamara

> ... was represented as an Irish Duellist who never missed his mark. The cause of the quarrel was really puerile, but the parties seem to have been equally expert marksmen at 12 long paces distance, as they were both wounded at the first and only fire. Notwithstanding the charge given by the judge to bring the verdict of Manslaughter the Jury after retiring for half an hour delivered their verdict Not Guilty. They appear to me to have been actuated in this instance by an indignation against the fashionable cry.

Macnamara made an eloquent speech in his own defence, arguing that as a Gentleman and the commander of seamen he had to be fearless and resolute – and that this had meant standing up to Montgomery's assault. The speech may well have swayed the jury. So may the fact that four admirals (including Nelson), five captains, Lord Minto and General Churchill all turned out to give Macnamara supporting testimonies.[122]

Meanwhile the naval armament had been continuing, though there was considerable secrecy about certain elements of it. It was known, however, that a squadron of ships of the line was being assembled at Torbay, though most of the ships in it were short of complement. Moore observed these developments with mixed feelings. He had no great inclination to return to sea, but knew that his duty lay in that direction. However, until war was declared he thought he would bide his time;

> Why then should I sacrifice any more of my best days before honour and what I owe my country calls upon me to do? I will not. I will follow my bent while it is not unbecoming.

On 14 May, the whole of London seemed to be waiting anxiously to hear the outcome of negotiations with Bonaparte. At Richmond, Moore waited along with the rest;

> If it is for War, I immediately solicit a ship and prepare for embarking. I go to it with no alacrity but with determination. I wish for Peace.

Later that day the news came. Lord Whitworth had terminated discussions with the French. It was to be war. The next day, true to his resolution, Moore presented himself at the Admiralty, though not without some misgivings. As an experienced commander, he knew that when he did return to sea, he was almost certainly going to have to command a ship full of deeply discontented seamen. Not only those who hadn't been released from the service when peace was declared, but others who were being pressed as part of the re-armament. He truly wished that the government could consider some other means of manning ships than by impressment:

> While that violent practice is resorted to that class of men, the seamen, have much to complain of. The Country loves them and is fully sensible of their merit and of their importance, then is it not worthy the attention of Government to conciliate the affection by rendering more comfortable the lot of this meritorious but hard used body of men.

Moore, along with many other unemployed officers, waited on the First Lord, to solicit some form of employment. At least Moore was given an interview;

> He told me I was too old a captain for a frigate and that he would appoint me to a Line of Battle ship as soon as he had an opportunity. The same day, having informed myself at the Navy Office what ships were coming forward, I applied by letter to the 1st Lord for the Monarch, but in his answer he declined an engagement for an Appointment to any particular ship. Perhaps it may be some time before I get a ship.

Moore had really wanted a frigate but would not have been surprised at the outcome of his discussion with Earl St Vincent. He was over thirty-nine years of age, had been a Post Captain for ten years and had been in command of a frigate for a total of more than seven years. It was extremely rare for a captain to continue commanding a frigate when he had more than eleven years of seniority – and the great majority of captains – if they commanded frigates at all – did so for an average of four or five years. There was also a considerable number of captains applying for a much smaller number of ships, so some were bound to be disappointed. Moore's career as a frigate captain had already lasted longer than most, and both the ships and the stations to which he had been appointed, indicated that he was well favoured. Now he had to reconcile himself to disappointment, so he accepted an invitation from Currie to stay in Liverpool for a few days. He travelled up by the mail coach and stayed ten days. Ironically, now that it appeared that he was being overlooked for employment, he was keen to get back to sea. Immediately upon his return to London, he applied for a meeting with one of the Lords of the Admiralty with

233

whom he was acquainted, and asked him to intercede with the Earl St Vincent. The Lord of the Admiralty

> *... asked me if I would like a 50 gun ship. I told him I did not like a 50 gun ship so well as a 74 but that I wished to serve, as we were at war, and I would accept of any ship the Admiralty thought me entitled to command ... I am now very anxious to be employed.*

A week or so later, Moore wrote to St Vincent once again;

> *Perhaps I may not get a 74 which, next to a good frigate, is the class of ship I would like to command, and even if I do there is a great risk of my being continued in the command of her after the war is over, which I do not believe will last too long. Nothing but war can make me wish to be employed at sea.*

The response from the Admiralty was a complete surprise.

14

The Star Captain
(July 1803 – June 1805)

On the 8th of July I was appointed to the command of the Indefatigable *of 44 guns, very much to my astonishment as the first Lord had informed me that I could not have a frigate. I was pleased much with my appointment and set off a few days afterwards to take the command of the ship. I arrived here [Plymouth] on the 17th and found the ship by no means in the forward state that I expected, a great deal of the carpenter's work being in an unfinished state and the copper on her bottom so very foul that I immediately wrote to the admiralty to have her hauled into a dock to wash it down.*

The *Indefatigable* was one of the navy's most highly regarded frigates. Originally she had been a 64-gun ship, but in 1794 she, along with two others[123], had been cut down or 'razeed' to convert them into heavily armed 'super-frigates'. Her first Captain had been Sir Edward Pellew, the commander of one of the frigate squadrons and one of the navy's finest ever frigate captains. If Moore had wanted confirmation of the high esteem in which he was held, the appointment to the *Indefatigable* was it.

He now had a very fine ship, but the same could not be said of her complement. A month after joining the ship he was still desperately below complement; *'I have about thirty working men, of which not more than three can be called Seamen.'* Any available or potential seamen around the coastal ports were immediately being pressed and sent off to man the line-of-battle ships. Ordinarily, an officer like Moore, a frigate or the *Indefatigable* in particular, could rely on willing volunteers. But this time he could not even get

. . . those volunteer sailors who enter at the different Rendezvous for the Indefatigable. *We have a very poor prospect of being manned, and*

235

I am glad to take very indifferent Landmen in order to make any shew at all.

In one of his rare surviving letters, he wrote of the situation to his friend Creevey:

. . . I never had to do with a new ship's company before made up of Falstaff's men – 'decayed tapsters', &c., so I do not bear that very well and I get no seamen but those who enter here at Plymouth, which are very few indeed. The Admiralty will not let me have any who enter for the ship at any of the other ports, which cuts up my hopes of a tolerable ship's company . . . I am convinced the French can make no progress in England, and do not believe now that they will attempt it; but how is all this to end? However that may be, as I am in for it, I wish to God I was tolerably ready, and scouring the seas.[124]

Around 6 September, Moore was able to move the ship out into Cawsand Bay. To his surprise he had suddenly been sent a very reasonable draft of men to help complete his crew and he thought them

. . . capable of becoming a very good ship's company with a little practice and experience.

Although he received orders to make the frigate ready for sea instantly he was still waiting for operational orders ten days later. He expressed his frustration and fears in another letter to Creevey:

. . . It has pleased the Worthies aloft to keep us in expectation of sailing at an hour's notice since Sunday last. This is very proper, I am sure, and rather inconvenient too. I hate to be a-going a-going. It is disagreeable to Jack, because I have sent all his wives and his loves on shore, and altho' I have made him an apology, he must think the Captain is no great things. The blackguards will know me by-and-by. They seem a tolerable set, and I am already inclined to love them. If they fight, I shall worship them . . . There is another very fine frigate here, as ready as we are – the Fisgard, commanded by a delightful little fellow, Lord Mark Kerr. He is an honour to Lords as they go . . . If there is to be a war with Spain, it would be well to let us know of it before we sail, as money – altho' nothing to a philosopher – is something to me. I am growing old, and none of the women will have me now if I cannot keep them in style, and you know there is no carrying on the war ashore in the peace, when it comes, without animals of that description . . . The most cheerful fellow on politics is my brother Jack; you'll hear no croaking from him. He says it's all nonsense .[125]

Eager to get the frigate and her crew shaken down, Moore obtained permission to exercise in the Channel and for the next ten days he cruised between Eddystone and Plymouth Sound, putting both the crew and ship through their paces. When his orders did arrive, they were simply to continue patrolling as he had been, to protect Plymouth. It was frustrating, but he was aware that with serious fear of imminent invasion, the Admiralty was unwilling to let the *Indefatigable* cruise very far from the coast. It was doubly frustrating, because as he cruised along the north side of the Channel, a number of prizes, taken by frigates further out to sea, passed by on their way to Plymouth. It was particularly exasperating for the crew; '*Seeing the prizes go under our noses creates a good deal of impatience among our fellows.*' It could create discontent and Moore was already aware that although the great majority were well affected, there were '. . . *some very great rascals in the ship.*' This sort of cruising wasn't doing the ship any favours either, for Moore was convinced that the copper of the hull was already fouling up. And as if this wasn't enough, he was growing increasingly anxious that his health would not stand up to a winter in the Channel. But there was more to it than this. The role of a naval captain was a demanding one and some of the duties required a particular hardness of character – or at least the outward appearance of toughness. Moore had always found this difficult, but he was finding as he got older and as his experience grew, that this was becoming harder to sustain;

> There are a number of details which a man must shut his eyes to, in order to execute with effect the duties which the situation of an Officer imposes on him. As Lady MacBeth says 'Think not so brain sickly of these things, else 'twill make us mad'. Pressing seamen, Discipline &c &c. The worst of all this is, there is no remedy. If a man retires, such is the constitution of things that he owes his comforts and his security to the protection afforded by this System which has revolted him and which he vainly thinks to wash his hands of – No man who eats Mutton has a right to tax the Butcher with cruelty. Ye are all Butchers.

At the end of October, Moore was ordered to join Admiral Cornwallis' squadron off Brest. Despite his misgivings, the weeks at sea had gradually toughened his constitution, and he was generally feeling in better health. He was also heartened by the fact that the crew of the *Indefatigable* was now complete. Few of the men were stout, hardy seamen – there was a high proportion of inexperienced

237

landsmen amongst them – but they were mainly young and that was promising.

Cornwallis ordered Moore to cruise for six weeks in the Bay of Biscay and he sailed with a gale blowing in his teeth and a considerable sea running. As the frigate battled her way south-east towards Lorient, it was clear that the dockyard workers had made a poor job of her repairs. The decks leaked badly with the result that the 'tween decks were as wet as the upper deck. Furthermore,

> ... *our people are very uncomfortable at present owing to being badly cloathed and much exposed to wet for these three days past.* Moore was also a little wary as ... *neither myself, the master nor any of the officers are acquainted with this part of the coast.*

Heavy squalls soon set in which tested the inexperienced crew severely. In these conditions Moore soon discovered that the *Indefatigable* could also carry a press of sail better than most English men-of-war, and this was to her advantage in squally weather but she drifted a great deal to leeward when under light sail or hove to.

The crew, though, were still incompetent. This was brought home to him during an incident off the Cordovan Light in the second week of November. As the crew hurried aloft to make more sail in chase of a French vessel, one of the topmen fell overboard. Then the boat, lowered to try to save him, capsized. By the time the men had been recovered the chase had vanished. Moore could only note wearily in his journal:

> *We are very indifferently manned, and it will be a long time before this ship's company will become tolerably expert. She is by no means a safe ship to get into an intricate Navigation or to trust on a lee shore.*

The weather continued wild and squally and Moore's gloom continued. He could find no interest in his profession and began to find fault with himself and his ability to command:

> *I hate to punish and I am indolent and too easy ... I have here no Society. No Women. My life passes away like a dream.*

What was worse, he was again having problems with his right eye and now began to fear that he might lose the sight in it completely. The possibility that he might be forced again to give up the command of another ship, and in particular the *Indefatigable*, mortified him:

238

She is the last thing in the shape of a frigate that I am likely ever to command, and I do not expect to be allowed to keep her above a twelve-month even if I preserve my health.

As the days passed, Moore's depression grew deeper. The crew were almost all badly clothed and they had been perpetually wet for the last three weeks. It was hardly surprising that they seemed to have little spirit and Moore knew well the dangers that lurked in this situation;

I would not lead them into action with any great confidence . . . though he conceded that *they are probably at least as good as those we may have to encounter.*

He was cheered somewhat when, on 17 November, the *Indefatigable* was joined by the frigate *L'Aigle*, commanded by Captain George Wolfe, an extremely capable frigate commander who, although nearly Moore's age, had not been promoted to Post Captain until the end of 1800.[126] Fortunately, Moore's health remained generally good, which was just as well because they were experiencing '. . . *very bleak, raw, uncomfortable weather, the wind at south east'*. As ever the commander's isolation grew, and occupied his thoughts:

It is very curious that, although I am very tolerably off for Officers and on very good terms with them all, I have very little pleasure in the conversation of any of them. Is it the Naval Discipline which occasions this, or are we ill suited to each other for social intercourse? Both these objections may operate. I have a real regard for some of them and would really exert myself to serve them, but their conversation is taste-less to me. I have recourse to my books and to my memory for solace and for pleasure. I am tired of commanding and of obeying.

It occurred to him that he could consider resigning, but the thought appalled him:

What right have I to shake myself clear of it more than the Captain of the Forecastle whom we pressed – Poor Fellow! I am tired of it but I will go on, we must do something.

The spell of bad and wet weather continued. Moore was keeping station close to the land with difficulty and was all too well aware of the great danger that they stood in on occasions. Twice the frigate had been taken aback in a most hazardous fashion, but they had been fortunate to escape without injury to the ship. Equally badly, the

239

weather was preventing any improvement in the general efficiency of the ship. Moore was torn between the need to put his men under pressure and consideration of their wellbeing;

> I have had no opportunity of practising them at the Guns. We must not worry them too much, poor fellows.

This, and the growing sick list made him despondent about his ability to achieve anything. His crew was still inexperienced, and in his depression Moore turned to blaming himself as much as they:

> I do not think the fellows I have with me would cut any great figure in a struggle. The ship runs away with them. We have too few seamen. I do not know if other men take themselves to task as I do, or if I am blind to the faults and weaknesses of the people around me as much as many of my friends seem blind to mine. But I certainly do not stand high in my own opinion . . . I do not wish for more reputation in the world than I believe I have, because I believe I have my due. I wish to _deserve_ more.

The problem was highlighted on 24 November, when the _Indefatigable_ went to quarters on sighting two strangers who turned out to be British men-of-war;

> The People appeared to me to shew a good countenance but there was a good deal of confusion. A line of Battle ship and a frigate are not to be trifled with, especially in the state we are in, with so many raw hands.

However, he was at least cheered by the spirit shown on this occasion:

> On the whole they are the best I have ever had. Exceedingly well disposed and all willing and active.

Towards the end of November, Moore received another reinforcement in the form of the frigate _Doris_, commanded by Captain Patrick Campbell. A few days later they sighted a convoy sailing under the escort of a frigate and gunboats between the Isle de Groix and the mainland. Seeing the two English frigates, the convoy began to anchor under the protection of shore batteries on the island and nearby mainland. Moore hauled off for the night and, at first light, sent in boats to try to cut out several of the vessels; however the boats came under heavy fire and, rather than expose the frigates to the guns of the shore batteries, he called off the attack. Although the two frigates had failed in their attempt to take any of the French convoy, Moore was far from dissatisfied with the event, as he recorded on the following day:

Yesterday afforded tolerable exercise to our people, as we have had so much necessary business to do in the ship, when the weather was tolerable, that the men have had very little or no useful practice at the guns, and when they have an Enemy to fire at and the shot are whistling about their ears it does them ten times as much good as the more common affair of exercising the guns. A shell yesterday burst so near us that a splinter from it struck our Mizzen chains. They fired a great many shells from the batteries on both sides at the ship. Captain Campbell of the Doris *came on board and dined with me after we stood off, and, as he is a remarkable gallant fellow, I was exceedingly happy that he was perfectly of my opinion with regard to the imprudence of attacking them, situated as they were.*

Soon afterwards, the *Doris* sailed to rejoin the Channel Fleet and the *Indefatigable* was left alone once again. The sea became almost devoid of ships and Moore came to the conclusion that a continental embargo had been imposed. December drifted past in dismal inactivity and Moore found himself with little else to note in his journal:

This has been a most gloomy, cheerless, inhospitable day, damp and dreary, and powerful were the effects of an opening in the clouds and a burst of evening sun shine on my spirits.

On Christmas Eve, the *Indefatigable* fell in with the *Defiance* (74), commanded by Captain Philip Durham, an old friend and shipmate of Moore's. The weather, though, was too bad for any social visiting and in any case, Moore's attention was too closely focussed on his own crew, for it was a bad day. Firstly, because of the rough sea, one of the seamen broke his leg whilst working in the hold, then two men fell from the main yard onto the boats on the booms. One broke his thigh and the other was badly bruised.

The following day, Moore wrote in his journal:

This is Christmas, a day on which one naturally likes to think of our home and of our friends. I have been drawing groups of them in my mind, certainly thinking sometimes of their Old Companion and guessing where he might be and how differently employed from them in the 'Hall, where beards wag all' . . . Many a rough and unsociable Christmas have I spent on the waves. Well I am here on my Post . . .

There wasn't long for relaxation; on 28 December, at 4am, the wind suddenly shifted seven points from the south-west to north-west by west, and blew up a perfect storm. Luckily, the frigate was already carrying only a close reefed main topsail and foresail;

We got the courses furled with great difficulty and the Main and Mizen top gallant masts struck, but the fore top gallant mast was blown away and the main top sail split to pieces. If the gale had continued with equal violence we should probably have been in a damned scrape as the few seamen we had could only do one thing at a time and the half seamen were afraid to do any thing aloft. We are very weak indeed in seamen, but we must make the best of it, the weather was very trying, but I was very much chagrined at their spiritless and awkward behaviour.

That same day, the sailor who had broken his leg falling from the main yard died. As always, Moore was genuinely sorrowful:

The poor young fellow had been delirious almost ever since, and when not in that state appeared to suffer much; the other man is likely to recover without any permanent ill consequences.

He felt as sincerely about this as indeed he did when he was forced to order a flogging:

The necessity of inforcing the most necessary regulations by punishment is exceedingly disgusting to me and yet it is absolutely unavoidable as the class of men we have to deal with are some of them so brutified that only corporal punishment can restrain them from drunkenness and other vile excesses which from their dangerous effects are unpardonable crimes at sea. The love of grog gets the better of the fear of punishment with some of them and the punishment of these determined sots deters the rest in some degree but scarce a week passes that I am not obliged to punish some men for this baneful vice. It weighs down my spirits to be forced to these degrading exhibitions of human Nature. Discipline is a very necessary evil, but it is one. Perfect Liberty is inconsistent with any state of society, but I am always for imposing no restrictions but those that are clearly necessary for the good of the whole.

Although the problem of drunkenness was a ubiquitous problem in the Royal Navy, Moore had never had to deal with it to quite the same extent as he did now. To a large extent his previous crews had been composed of volunteers or experienced frigate seamen, with a few hard cases thrown in. The crew of the *Indefatigable*, as we have seen, was composed of a largely inexperienced draft of men. Despite Moore's best efforts it was taking time to weld them into an efficient and conscientious team – and until that was achieved, many of them would continue to find comfort and escape in alcohol. There was, however, a more insidious problem. A number of the crew had ganged together and were bullying or terrorizing the more peaceful members of the crew. Among the gang was an Irishman who had been entered by the civil powers as an alternative to a custodial sentence. Moore was already aware of this man,

> . . . *a most infamous character and one of a gang of ruffians we have on board that require looking very sharp after. They are few in number but I believe are capable on any atrocity.*

One night when he should have been on deck, a seaman challenged the man after he had disturbed the watch in their hammocks. Drawing a knife, the Irishman slashed the backs of the other man's legs, cutting his tendons. Moore was both aghast and furious:

> *The man's leg has been dreadfully cut but the Surgeon has hopes he will not be lame, one of the Arteries was divided and obliged to be taken up.*

The culprit was immediately seized and put in irons, but no witness would come forward;

> *It seems curious that a few fellows of this description should make themselves formidable in a ship, but so it is. The seamen although they know them to be villains and cut-throats are very averse to peach against them, they wish to have nothing to do with them. These fellows herd together and support each other, while the rest of the men act separately, by which means and by talking big they make themselves feared. These fellows have been heard to use the most mutinous expressions, but all the information I have yet heard has been general, they hear the expressions but they pretend they do not know who used them, it was in the dark.*

Although Moore had an informant among the crew, the man did not wish to put himself at risk and Moore certainly had no desire to expose him.

On 11 January, Moore headed north for orders from Cornwallis. Violent gales had set in and one night, just as Moore was getting into his cot, the frigate was hit by a violent squall. Almost naked, he ran on deck to supervise the taking in of sails, which was eventually achieved, but with great difficulty. Cornwallis ordered the *Indefatigable* back to Plymouth. She entered the Sound in a gale

243

having lost her fore topgallant mast, which was blown overboard to the great alarm of the men who were in the process of striking it at the time. Fortunately, no-one was injured. The frigate anchored in the Sound but the wind began to blow even harder. As Moore stood on deck watching the worsening conditions, the frigate *Boadicea* at the outermost edge of the moorings, parted a cable and ran athwart the bows of the frigate *Loire*, carrying away her bowsprit. The *Loire* then drove down onto the *Indefatigable*. As she did so her foremast collapsed onto the bows of the *Indefatigable*, springing her bowsprit in turn and shattering the cutwater and head. The crews managed to disentangle the frigates, but the *Loire* was unable to pull far ahead of the *Indefatigable* and both ships rode out the gale in a highly perilous situation as the former rode on the *Indefatigable*'s larboard cable,

> *... striking against our small bower with her rudder so that we expected it to part every instant. Had we gone on shore, which I expected, I think most of us must have perished as the wind was right in, blowing most violently and a tremendous sea.*

Happily, the gale moderated next morning and the two frigates limped into Hamoaze.

The *Indefatigable* was docked for a month, during which time she was repaired and re-coppered, and Moore took a month's leave. He returned to the frigate much revived, writing breezily to his friend Creevey:

> *If they do not take my men, we shall soon be ready for sea again. New copper, my boy! We shall sail like the wind ...*[127]

However, he was less happy to receive orders to join the inshore squadron blockading Brest. The *Indefatigable* was a difficult ship to operate close to the shore and Moore knew that the station was going to be trying for both officers and crew. He was perhaps less optimistic because of the recent loss of the frigate *Hussar*, wrecked on the Saints:

> *This is the fifth capital frigate we have lost since the commencement of the war. One, La Minerve, which ran on shore on the Dique at Cherbourg was got off by the Enemy without much damage, the other four were totally lost.*

He was also concerned about the health of his crew, who had been housed in very poor accommodation in one of the hulks while they worked hard refitting the ship. Many of them now had colds or fevers and, of course, there had been no chance of any of them getting the shore leave he liked to grant them. Moore was particularly sensitive to this latter issue:

> I think there is too little attention to people's feelings and propensities. They cannot help feeling by degrees a disgust to their business, which affords them no relaxation, no time to attend a little to their own family concerns.

Sent to join Admiral Graves' blockading squadron, he soon decided he did not approve of the Admiral's tactics. His concerns were justified on 22 March when the squadron sighted a 22-gun ship close to the shore in the Bay of Conquet. Captain Jervis of the 74-gun *Magnificent* was sent inshore to see if the ship could be cut out. Moore thought that, unless she could be taken by surprise, the cost in life and injury would be too great to justify the attack. The ship would be strongly defended as her crew probably numbered around 200 and the French could ferry as many soldiers as they wished on board during the night. Despite his misgivings, the following morning, Moore was ordered to join Jervis and Captain Robert Otway of the *Montague* (74) on the island of Beniquet, from where they could reconnoitre the ship in more detail. From the island they could see that she was supported by three gunboat brigs and other smaller vessels, all of which had been hauled close under the guns of a battery. Jervis, put in charge of the operation, was determined to launch an attack using between 500 and 600 seamen and marines who would be carried in twenty to twenty-five boats. At 8pm the following evening, the boats all rendezvoused alongside the *Magnificent*, with a view to attacking at 2am the following morning. After all these preparations, before the attack could be launched, the wind changed and the attack had to be abandoned. As the squadron began to weigh to fight their way off shore, the *Magnificent* hit an outcrop known as the Black Rock. Moore and his crew quickly realized what had happened, and put about to give assistance to the stricken ship, for they could see that she was already sinking. *Indefatigable* was soon joined by Wolfe in the *L'Aigle*, and both frigates sent their boats across to start rescuing the crew. These were soon joined by other boats from the squadron and the rescue operation continued until the *Magnificent* settled with her gunwale just out of the water. As if the attempted attack had not run into enough difficulties – another disaster now began to unfold. The wind changed direction and began to blow stronger and a number of the squadron's boats, loaded with rescued seamen, were blown towards the shore. Moore got the *Indefatigable* underway, and began collecting both boats and men, until he had nearly 300 of the *Magnificent*'s crew on board. Despite his efforts, they could only watch helplessly as a number of boats were driven ashore into the arms of waiting French troops.[128] Moore was quietly seething about the whole operation:

> We sometimes make too free with this Enemy's coast and on this occasion, there certainly was no more enterprise and hardihood than I am equal to when the object to be gained did not seem to me to be proportioned to the risk we ran. On the projected attack on the Vessels in Conquet, some of the Boats must have had to row near 12 miles before they could reach the point of Attack and the least distance that any of them could have had to row was 8 miles. Where the ships lay they were so much exposed with the wind any way from the westward that they could not ride, and the boats must have had the greatest difficulty in pulling back to their ships. There was no probability that the ship and brigs in Conquet could be taken by surprise, as they must have seen Officers reconnoitring them from Beniquet, and they had every reason to be on their guard . . .

As an officer, he could not help feeling sorry for Jervis, for the *Magnificent* had been in admirable order and

> . . . his personal loss is I am convinced between two and three thousand pounds. He lost in the ship about £1,700 worth of plate.

On 16 April the *Colossus* arrived, delivering two bullocks and a large quantity of fresh vegetables for the *Indefatigable* and with her came the frigate *Acasta*, who had also been ordered to join the inshore squadron. Within days the wind turned raw and sharp. The *Indefatigable* was still suffering with thirty men on the sick list, most of whom had been stricken with an inflammatory fever of the chest, of which one man had already died. Fortunately, nine of the *Magnificent*'s seamen had applied to be taken on the frigate's books and Moore had accepted them as they were '. . . *in general, very fine fellows*', although he knew that there was every likelihood that he would eventually be ordered to give them up. Still, he was disappointed when the order came because the men were

> . . . all seamen except one who is a shipwright and therefore as valuable, and what made it the more grievous to me was the circumstance of their wishing exceedingly to stay in the ship, they were therefore

more to be depended on than any we can get. We are considerably short of our number now, and the ship is on the whole ill manned.

There was just one possible consolation:

We are teased and worried by being kept constantly at sea, but the consequence must be rendering the crews more and more expert and the superiority of skill more decidedly with us.

Experience had long taught him that this was the case – it all depended on being fortunate enough to avoid disaster for long enough. At the same time, much depended on his own enthusiasm as commanding officer, and nothing that had happened recently seemed to prevent this from draining away. It was not just Moore;

. . . there is at present a degree of dullness and insipidity in our processional business which is heavily felt by all the navy officers of my acquaintance. There is a great difference in the way things are carried on now and during the greater part of the former war. Formerly when a ship came in from a long cruise there was a little relaxation allowed while the ship was refitting. The seamen had, to a certain extent, leave to go on shore, the Officers had sometimes leave of absence on their private affairs, in short, it was to a certain degree expected that the Officers and ship's companies should have some amusement provided the duty of the ship was in no respect neglected. Now the system is for the ships to be, if possible, eternally at sea. When it becomes absolutely necessary for a ship to go into port, the men are worked and jaded off their legs to get her ready again and the instant what is indispensable is completed she is out again to remain as long as possible. . . . All this might be supportable if there was the spur of danger or the object of meeting and fighting the Enemy but it is to cruise eternally off their ports and never see them but within their harbours and out of our reach. This is wearing to officers and men and the most tiresome of all service. The question is, is this necessary? I believe not, and I do not think it can go on so.

When he returned to his station off Brest, Moore received orders to take the *Indefatigable* into Plymouth for provisions and to 'refresh' the crew. He was strictly warned to spend no more than seven days in port – which effectively ruled out any possibility of a visit to London. Nevertheless he must have been glad to give his crew a rest. Eight men, including his cook had now died from the inflammatory fever.

When she sailed again, the *Indefatigable* was heavily encumbered with stores for the Ferrol Squadron. Moore, like many other frigate commanders who had been in this position, surveyed the state of his ship with dismay. The stores were

> *... so numerous and so bulky that the ship is excessively lumbered with them and two guns on each side on the Main deck are blocked up completely, and several of the Quarter deck guns are very much embarrassed by them.*

Having delivered the stores, Moore was ordered to escort the damaged *Spencer* (74) back to the Channel and then cruise off Cape Penas. When he finally reached his cruising ground, the only ships to be found were either American or Spanish neutrals. Now that they were in warmer weather, the health of the crew was generally improving and they were, with practice, welding together more as an efficient fighting team. On 3 July, for example, Moore put the gun crews through their paces, firing at an empty cask;

> *I was very well pleased with their accuracy, most of the guns were exceedingly well pointed. This ship well manned is a most formidable battery; our people are exceedingly improved but they are still but a very indifferent ship's company; the weather has been so fine these five weeks that they have suffered nothing, and now that they know each other better there is much more joviality and fun about them. In short they are scarce the same men they were six months ago.*

The quiet time again enabled Moore to ponder his future because he knew that he would not be allowed to remain in a frigate for much longer;

> *I expect soon to be appointed to a 74, not from any application of my own but because I am so high up on the list that I think it not likely that I shall be allowed to remain in a single decked ship much longer. If this war were like the last I would prefer this ship [the* Indefatigable*] to a ship of the line but as it is I will quit her without much regret. She is however, in an active war, a most desirable ship to a man in good health as she is a most powerful man of war and in general sails very well.* [Although] *Her accommodation for the captain are inferior to those of a small frigate.*

And she was still a desirable ship because Moore was in generally good health, though he was finding that even walking on the quarter-deck for any length of time was exhausting him.

With little activity, Moore decided to shift his cruising ground northwards near the Gironde. Here though he could only watch with dismay as large numbers of neutral vessels came and went. How, he wondered, was a frigate commander to know what to search and what to ignore, and then how could he prove a contraband cargo when he saw it? It was, he concluded, an impossible task – maintaining a blockade under these circumstances. The lack of profitable activity was also leading to a growth in drunkenness among the crew, as they drank to relieve boredom and low morale. Moore loathed it, but all he could do was punish occasionally – which he hated more – and rail in his journal:

> The great and prevailing vice among seamen is drunkenness, the absolute certainty of corporal punishment cannot altogether prevent it even in some of the finest fellows in other respects. It is a most irksome and disgusting circumstance to be under the necessity of ordering a shameful punishment to be inflicted on a gallant and, in other respects, most respectful seaman, for this baneful habit. Nothing but punishment can at all check it, for talking to them on the subject is mere prating, they are conscious that it is not a thing to be suffered at sea yet they cannot resist the temptation of getting drunk occasionally.

There were many Post Captains who shared this same weakness.

On 25 August, the *Indefatigable* was ordered to Plymouth again to reprovision. Moore was determined that this time he would reward his crew, believing that it would pay in the longer term;

> While we were in the Sound I ventured to let one Division of the ship's company go on shore on leave at two different times, by which I lost three men by desertion, which however will not deter me from giving the same indulgence to the seamen when next we return into Port to refit. I expect, by this means, to lose fewer men on the whole than if I gave no leave. Besides that I cannot bear that the ship should be considered by the men as a Prison. We should consult the comfort and happiness of the Seamen which is not to be effected by mere feeding and clothing them. They must have some relaxation, some amusement.

The *Indefatigable* was back on station off Brest by 10 September. Four nights later, while Moore was giving dinner to Captain Campbell of the *Doris*, the weather became misty and squally. Groping their way cautiously through the darkness to avoid the Parquette Rock, the *Indefatigable* ran onto a rock known as La Vandre. The hull of the frigate struck the rock twice and then passed over it, leaving several pieces of her false keel behind. Although the ship began taking on water, it was hardly serious enough to warrant returning to port. Then, on the evening of the 22nd, Moore received urgent orders from the Commander-in-Chief off Ushant, to proceed immediately to the west of the rocks known as The Saints, and open a packet of secret orders. When he opened these, he found that the order

> . . . *directs me to proceed off Cadiz and the mouth of the Straits, with all possible dispatch, and in conjunction with any ships I might find there to use my best endeavours to intercept two Spanish frigates with treasure from South America and to detain them until further Order. This is secret I do not know whether or not I may thank the Commander in Chief for giving me a preference or if he had no choice. The* Indefatigable *being, perhaps, the only disposable ship. In the meantime, however, I am in charity with the old gentleman and willing to believe he has selected me for this service.*

In a state of great excitement he set off across the Bay of Biscay, and by the evening of the 25th he was running down the coast of Portugal. He already knew that there was a very strong prospect of imminent war with Spain and the *Indefatigable* was going to be in the best possible position to take advantage of the outbreak of hostilities.

The next day, a confident Moore began patrolling between the Rock of Lisbon and Cape St Vincent; *'For action, I think we are pretty strong and the ship's company, on the whole, of good composition.'* By the 28th, Moore had seen a number of Spanish vessels and it seemed that they had no idea that there was the possibility of a war with England but he was also becoming anxious about finding any other British cruisers for, without some support, he might not be able to take on a couple of Spanish frigates. His concern increased when he looked into Cadiz harbour and saw a number of French and Spanish men-of-war preparing for sea. He was therefore very happy when, on 30 September, the frigate *Medusa* arrived, commanded by Captain John Gore, from the Mediterranean Squadron. When the two officers met, Moore immediately had to make a tactical decision. Gore reported that the 74-gun *Triumph*, commanded by Robert Barlow, was about to sail from the Mediterranean for Cadiz, to provide an escort for any English merchantmen needing a convoy. Without warning, she could sail straight into a trap if the Franco-Spanish fleet left Cadiz. It was agreed that Gore should sail southwards where it was thought the frigate *Amphion* was cruising in the Straits of Gibraltar. He would have the *Amphion* go in search of the *Triumph*, and then rejoin him immediately. Moore could only hope and wait – but he was also worried. In responding to the threat to the *Triumph*, he had had to share the content of his secret orders;

> *I have acted for the best in revealing my orders for the information of Sir Robert Barlow, but I do it at some risk and am not quite at my ease on the occasion. Curse mystery and secrecy! I never like to have any thing to do with either.*

On 2 October the frigate *Lively* arrived, commanded by Captain Graham Hammond,[129] who had been ordered to follow Moore's instructions. Moore had hoped that by this time he would have received news of war with Spain, for they had seen enough Spanish ships sail past to have made their fortunes from prize money. The following day, the frigate *Medusa* returned with the *Amphion*. Moore was now in command of a reasonably powerful frigate squadron and he set sail for Cape St Mary, this being the usual landfall ships made for before turning for Cadiz. Moore now had to give some thought about how he would deal with the Spanish frigates if, indeed, they did turn up:

> *If we fall in with these frigates it will be proper to go through the ceremony of speaking [to] them, but the business must finally be decided by fighting as it is impossible to believe that frigates will suffer themselves to be examined or detained without resistance, I would not like to begin by firing into them, but it must end with firing on both sides, end as it may. Well I wish to God we may meet them and soon. I am not well.*

This rather limp comment reflected the fact that, at this crucial moment, Moore had developed an ailment that was preventing him from walking properly. Even when forced to stand around on deck on lookout or during a chase

> *. . . it is exceedingly distressing to me. If I cannot get better after taking advice in London I must go on shore and give up the ship, otherwise I must give up all comfort for the rest of my life.*

On the morning of 5 October, when the squadron was some nine leagues south-west of Cape St Mary, the *Medusa* signalled to indicate four sail bearing west by south. Moore immediately ordered a general chase and the squadron instantly made all sail. It was soon apparent that they were bearing down on four large Spanish frigates;

They formed in Line of Battle ahead as we drew near, the Van ship bearing a Commodore's broad pendant, the next, being the largest and a beautiful frigate, carried a Rear Admiral's flag. They carried a press of sail on the wind steering in for Cadiz. The Medusa, *being the headmost of our ships, as she drew near took in her studding sails and hauled up close on the leading ship's weather beam. The* Indefatigable *took a similar position close to the Rear Admiral, the* Amphion *and* Lively *each, as they came up, formed opposite to a Spanish ship. I had previously made the signal to prepare for battle. I now hailed the Spanish Admiral. From whence came you? South America. Where are you bound to? Cadiz. I then desired them to bring to, as I wished to send a boat on board, but they either did not or would not understand me but continued to carry a Press of sail. I then fired a shot across the Admiral's hawse on which he shortened sail and I sent Lieut. Ascot on board with a verbal message that I had orders to detain the Spanish Squadron and carry them to England, that I earnestly wished to shed no blood in the execution of them, but that his determination must be made instantly. The Admiral called the Officers together, wished to gain time &c. After waiting some time and seeing they were all ready and pointing their guns at us, I made the signal for the boat to return and fired a shot ahead of the Admiral. As soon as Ascot returned and informed me they had treasure on board, I bore close down on his weather bow and fired another shot ahead of him. At this moment I observed the Admiral's second astern fire into the* Amphion, *the Admiral fired a shot at us, I made the signal for close action and in an instant we were engaged from van to Rear. Captain Sutton of the* Amphion *had just before this placed himself close to the leeward of his opponent, which I was very glad to see. In less than 10 minutes his opponent blew up with a horrible explosion and in less than half an hour the Admiral hauled down his colours as did the rear ship opposed to the* Lively. *The Commodore was still engaged with the* Medusa *but was carrying a great deal of sail and seemed to outsail the* Medusa, *on which I made the signal for the* Lively *to chase and, as she passed, hailed Captain Hammond and desired him to make all sail to the assistance of the* Medusa. *She accordingly passed on and as soon as I had sent a Division with 2 Lieutenants to take possession of the admiral's ship I made sail towards the floating remains of the unfortunate Spanish ship that had blown up, in hopes of saving some, but nothing remained on the surface but a few dead bodies, floating pieces of the wreck and quantities of ashes! The* Amphion *had saved 40 men one of whom was the second captain, all the rest perished. While we were securing the two ships that were taken, a running fight continued between the Spanish Commodore and the* Medusa *which, as it appeared to us, would have probably ended in the Spaniard's escape had not the* Lively *come up to windward and forced him to surrender, late in the afternoon, and when we could only discern them from the mast head. I do not know how the* Medusa *allowed herself to be thrown out in that way unless it was that they were so fond of playing on their antagonist's quarter (which I think very silly, with a ship of equal force) that the other by steering a steady course got to windward of her and ahead withal. We shall know hereafter for I have seen nothing of them since. This squadron consisted of the* Medee, *the admiral's ship of 42 guns, 28 eighteen pounders on the Main deck, on the quarter deck and fore castle long 9 pounders and 24 pounder carronades; the three others were 36 gun frigates carrying 12 pounders on the Main deck. La Medee had about 300 men, the three others viz La Fama, La Clara and La Mercedez, which last ship blew up, had each from 280 to 300 men. I have not yet been able to determine the amount of the Specie on board this squadron but the most modest account gives it at about 3 million and a half of Dollars on board the three captured ships and about eight hundred thousand on board* La Mercedez *which blew up.*

The *Clara* and the *Fama* had sailed from Lima, while the other ships had come from Montevideo. The Spanish Admiral informed Moore that *La Medee* had suffered two men killed and ten wounded during the engagement,

. . . owing to my giving orders to fire particularly at the rigging, for the purpose of preventing their escape, Cadiz being so near. She was accordingly a good deal cut up in the masts and rigging. The Indefatigable *with her usual good fortune in that respect, did not lose a man, she suffered a little in the sails and rigging.*

Moore was immediately anxious to get such valuable prizes away from Cadiz, from whence the Spanish fleet could issue in overwhelming force. The problem was that the rigging of *La Medee* was badly damaged and it took the remainder of the morning to carry out adequate repairs. The *Lively, Medusa* and *Fama* had disappeared over the horizon, so Moore began to make his way back to England with his two captives and the *Amphion.* But progress was slow because, for several days, the wind swung round to either the north or the east, blowing directly against them;

I have the Spanish Captain of La Medee *and about 300 Spaniards on board here. My first Lieutenant John Gore[130] with the two Mates and*

253

a Midshipman and about 70 Indefatigables has charge of La Medee. The Spanish admiral, at his own request remains on board La Medee, with some of his staff among whom is the Major of the Squadron, whose Wife, a very fine woman, with four Daughters and three sons perished in La Mercedez. I have not yet seen any of them as the weather has been rough and I did not think my company could be acceptable so soon after so melancholy an accident. I have no uneasiness for the other ship La Fama as there were two of our ships, the Medusa and Lively, to look after her alone.

The ever-sensitive Moore was clearly not looking forward to his meeting with the Spanish Admiral, and he was dreading the prospect of meeting the Major whose family had been so savagely destroyed in *La Mercedez*. A few days later, he plucked up the courage to visit the Admiral;

He was in bed and very ill. I had a good deal of conversation with him. I endeavoured to console him and to sooth his feelings by telling him that even before his second blew up the force of our squadron was much superior to his, that I was extremely distrest at the dreadful misfortune that had happened and that it was with much regret & very painful to me to be obliged to fire upon the Spaniards in the execution of my orders. He seemed to be a sensible man, said he was satisfied with my conduct but thought it a most extraordinary proceeding on the part of the English Government, wished to know if I considered the Spanish ships as prizes and if I would hoist English colours on board of them when we arrived in England. I told him that my orders went to detaining them, that I had no orders to make Prizes, that his own Flag and Spanish colours should be hoisted when we met the fleet or arrived in England and that the rest would depend on our Government.

Then came the moment that Moore was dreading:

He introduced me to his Major, a most respectable man in appearance, between 50 & 60 years of age, an old captain in the navy, who had been 30 years in South America, employed by the Government in different situations on shore and last in settling the limits between the Spanish and the Portuguese possessions in America. His wife, who was from Paraguay where he had married her, with all his children, five daughters and three sons, who were on board La Mercedez, one boy remaining with himself on board La Medee, perished before his eyes! The wife was very amiable, the daughters beautiful, the eldest only

254

eighteen. This unfortunate officer seemed to feel his terrible loss with the sensibility of a man and the resignation of a virtuous and pious Christian. I could scarce bear to look in his mild and benevolent countenance. He presented me his only remaining boy 13 years of age. There, he said to me, Sir, is all that remains to me.

By the 13th, the wind had swung in their favour and they were able to make better progress. Running up past the Bay of Biscay, Moore kept a close lookout for the Channel Fleet, hoping that they might escort him to Portsmouth. But no ships were to be seen, so he headed straight for Plymouth, arriving there on 19 October to find the *Lively* and the *Fama* already there. The remaining Spanish frigates were run straight in to Hamoaze, rather than anchoring in the Sound. The *Indefatigable* followed them in, because she was still leaking and repairs could be delayed no longer. However, if her crew were hoping for shore leave, they were to be disappointed. Some of the Spanish sailors were still suffering from fever they had contracted in the West Indies, so everybody was placed in quarantine – everybody, that is, except Moore who managed to get ashore before the Customs Officers came on board. Moore's ailment, which had become rather serious, resulted in his being given immediate permission to travel to London to seek urgent medical advice. Whilst there, he began to feel the glow of his success:

My conduct has been approved of by the Admiralty and I have received from all quarters congratulations on our success and good fortune. The answer from the Court of Spain had not been received when I left London, the question of Peace or War with that country is still un-decided and on that question depends our chance of riches. There has been great delay in the Public Offices with respect to landing the trea-sure, not that it was not intended to be landed and lodged in the Bank of England from the first, but merely from dilatoriness and want of arrangement as to the execution of what they intend.

The news of Moore's success was also causing something of a stir at home. General Moore wrote from Sandgate to his mother:

I think I see the spectacles jumping off your nose, in reading the account of Graham's success. We shall hear no more of his being relaxed.[131] Depend upon it, that since the 5th instant, the day he fell in with the Spaniards, he has been quite well. Everybody rejoices, I believe that this good fortune has fallen to the lot of Graham Moore. I have no less than three letters this morning to announce it. We shall have Graham's letter

255

in to-morrow's Gazette. I am impatient to read the particulars of the action. I am with him, and I may add with you, more eager for his fame than his riches.[132]

When Moore returned to Plymouth on 13 November, he learned that the damage inflicted on the *Indefatigable* when she struck the Vandre Rock had been very serious indeed. So much so, in fact, that another slight knock would have sunk her outright. Nevertheless, two weeks later she was ready for sea again and, to Moore's immense pride and joy, he was ordered to take General John Moore on board and carry him to meet Rear Admiral Cochrane, where they were to discuss the feasibility of an attack on Ferrol. The *Indefatigable* found Cochrane's squadron off Ferrol on 15 December, where it was agreed that the Admiral, together with both General and Captain Moore, should be landed covertly to reconnoitre Ferrol from a nearby height, disguised as a hunting party. The operation nearly ended in disaster when Spanish troops spotted them and intercepted the boats. As it was, a Midshipman and two sailors were captured. By the time that the *Indefatigable* set sail again, General Moore had already concluded that such an attack on Ferrol would be near impossible*. The anchorage was inadequate for an expeditionary force, and there were too few landing places. The Spanish batteries were well designed and were protected from the rear so that the only possible means of attacking the town would involve troops travelling extremely long distances, with all the risks that that involved.

Having returned the General to England, the *Indefatigable* sailed back across the Channel to rejoin Cornwallis. Falling in with Cornwallis' fleet, Moore went aboard the *Ville de Paris* to report to the Admiral, '. . . *and the Old Lad received me, as he has ever done, exceedingly well*'. Cornwallis gave Moore command of the inshore squadron watching Brest, '. . . *among them I find my old favourite the* Melampus'. Moore was pleased at this recognition of his abilities, but he may have begun to wish that his days on blockade duty were over: '*The weather is dismally cold and we are all very uncomfortable. I am cramped up with Rheumatism and Chilblains.*' With appalling weather setting in again, the entire squadron was forced to cut their cables and run off the land as best they could. They all escaped being blown onto a lee shore, but Moore knew that it had been a close run thing:

* There had been a previous attempt to take Ferrol in 1800. This had failed.

What remains of this cruise I look to as of time to be got through as well as we can and the sooner the better for I expect no kind of comfort or satisfaction in it . . . This cruise has been severe upon us all.

The *Indefatigable* too was sustaining wear and tear. Most worryingly, the gammoning on her bowsprit had worn through in several places and could not be repaired whilst she was at sea.

On 23 January 1805, the cutter *Nimble* arrived with dispatches, including an order which Moore had hoped might arrive sooner. They were to seize or destroy all Spanish ships that they fell in with. Moore wondered how this might effect the Spanish frigates and treasure he had captured;

If Government behave tolerably fair to us with respect to the Frigates we took we shall not be very badly off as to our share of prizes.

Cochrane ordered Moore to take up a position off Corunna, just in case the Rochfort Squadron (which had actually already sailed into Brest) should try to enter that port. The weather had turned agreeable, and although it was only February it was as warm as an English summer;

If I were in good health I should enjoy this work and the whole of our prospect, as it is I feel tolerably cheery. The face of the country of Spain is agreeable to me, the mountains seem rocky and barren, but the valleys smile and the delightful spring already makes its appearance. No season is so cheering to me as the Spring. I love to see the youth of Nature.

It was a long time since Moore had written so lightly in his journal.

On 1 March, Admiral Calder arrived to take command of the Ferrol Squadron and Cochrane was ordered elsewhere, taking the more powerful ships with him. Moore speculated that the Rochfort squadron had perhaps not made it into Brest after all, and that Cochrane was being sent to look for them. He thought that, as the Rochfort Squadron was reportedly carrying troops, they might have made a dash for the Leeward Islands, in a move designed to draw an English expeditionary force after them. Calder ordered Moore to take the *Indefatigable* close in to watch Ferrol, while he took the rest of the squadron further out to sea. It was a potentially vulnerable position for the frigate, which Calder may have been using as bait to try to draw out French or Spanish men-of-war;

In my opinion the admiral keeps a great deal too far out, we did not see him all yesterday and both yesterday and today the wind was favourable for the enemy coming out. The Blockade is a complete farce, but it might certainly be much closer . . .

There was not even the consolation of prize money:

We have entirely lost our chance of Spanish Prizes now, they all now must know of the war, and besides this is now bad cruising ground for any thing but Men of War and of them I think our chance very indifferent. If Government act towards us according to the usual custom with regard to the ships detained by Order, previous to hostilities, we shall have been very lucky.

By the end of March, the neutral vessels that Moore was stopping and searching on a regular basis began reporting that the ten or twelve Spanish ships of the line in Ferrol were preparing to break out. Calder's squadron, though, was soon reduced to six ships of the line and Cornwallis was replaced by Lord Gardner as Commander-in-Chief of the Channel Fleet. On 16 April, Moore's old favourite, the *Melampus,* appeared bringing news that the French Toulon fleet had escaped through the Straits of Gibraltar on the 9th – and what later became known as The Campaign of Trafalgar, had begun. The two frigates immediately made all sail to warn Calder who, in turn, sent the *Melampus* north to warn the Ushant squadron. Calder, having withdrawn the *Montague* from her inshore station, now had seven ships of the line and the *Indefatigable,*

. . . which he has informed me he means to take into the line as he expects to be outnumbered by the enemy if he meets them . . . We shall have hot work this Summer, I think.

It was now known that the Rochfort squadron had arrived at Martinique in late February; but the destination of the Toulon squadron remained a mystery until 27 April when it was reported that Sir John Orde had seen the Toulon squadron enter Cadiz. Calder dispatched the *Indefatigable* to Cape Finisterre to watch in case the French should try to break out of Cadiz and head north. Moore took up his position in thick, rainy and unsettled weather. He had managed to obtain London newspapers and read that there, public attention seemed to be entirely focussed on the prosecution of Lord Melville[133]. Moore strongly approved of

. . . those who have abused their trust and connived at, and perhaps profited by, the corrupt practices of those under them [being] *detected and exposed.*

He believed such prosecutions had

. . . a very good effect. I believe Mr Whitbread's motive was perfectly just and honourable and I think he conducted the charge he made against Lord Melville with great discretion and in a very open and manly style.

Meanwhile, off Finisterre, a Portuguese brig reported that the Toulon squadron had already sailed from Cadiz, taking the Spanish fleet from that port with them. If they managed to unite with the Ferrol Squadron, which was reported to consist of twelve or thirteen ships of the line and five or six frigates, Calder's small squadron wouldn't be able to meet them. Moore noted in his journal: *'We have heard nothing yet of Lord Nelson'*, adding sarcastically, *'. . . another instance of the efficacy of Blockade'*.

Then at 10pm on the night of 14 May, Calder's squadron was considerably alarmed by the arrival of a frigate firing rockets and burning lights. It was the *Loire*, commanded by Captain Frederick Maitland. He reported that three days earlier he had been chased by five French ships of the line and three frigates, steering a course for Rochfort. By his calculation, they would now be ten leagues north by east of Calder. Moore thought this might be the Rochfort Squadron on its way back from the West Indies and was convinced that Calder should give chase or *'. . . I shall have no opinion of him'*. However, Calder simply returned to Ferrol. Moore was furious and frustrated at the growing inefficiency of the blockade that he witnessed all about him. Calder did not have the strength to meet the Ferrol Squadron if it came out but, the wind being westerly, he was in a perfect position to intercept the Rochfort Squadron. Moore was *'Sick and disgusted with the scene I am engaged in, to which I see no end.'* And there was still no news of Nelson's whereabouts.

On 30 May, the *Loire* returned with dispatches for Calder. Privately, Maitland informed Moore that after he had left Calder on the 15th, he had fallen in with a ship that had confirmed the position of the Rochfort Squadron. If Calder had given chase, he would certainly have caught them. It was, for Moore, virtually the last straw: *'O lord! O Lord! I wish with all my heart we were ordered in.'*

The anxious waiting continued but then, on 2 June, came news that Nelson had taken the Mediterranean Fleet to the West Indies in pursuit of the French;

I am very glad he has taken this decided step of pushing for the West Indies where they are most probably gone as it is there where we are most vulnerable at present. I understand that he has taken the whole of this measure on his own shoulders having received no orders from England. His fleet are of excellent composition, in the best order and extremely attached to Nelson who has the good sense and rare talent of keeping up good discipline while at the same time he is esteemed and liked by all under his command.

This was honest praise from one who had always been conscientious about his duties as a commander. Unfortunately for Moore, his health had broken once again, and his spirits were hardly less in a state of collapse. At this critical moment in the history of the war, he was compelled to write to Lord Barham, First Lord of the Admiralty, requesting two months leave of absence to recuperate, and also saying that he hoped he would not have to leave the *Indefatigable* permanently. The reply, when it came, bore the news that he had been anticipating and fearing for so long.

I have received his [Lord Barham's] answer stating that he has set his face against appointing acting Captains for [a] time, that therefore he could not comply with my request but that if I was obliged on account of my health to give up the command of the Indefatigable *he would do all in his power to appoint me to a good ship as soon as I was recovered . . .*

Because the inescapable fact was that

I am so high up the List of Captains that it is more becoming for me to command a ship of the Line than a frigate.

It was the end of Moore's career as a frigate commander. As though reluctant to bring this to a close, he did not remind Calder that the *Indefatigable* had been sixteen weeks out of port, and was therefore overdue for reprovisioning. However, the end could not be avoided. On 14 June 1805, Admiralty orders arrived ordering him to take the *Indefatigable* to Plymouth, and there in the first week of July, Moore handed the command of his frigate over to Captain John Rodd. For the first time, he made no reference in his journal, of his farewell to his crew.

15

The Long Decline
(1805 – 1843)

Moore arrived at Plymouth in broken health and with his frigate career at an end, but while he was unquestionably sad about this, his naval career was far from over. His immediate concerns, however, were to recover his health. He travelled to London via Bath and within a few weeks had undergone some form of surgery. He spent August 1805, recuperating at Marshgate House, but with the wound from the operation healing well, he could barely contain himself from applying to the Admiralty for new employment. At the end of August he was given command of the new *Fame* (74), though, as she had not yet actually been launched, he was allowed to retain nominal command of the *Indefatigable* in order to receive full pay.

The following month he travelled down to join his brother John at Sandgate, where he was able to take advantage of the sea bathing:

I go into the sea every morning at day light, but I still am not recovered from some of the effects of the operation. Which, however, I believe has succeeded in removing the complaint I was troubled with.[134]

It was almost certainly whilst he was at Sandgate that the sad news came of the death of his old friend Dr Currie.

The *Fame* was launched into the Thames on 8 October and taken to the Woolwich Dockyard to be fitted out. Moore formally joined her at the end of the month, accompanied by Lieutenant John Gore from the *Indefatigable*. In January 1806, she received a draft of 100 men from HMS *Victory* [100], though Moore was disappointed as to their quality.[135] The *Fame* was quickly ordered to join the Channel Fleet but within a few months, Moore's health had weakened again and he realized that the operation he had undergone had not removed his complaint. He was finding walking difficult, and once again had to consider whether he should resign his command. By May the decision could be put off no longer, and he formally requested to be superseded.

There may have been another reason for his resignation; he had just purchased a new estate with the proceeds of his accumulated prize money. As he had previously indicated, and despite his brief flirtation with properties in Scotland, he wanted to live in Surrey. The estate he purchased was Brook Farm, just outside the village of Cobham. The house itself had been built in 1800 in the new 'villa' style, as an elegant, smaller version of the country house. It had stables, a patent water closet upstairs, and was described as

> ... commanding most delightful and extensive prospects: Pains Hill, richly embowered, forms one of the many picturesque objects on the one side.[136]

There is no doubt that Moore dearly loved the place. In June, he confessed contentedly to his journal:

> I am remaining quietly at home in the beautiful part of the country which has always been a favourite spot with me. My health very indifferent . . . I have involved myself, perhaps rather imprudently in farming, of which I am totally ignorant, but I have a bailiff to whom I am obliged to trust the management of the land and of whom I have had an excellent character. I shall try how this does for a year or two when I must decide whether to go on or not. In the meantime, I certainly have had great satisfaction in this purchase.

His mother and sister were quickly brought there to live with him and also, to his great joy, his brother John, whenever he was not employed militarily.

But Moore had not altogether abandoned his naval career. In February 1807, Grenville, the First Lord of the Admiralty, offered him the command of another new 74-gun ship of the line, but Moore was still unconvinced about the strength of his health. He took to travelling to the Malvern Hills to help regain his fitness and fell in love with the area. He also spent time visiting his old friend Admiral Sir Harry Neale at his estate near Lymington. The two were to remain close friends until Neale's death in 1840. At the end of July, Moore was again offered a ship and given the choice of several new 74-gun ships. On the advice of Sir William Rule, Surveyor to the Navy, he chose the *Marlborough* (74). Again he was joined by his old shipmate Lieutenant John Gore, and now also by the former Second Lieutenant of the *Indefatigable*. For a crew he was given the entire crew of the frigate *Mermaid*, and 136 men from the *Lancaster* (64), which had just returned from years serving in the East Indies. True to his previous form and beliefs, Moore could not simply pack them all off to sea again. He insisted on every man receiving all the pay that was due to him, and then promptly gave them all three weeks leave to go home. The fact that all bar about twenty of them returned voluntarily and on time from their leave, illustrates the extent to which old fashioned beliefs in sailors' attitudes to service in the Navy was wrong. Moore himself knew what it meant to have to leave family and friends. The pain had not grown any less in more than twenty years of service:

> *I cannot leave my family and some friends, without feeling low and dejected. This has been the case with me ever since I first went to sea. I never have been able to harden myself to these separations. I believe it is better that I should remain away [from home] after I have once been appointed to a ship, for I find every time I go among my friends I experience the same degree of dejection at quitting them again.*

Towards the end of the year, the *Marlborough* was sent to the Tagus where Portugal was being threatened by the French. Ordered to carry the Portuguese royal family to safety in Brazil, Moore found himself once again under the orders of his old commander, Sidney Smith. Smith was unchanged;

> *Sir Sidney is . . . , as full of business and with as much parade and stage trick . . . I know all that he is about, and what I know does not by any means improve the idea I entertain either of his judgement or his zeal for the public service . . . I always am on good terms with him, which, you know is easy enough, he is so good tempered. I believe he is not ignorant that I approve of none of his plans, and, thank God, he seldom communicates them to me so we go on smooth enough.*[137]

Moore's next posting also took him back to join another of his old commanders – Sir Richard Strachan – this time for the expedition against the Schelde. Moore still maintained the highest regard for Strachan, even after the expedition faltered and ground to a halt, at the cost of the lives of over 4,000 men from Walcheren Fever alone. By September 1809, Moore was back at Brook Farm, commenting ruefully to his friend Creevey: '*I hope Walcheren will be evacuated before we lose any more of our invaluable men.*'[138] In fact, it was Moore himself who was employed to bring off the last British troops three months later.

In 1811 Moore was offered command of the yacht *Sovereign*, a sinecure which was often offered as a form of quiet reward to the more senior officers or perhaps those suffering from weakness caused by injury sustained in action. Moore declined the situation, fearing that it might truly put an end to his career. It was an astute move, for in 1812 he was given command of the *Chatham* and at the end of the year, promoted to the rank of Rear Admiral and made Commander-in-Chief in the Baltic. Leaving England this time may have been much harder for, in March 1812, he had married Dorothy (Dora) Eden, the daughter of Thomas Eden, auditor of the Greenwich Hospital and brother of Lord Auckland.[139] She was twenty-two years of age, whilst Moore was now forty-eight. Moore's health, his frequent absence and the age difference between them may have contributed to the fact that only one child survived from their union. This was John, named after Graham's beloved brother, who was born in 1822.[140]

By the end of the war, Moore was serving as Captain of the Channel Fleet under the command of Admiral Lord Keith. Immediately after the war he was awarded a KCB, and when Napoleon escaped from Elba, Moore was given the *Caledonia* (120) and appointed second in command in the Mediterranean.

The post-war years continued to be fully active ones for Moore; in 1816 he was called to the Board of Admiralty and, after three years service there, was promoted to Vice Admiral and given command of the Mediterranean station. Further honours were awarded him for his role in attempting to mitigate the worst excesses of the war between Greece and Turkey. By 1837, Moore was both Admiral and a GCB (Grand Cross of the Bath), but his ever unreliable health had taken too many blows. In 1839 he accepted the appointment as Commander-in-Chief at Plymouth, in the hope that the duties would be less demanding. However, his friends had already begun to see a marked physical deterioration in him and he retired to the peace of his beloved Brook Farm, where he could rest in financial security. His will, drawn up in March 1841, reveals something of the life that he led. His servant, William Mayford, may well have served with him in the navy, following him from ship to ship. His possessions not only included the usual stuff of the country gentleman: household furniture, linen, plate and china, carriages, horses, wine and liquors, but also items that we would expect to belong to the old naval officer: books, swords, pistols, charts and maps.

Although in failing health, Moore still managed to travel and keep in touch with his old comrades. One of his last letters to Admiral

Thomas Byam Martin, written from a hotel in Brighton, provides a deeply poignant illustration of Moore's final years:

My dear Martin, Thanks for your letter from Harrowgate, which caught me at Brook Farm the day before we started for this, which was yesterday. We were obliged to leave the house to the painters for a fortnight, much against my will, as I am now degenerated to be qualified to be President of the Never Wag Society. I wish this may capture you before you see Curzon[141], for whom I have always had a great esteem and regard, which you may tell him, if you like, though I fear I used to be rather more of a blackguard than he approved of when we were messmates on the old Adamant.

I give you carte blanche to assure him how much I am reformed since those days. I inquired after him from Bob Curzon when I was last in town. There are not many of that mess now in existence besides him and me, if any. We must be, at least, a fortnight away, and I intend to pass it here, as this place is a very favourite one of my wife, and you know that decides the matter. You are a young fellow[142] and may go anywhere (I think) either by sea or land, but I am, in spite of your flattery, very shaky. It annoys me to feel my powers decay, mentally and bodily: but I have no right to grumble, neither do I. You are now almost my only correspondent, and I used to have many. It is half a day's work now to write a letter . . . I had entertained some hope of finding you here, which would have cheered me up not a little . . . I write now in gratitude for your most welcome letter, and not from having any cut-and-dried matter to communicate, for I am dull and foggy this morning, which is now often the case with me, but I am as much attached to my old friends as ever, though sad to see them dropping off too fast.[143]

Moore returned to Brook Farm, but in the following year his health became noticeably worse. By the summer it was clear that his constitution had reached an irrecoverable position, and he finally died on 25 November 1843. His body was interred beneath a sturdy stone tomb near the south door of the mediaeval church at Cobham. It lies there now in the company of his beloved Dora, and his son John, beneath the trees of the quiet Surrey countryside that he loved so much.

Appendix 1

The Identity of Miss 'M'

Even during the final proof reading of this book, the identity of Moore's mysterious love continues to intrigue. Since another may also be tempted to look into this – and I hope they will – I feel it important to mention one strong possibility.

In the Duchess of Sermoneta's book, *The Locks* [sic] *of Norbury*, it is claimed that between around 1794-1804, Graham Moore maintained a romance with Augusta Locke, the eldest daughter of William and Mary Locke. As the author of this book is a descendant of the Locke family, there is clearly both family tradition and, apparently, some slight evidence that Augusta Locke might be Moore's mysterious love. This could certainly tie in with our first introduction to her in his journals (see page 90), for Augusta Locke was actually eleven years younger than Moore (near enough to his estimated nine or ten years), and the 'friends' which he refers to in the journal extract could well be the Lockes, since he was certainly intimate with the family before early 1791.

The problem lies in the circumstances of the end of the relationship. According to Moore's journal, he is rejected (in June 1799) because she does not feel prepared to leave her parents establishment. He then learns, months later, that she has accepted a proposal from another, whereas Augusta Locke did not finally marry until 1815.

According to the Duchess of Sermoneta and her evidence – a letter written by William Locke senior in 1806 – the affair between Graham Moore and Augusta Locke had been going on for ten years, ending around 1804. We know that Moore's second love affair ends in 1803, but it would be stretching the evidence to suggest that this might be a reference to Augusta.

However, it is curious that Moore blames the failure of this second relationship on the opposition of his betrothed's family, especially since he also mentions the problem that ended his first relationship – that

266

being his inability to provide a degree of comfort and lifestyle comparable to that provided by the young woman's parents.

However, according to the Duchess of Sermoneta, it was Moore's mother who gave the reason for the failure of the suggested relationship between Augusta and Graham: '. . . *the difficulties and hazards he foresaw in taking his wife with him in any service he might be called to, or the pain he should feel in leaving behind him a woman who wished to share all his fortunes . . . had prevented his marrying and would probably continue to do so as long as the war lasted.*' (*The Lockes of Norbury*' p.241).

Whilst one feels in danger of straying into not altogether desirable territory, it has to be questioned whether these relationships were in fact broken by family interference. We know that Moore tended to entrust his love letters to his mother, but it is also clear that the Lockes were a particularly close family. So close, in fact, that some found it claustrophobic, especially under Mrs Locke's direction.

There is also another possibility – and the only one which would fit in with the tradition of the Locke family – which is that Moore's first love did not actually marry another and that there was a reconciliation which lasted until 1803. However, Moore does not tell us this in his journal and without real evidence, such a romance is beyond the intentions of this particular book.

Tom Wareham
March 2004.

Notes

1   Dr Moore's other works included an updated edition of *Society and Manners* in 1781, which included Italy; the novel *Zeluco* in 1786; *A Journal During a Residence in France*, 1790; the novel *Edward*, 1796; and the novel *Mordaunt* in 1800.

2   Debrett's Complete Peerage, 1834.

3   R. Parkinson, *Moore of Corunna*, p.6.

4   Moore, Journal, Vol 12, 30 July 1798.

5   Moore Family Papers, British Library, ADD57321.

6   Capt. Molloy was eventually dismissed from the navy in 1795 following criticism from Lord Howe of his conduct during the Battle of the 1st June 1794. He died in July 1814. See James, *Naval History of Great Britain*, Vol I, p.201.

7   John Moore to Dr Moore, 7 Jan 1780, Moore Family Papers, ADD57320.

8   Ibid.

9   Moore, Journal, Volume 11, July 1797.

10 For example, Robert Barlow, Richard Bowen, Edward Buller, Michael de Courcy, John Hancock, Richard King, Josias Rogers, John Borlase Warren.

11 Old DNB, entry for Isaac Coffin.

12 In such executions, several seamen from all of the ships assembled were given the task of hauling on the rope by which the victim was hanged.

13 The poet Thomas Gray.

14 The naval area of Plymouth – now known as Devonport.

15 'Crimps' encouraged seamen to get drunk, and then sold them to merchant vessels in need of a crew, the Crimp pocketing a substantial bounty in the process.

16 A Blue Ensign with a harp and crown.

17 To those already mentioned should be added Lord Hillsborrow, who invited Moore to dinner one night after the *Perseus* had ferried him across to Carrickfergus.

18 French armed forces were mobilized to support a 'rebellion' in Holland. England mobilized naval forces in response to an appeal from her ally, Prussia, who was also allied to Holland. The French fleet was also mobilized in reaction to the English naval armament, but on October 27, the French and English governments came to a peaceful settlement. See W. Laird Clowes, *The Royal Navy*, Vol IV, p.102.

19 Flagship: the ship bearing an admiral.

20 Here then was another advantage of interest. It could be used in such a way

as to give the appearance that an officer himself was innocent of any approach made on his behalf.

21 Unfortunately, a page has been cut from the diary at this point, seemingly just as Moore was about to expand his thoughts on this issue.

22 A stroke.

23 In 1790, the Spanish laid claim to Nootka Sound, on the western seaboard of Canada. A fleet was assembled under the command of Lord Howe and a second fleet under Admiral Cornish was sent to reinforce the West Indies.

24 Norbury Park or House, in Mickleham.

25 Now Dinefwr Park.

26 Moore was a devotee of *The Ossian*. Published during the 1760s, *The Ossian* consisted of a series of ancient Scottish poems and tales collected by James Macpherson. By the 1790s, controversy was raging as to whether these were genuine or not. Although it was eventually accepted that the work was a fake created by Macpherson himself, *The Ossian* became a literary gem in its own right.

27 Interestingly, another young officer who was shortly to become a famous frigate captain, Thomas Byam Martin (also a close friend of Moore's) also knew Riou and described him thus: '*A pleasing gloom hung over his manly countenance, unlike anything I ever witnessed in any other person. His eye was peculiarly striking, beaming with intelligence, while every feature seemed to indicate all the qualities that most exalt and adorn our nature . . . There was a pensiveness of look and a reserve in his manner which sometimes made strangers regard him as cold and repulsive, but this first impression was soon removed, and all who knew him loved him.*' Letters & papers of Sir Thomas Byam Martin, I, pp.43–44. Riou was killed in 1801 at the Battle of Copenhagen, cut in two by round shot.

28 Shortly to inherit a Baronetcy and change his name to Harry Burrard Neale.

29 The Third Mysore War 1789–1792.

30 This could obviously have been a euphemism, but the journal gives no suggestion that this was the case.

31 See, for example, Anselm Griffiths, *Observations on Some Points of Seamanship with Practical Hints on Naval Economy*, 1828.

32 For a comparative view on the degree of autonomy which should be given to the First Lieutenant of a frigate, it is worth looking at the Standing Orders issued by Moore's friend , Edward Riou, when he was captain of the *Amazon*. See B Lavery, Ed., *Shipboard Life and Organisation 1731–1815*, NRS, 1998, pp.127–129.

33 This was a levy, which appears to have been charged on the merchants of Newfoundland for the presence of naval vessels deployed to protect their interest.

34 Which was manned by the 4th Regiment.

35 In fact Moore was ignoring the fact that Maude had been promoted to the rank of Post Captain in 1790 and was, therefore, significantly senior to him.

36 The French government formally declared war on both the British and the Dutch on 1 February, but Murray's Squadron does not seem to have been immediately aware of this.

37 Thomas Maxtone was promoted to Commander in February 1796, but was drowned in the following September when his brig sloop, the *Bermuda*, disap-

peared without trace in the Gulf of Florida. It was assumed that she must have foundered.

38   i.e. a 32-gun frigate.

39   See James, *A Naval History of Great Britain*, Vol I, p.110.

40   Edwards never fully recovered. He was promoted to the Rank of Commander in June 1795, and died as a result of the long-term effects of his wound in January 1823, the same month in which Brenton's accusation was published.

41   Clerk's work was published in 1782.

42   Presumably Moore means 'on the quarterdeck' here.

43   Marshall, Vol 2, p.195.

44   See Lyon, *Sailing Navy List*, pp.149–150.

45   See Hepper, *British Warship Losses in the Age of Sail, 1650–1859*, p.78.

46   Despite some effort in trying to identify the object of Moore's passion, I have been unsuccessful. There are a number of clues to her identity but these are inconclusive. Tantalizingly, in January 1796, Col. John Moore wrote two letters to his mother in which Graham is referred to in connection with the youngest daughter of the Minchin family who were, on that occasion, visiting Newport on the Isle of Wight. It is possible, therefore, that Miss Minchin was Moore's 'secret' love.

47   This explanatory comment suggests that Moore did intend that his journal should be read by others at a later point.

48   See Duffy, *Soldiers, Sugar and Seapower*, p.106 et seq.

49   The action took place on 13 June. See James Vol I, p.369.

50   Susan Gordon, daughter of the Duke of Gordon. She had married William Montagu, Duke of Manchester, in 1783.

51   Moore is referring to the engagement with the French private frigate *Citoyenne-Francais* in 1793. See James, Vol I, p.101.

52   *Melampus, Diamond, Syren* and the sloop *Cynthia* were all present during this capture.

53   There is a discrepancy here with the punishments recorded in the First Lieutenant's log. According to this, two men were punished on 7 September for drunkenness, but no more after that until 10 October when the marine Henry Sillard received twelve lashes for insolence. It seems quite probable that the First Lieutenant wrote up his logbook at some period after the events recorded – and that he was unable to recall the punishments accurately.

54   The battle took place on 14 February 1797, but Moore doesn't refer to it until around 17 March.

55   In fact, almost by the time that news had reached London, John Moore had been struck down with a much more severe attack of the fever, and had to be invalided home.

56   That is, goods or provisions belonging to the royal party.

57   This could have been meant literally. All of Moore's money at this time was in public funds.

58   James, *Naval History*, Vol II, p.103.

59   Moore used the term 'civil war' in his journal – which suggests that this was the phrase used by the Master of the Irish vessel.

60   Moore subsequently learned that this included the 100th Regiment.

61   i.e. from the *Endymion*.

62   It is worth noting that, rather cleverly, by referring to the victim of the abuse in this way, Moore had cleared him of any suspicion of 'telling tales'.

63   Here, as on so many other occasions, Moore was prophetic without really seeing the irony of his remarks.

64   i.e. Whitehouse Bay.

65   Dr Johnson had accused Macpherson of being a charlatan in his *A Journey to the Western Islands of Scotland*, published in 1753. Macpherson died in 1796 without ever really refuting Johnson's claim – which in a sense would have been impossible.

66   Curiously, Moore's thoughts had turned to Nelson just five days after the Battle of the Nile had taken place.

67   Lord Ranelagh, The Hon. Charles Jones (1), was the eldest son of the Irish 4th Viscount Ranelagh.

68   i.e. sailing as close as possible towards the wind.

69   i.e. sailing with the wind from nearer the stern.

70   The force consisted of four frigates under the command of Commodore Daniel Savary. See Laird Clowes, *The Royal Navy*, Vol IV, pp.343–344.

71   The force actually consisted of a 74 and nine frigates. They sailed from Brest on 16 September, but were shadowed by a frigate squadron under the command of Richard Goodwin Keats in the *Boadicea*. See Laird Clowes, Vol IV, p.345.

72   The Franco-Irish force under General Humbert defeated Hutchinson's much smaller force on 27 August. Hutchinson's force consisted largely of militia, who lacked the spirit of the small but well disciplined body of French troops.

73   This was erroneous, as Savary's squadron returned to Brest without hindrance.

74   This was possibly the Third Lieutenant, Cuthbert Ellison. He was never promoted to Commander, and died in 1801.

75   *An Authentic Account of An Embassy from the King of Great Britain to the Emperor of China*, published in 1797.

76   Humbert had not received the support he had expected from the Irish, and by the time he reached Ballinamuck, his army was down to less than about 2,000 men. He was surrounded, and after a brief engagement, surrendered honourably to vastly overwhelming forces.

77   For a full account of Warren's action, see James, Vol II, pp.139–163.

78   For a more detailed explanation of this see Wareham., *The Star Captains*, Chapter 2.

79   Actually a pretty good £65,000 at modern-day prices.

80   Moore strikes an almost sarcastic note at this point because the *Nymphe* and *Melpomene*, simply by being in sight, could claim a share of the prize money. This was a common bugbear among frigate captains who had fought hard actions only to see another English ship turn up at the last moment. See for example the engagement between the *Amethyst* and the French frigate *Niemen*. See Wareham, *The Star Captains*, pp.186–192.

81   Thomas Grenville, Statesman, and brother of William Windham Grenville, the Foreign Secretary.

82   In fact the rumour was worse than the truth. The *Proserpine* was indeed wrecked, on 1 February 1799, near the Island of Neuwerk. After attempts to save the ship had been foiled because the ship was surrounded by ice, the 187 men, women and children on board set off to walk six miles across the ice to the island. All but fourteen made it to safety. See Hepper, *British Warship Losses in the Age of Sail,* p.90.

83   At this time, flag officers in command of the station to which a frigate was attached received one of the captain's three-eighth shares of prize money.

84   Second son of Baron Wodehouse. Interestingly, Wodehouse was given command of a frigate on several occasions, but never for very long. It is possible that he was deemed not quite suitable for this type of command.

85   Unfortunately, this was almost the only reference Moore made in his journal to his frigate's gun drill. Notwithstanding this, the evidence from the ship's logs indicates that the crew was exercised at both great guns and small arms on a regular basis. The logs also record that the great guns were fired at floating casks on several occasions. Regrettably, the evidence from the logs is not reliable enough for us to be able to estimate the frequency of these drills. In the *Syren*, the drills may have taken place on average twice a month. If this was to be confirmed, Moore's record for training his crews would be a good one.

86   See James, *Naval History*, Vol II, pp.273–275; also Wareham, *The Star Captains*, p. 205.

87   See James, *Naval History*, Vol II, pp.363–364.

88   Again, Moore was right. Smith organized the defence of Acre and held up Napoleon's advance for more than two months. See Laird Clowes, *The Royal Navy*, Vol IV, pp.400–404.

89   According to Moore, Bridport's frigates were now deployed as follows: Captain George Duff in the frigate *Glenmore* was off Cape Clear, with the frigates *Phoebe* and *Cerberus*. Captain Francis Fayerman, who had replaced Lancelot Skynner (who was drowned when the frigate *Mutine* was wrecked in 1799) in the *Beaulieu* after the mutiny, was cruising between the Skelligs and Loop Head. Captain Robert Stopford in the frigate *Phaeton*, together with the frigates *Clyde* and *Stag*, was off Tory Island to the north. Each of the squadrons was accompanied by a cutter which could speed back to Bridport at Bantry Bay if the French should appear.

90   Yet again Moore does not name him. Whoever it was, however, owned land in Ireland, but lived most of the time in England.

91   Eldest son of Viscount Torrington.

92   He was correct; the expedition was intended to lead to the reinstatement of the Dutch monarchy by a combined Anglo-Russian naval and army attack against the Walcheren.

93   John Moore was wounded during the expedition.

94   T. Mathias, *The Pursuits of Literature: A Satirical Poem in Four Dialogues, with Notes*, 1798.

95   L. Flammenburg, *The Necromancer: Or The Tale of the Black Forest*, published in London in translation in 1794.

96   J-H. B. de Saint Pierre (1737–1814), *The Studies of Nature*, 1784.

97   This action took place on 28 February 1799. See James, *Naval History*, Vol II, pp.365–371.

98   The losses were actually greater than this, and John Moore was wounded firstly in the hand, and then a few days later he received a bad head wound.

99   No relation.

100   See James, *Naval History*, Vol II, pp.405–411.

101   The fact that Garlies seems to have been an educated officer may have been one of the reasons why Moore found his company agreeable. Garlies, like

Moore, kept a collection of books in his cabin and had lent Moore a copy of Sir William Eton's *Survey of the Turkish Empire*.

102   John Hamilton Moore's *The Practical Navigator and Seaman's New Daily Assistant*. First published in 1763, this book was widely used and imitated.

103   George Dundas (2).

104   This action took place on 20 August 1800. See James, Vol III, pp.23–26.

105   The *Hermione* had become infamous after her crew mutinied, killing most of the ship's officers, including the extraordinarily brutal Captain Pigot, on 22 September 1797. She was subsequently recaptured by HMS *Surprise*, commanded by Captain Edward Hamilton, and renamed HMS *Retribution*.

106   Philip Cosby Handfield, Third Lieutenant of the *Melampus*.

107   The Dutch inhabitants of the Island had decided to surrender to Watkins in the belief that surrender to the British was preferable to possible attack from hostile French forces in possession of part of the Island. See James, *Naval History*, Vol III, p.39.

108   Brother of the more famous Captain Sir Edward Pellew.

109   In November 1800, Russia, Prussia, Sweden and Denmark formed the second coalition of Armed Neutrality – intended to prevent British warships stopping and searching their merchantmen. To a significant degree, this second coalition had been sparked off by an incident in which a frigate squadron under the command of Captain Thomas Baker of the *Nemesis* engaged a Danish frigate. The Danish captain refused to permit Baker to inspect two merchantmen he was escorting, and when Baker persisted, the *Nemesis* was fired upon. After a short but heated action, the Danish ships were seized, and a diplomatic row erupted. See Laird Clowes, Vol IV, p.426 et seq.

110   First published in 1800, the four volume set cost £1–11s–6d. By 1803, it was in its fourth edition.

111   The ship wrecked may well have been the schooner *Charlotte*.

112   Moore himself served in the *Edgar* (74) as a Midshipman, so it may be that Downie was known to him from this time.

113   This arrangement was also followed by the Gun Room officers of the two frigates though, interestingly, the respective pursers and marine officers decided not to join in.

114   The Isla de la Juventud.

115   Hayes was a superb seaman and later won the sobriquet 'Magnificent' Hayes, after saving the 74-gun HMS *Magnificent* from almost inevitable shipwreck on a lee shore.

116   This was true. The *Apollo* had learned about the wreck from a fishing boat from Vera Cruz.

117   Ann Radcliffe, *Mysteries of Udolpho*, published in 1794.

118   This attack took place on 16 August, achieved little and cost the Royal Navy forty-four killed and 126 wounded. See Laird Clowes, Vol IV, pp.444–445; also James, Vol III, pp.65–67.

119   Norbury Park was just a few miles north of the Denisons' estate at Denbies. Locke had purchased it in 1774, and he had the house built there. Curiously, adjacent to Norbury was Camilla-Lacey, where Mrs D'Arblay wrote *Camilla*.

120   Pitt resigned as Prime Minister in February 1801 after the King refused to support Catholic emancipation.

121   The Newfoundland dog seems to have been highly popular with frigate captains. Hardly surprising, as the Newfoundland is as happy in the water as

on land, and was said to be used for carrying lines from vessels to shore, and supporting men in the water. In addition to Macnamara, Captain David Milne had a Newfoundland on board his frigate, which on one occasion helped him to swim across to take possession of a captured French frigate. Graham Moore had a Newfoundland called 'Neptune'. The Newfoundland may also have been rather fashionable, because Lord Byron had a Newfoundland called 'Boatswain'.

122 Those attending were Lord Hood, Lord Nelson, Lord Hotham, Admiral Hyde Parker, Captain Thomas Byam Martin, Captain George Towry, Captain Charles Lydiard, Captain Waller, Lord Minto and General Churchill. See Marshall, *Royal Naval Biography*, Vol I, p.690.

123 *Magnanime* and *Anson*.

124 Moore to Creevey. Plymouth. *Indefatigable*. 7 Aug, 1803. Quoted in J. Gore, *Creevey*, London, 1948, p.12.

125 Moore to Creevey. Cawsand Bay. 16 Sept, 1803. Ibid., p.12.

126 See Marshall, Vol II, p.310.

127 Moore to Creevey. Plymouth Dock. 1 February, 1804. Gore, Creevey, p.16.

128 A copy of the *Moniteur* subsequently reported that seventy seamen from the *Magnificent* had been captured.

129 Son of the Comptroller of the Navy.

130 A coincidence!

131 An interesting and revealing aside!

132 Quoted in B. Brownrigg, *Life and Letters of Sir John Moore*.

133 Henry Dundas, Viscount Melville and First Lord of the Admiralty, was charged with corruption but eventually acquitted of many of the accusations against him.

134 Whilst we can only guess at the nature of this ailment, some form of rupture or haemorrhoid is suggested.

135 On 6 February he wrote to Creevey: 'They are not what you might expect from the companions of Nelson', adding tongue in cheek, 'but they will do with some whipping and spurring'. Ed. Maxwell, *The Creevey Papers*, 1923, p.78.

136 Quoted in D.C. Taylor, *Cobham Houses and their Occupants*, Cobham, 1999, p.8.

137 Moore family papers, British Library, ADD57321.; Graham to John Moore, 17 November 1808.

138 Moore to Creevey. 19 Sept, 1809. Quoted in J. Gore, *Creevey*, p.58.

139 Who happened to be the Director of Greenwich Hospital.

140 John followed his father into the navy, and reached the rank of captain, but died at the age of forty-four at Brook Farm, after a long illness.

141 The Hon. Henry Curzon, with whom Moore had served in HMS *Adamant*. Moore's generosity in not opposing Curzon's promotion had ensured their lifelong friendship. Curzon died in 1846.

142 Byam Martin was nine years younger than Moore and died in 1854.

143 Moore to Byam Martin, 2 October 1842. *Letters & Papers of Admiral of the Fleet, Sir Thos. Byam Martin*. Ed. R. V. Hamilton. 1901. Vol 3. pp. 1 & 3.

Bibliography

Primary Sources

Cambridge University Library

Journal of Admiral Sir Graham Moore, Add 9303, 1–37

British Library

Moore Family Papers, Add 57321
Letters of Colonel John Moore, Add 57320

National Maritime Museum

Lieutenants' Logs:
HMS *Melampus*, ADM/L/M/144
HMS *Syren*, ADM/L/S/624

Public Record Office

<u>Captains' Log Books</u>
HMS *Syren*, ADM51/1123
HMS *Syren*, ADM51/1147
HMS *Melampus*, ADM51/1233
HMS *Melampus*, ADM51/1267
HMS *Melampus*, ADM51/1338
HMS *Melampus*, ADM51/1399
HMS *Melampus*, ADM51/4474
HMS *Indefatigable*, ADM51/1472

Ships' Muster Books
HMS *Syren*, ADM36/11477
HMS *Melampus*, ADM36/11602
HMS *Melampus*, ADM36/14600
HMS *Indefatigable*, ADM36/16760

Secondary Sources

Brownrigg, B., *The Life and Letters of Sir John Moore*, Oxford, 1923
Duffy, M., *Soldiers, Sugar and Seapower*, Oxford, 1987
Farington, Joseph, *The Diary of*, ed. Various, New Haven & London, 1982, 16 Vols.
Gore, J., *Creevey*, London, 1948
Griffiths, Capt. A., *Observations on Some Points of Seamanship with Practical Hints on Naval Economy*, Portsmouth, 1828
Hamilton, Sir Richard V., (ed.) *Letters and Papers of Admiral of the Fleet Sir Thomas Byam Martin*, GCB, NRS, London, 1898
Hepper, D.J., *Warship Losses in the Age of Sail, 1650–1859*, Rotherfield, 1994
James, William, *A Naval History of Great Britain*, London, 1902
Laird Clowes, William, *The Royal Navy: A History from the Earliest Times to 1900*, London, 1997
Lavery, B. ed., *Shipboard Life and Organisation 1781–1815*, Navy Records Society. 1998.
Lyon, D., *The Sailing Navy List*
Marshall, John, *Royal Naval Biography*, London, 1823–30, 12 Vols.
Maxwell, The Rt. Hon. Sir Herbert, *The Creevey Papers*, London, 1923, *The Naval Chronicle*
Parkinson, R., *Moore of Corunna*, Abingdon, 1976
Ralfe, J., *Naval Biography, 1828, III, 206*
Sermonetta, The Duchess of, *The Locks of Norbury*, London, 1940
Taylor, D.C., *Cobham Houses and their Occupants*, Cobham, 1999
Wareham, T., *The Star Captains*, London, 2001

Index

230, Engagement broken off 231, Outbreak of War 232, Applies for command of *Monarch* (74) 233, Appointed to command the *Indefatigable* (44) 235, Joins Cornwallis' squadron 237, Joins Admiral Graves' squadron 245, Runs onto La Vandre rocks 249, Ordered to intercept Spanish treasure frigates 250, Action with Spanish frigates 252, Ordered to carry Gen. Moore to Ferrol 256, Hunt for the Toulon squadron 258, Resigns command because of poor health 260, Surgery in London 261, Appointed to command *Fame* (74) 262, Resigns command 262, Purchases Brook farm 262, Appointed to command the *Marlborough* (74) 262, Carries Portuguese Royal Family to Brazil 263, Schelde/Walcheren Expedition 263, Refuses command of the *Sovereign* yacht 264, Appointed to command the *Chatham* (74) 264, Marries 264, Promoted to Flag Rank 264, Commander in Chief of the Baltic Fleet 264, Awarded a KCB 264, Appointed to command the *Caledonia* (120) and the Mediterranean Station 264, Called to the Board of Admiralty 264, Promoted Admiral and awarded a GCB 264, Commander in Chief at Plymouth 264, Will 264, Death 265.

Moore, Jean, xii
Moore, John Hamilton *The Practical Navigator*, 201
Moore, Lieutenant Edward, 197
Morice, Captain Richard, 71
Murray, Admiral, 58, 63
Nantes 139

Nelson, Admiral Horatio, 75, 125, 136, 149, 152, 159, 169, 220, 223, 232, 259, 260
Newfoundland Banks 20
Newman, Captain James 170
New Ross, Ireland, 147
Norbury Park, Surrey, 225
Nootka Sound, 26
Nore Mutiny, 179, 230
Nore, The. (Sheerness), 56

Ossian, The 34, 155, 158, 159
Otway, Captain Robert Waller, 245

Palmer, Captain George, 2 et seq

Paris, 'The Terror', 53
Parker, Admiral Sir Hyde Parker, 197, 200
Pater, Captain Charles, 185
Paulet, Captain Lord Henry, 97
Pellew, Captain Israel, 210
Pellew, Sir Edward, 68, 84, 122, 123, 136, 139, 144, 235
Perry's Yard, Blackwall, 42
Peyton, Admiral Joseph, 133
Peyton, Captain Thomas, 100, 115
Pierrepont, Captain William, 188
Pine, Lieutenant, 89
Pitt, William (Prime Minister), 17, 231
Plampin, Captain Robert, 213
Poole, Dorset, 53, 180
Portland, Dorset 117
Port Royal, Jamaica, 199, 205, 211

Radcliffe, Ann *Mysteries of Udolpho*, 219
Rainier, Admiral Peter, 192
Ranelagh, Captain Lord, 159, 164
Reeve, Captain Samuel, xvi
Reynolds, Captain Robert Carthew, 122
Richery, Admiral Joseph de, 108
Richmond, Surrey, 224
Riou, Captain Edward, 35, 53
Rochfort 139
Rochfort Squadron (French), 257, 259
Rodd, Captain John, 260
Rodney, Admiral George, 3
Rowley, Admiral Bartholomew Samuel, xv
Rowley, Captain Bartholomew, 147
Rule, Sir William (Surveyor to the Navy), 262

Saint Pierre. *The Studies of Nature*, 191
Sandys, Captain Charles, 11, 25
Santa Cruz, Tenerife, 136
Saumarez, Admiral Sir James, 224
Schank's, Captain 85, 93
Seymour, Lord Hugh, 205, 212
Sheerness, Kent, 17, 82
Ships
    Acasta 40, 212, 217, 246; *Active* 38, 82; *Adamant* 50, 265; *Alcmene* 32, 196; *Amazon* 36, 94, 122, 143; *Ambuscade* 32, 177; *Amelia* 38, 164; *Amphion* 32 212–7, 221, 223, 250–254; *Anacreon* French corvette, 162; *Anson* 44, 164, 170, 172; *Apollo* 38, 81, 212, 219; *Aquila* Spanish armed vessel, 208;

282